C000213398

INFORMATION
WARRIORS

INFORMATION WARRIORS

WARRIORS

The Battle for Hearts and Minds
in the Middle East

Vyvyan Kinross

GILGAMESH

Information Warriors
The Battle for Hearts and Minds in the Middle East

Published by Gilgamesh Publishing in 2019
Email: info@gilgamesh-publishing.co.uk
www.gilgamesh-publishing.co.uk

ISBN 978-1-908531-65-0

Editorial: Joe Worthington
Design: Martin Humphries

CIP Data: A catalogue for this book is
available from the British Library

Author's Preface

The state of public opinion in and about the Middle East, both how it has arisen and evolved, is a subject that increasingly demands attention. More than anything, the processes inherent in the expression of public opinion make it central to the growth of free societies, including the development of constitutional political structures, economic models, mechanisms for social justice, civil and human rights and consumer choice.

Neither a politician nor historian, I have been part of a business whose purpose in shaping the perceptions and behaviours that drive public opinion is anchored in technical knowledge and applied expertise. To that extent I am a professional communicator who has worked with governments in the region to help them develop their information and communication capacity. Whilst this may sound abstract, it is specialist work through which outcomes exert a powerful impact on the way in which information culture, policy and systems are determined. This conscious engineering helps shape the mechanisms and content of a government's internal and external conversations and thus affects how it is perceived, factors which together constitute the building blocks of modern reputation management.

The idea behind *Information Warriors* first crystallised when I was working in the West Bank in 2015 as part of a team engaged with the Palestinian Authority (PA) to raise corporate governance standards and promote better relations between parts of the Authority and the people of the Occupied Palestinian Territory (OPT). This move reflects a wider trend amongst governments in the region, who want to talk both more directly and effectively to citizens, and is a political and social consequence of the Arab Spring of 2011. Amongst the outcomes of this cathartic event has been the elevation of the status of public opinion in the Arab world to a more pivotal position on the political stage and in turn its accelerated progress from the negative connotations of the old 'Arab street' towards a more contemporary force embracing expressions of identity, engagement and change.

In particular, the power vacuum left by the withdrawal of the United States from Iraq in 2011, the consequent advance of radical Islamism, an increasingly weaponised sectarian rift in the region and the transformative penetration of all corners of Arab dialogue by social and digital media have helped create a more polarised and active political environment in the Middle East. A central theme in this book is the tendency of states and movements to use information as part of a wider strategy to fully engage in conflict, an idea that has been floated since the 1920s as part of the analysis of how propaganda was successfully used by liberal democracies as a tool to achieve both military and foreign policy aims during the First World War.

A century has now passed since the world's major powers decided the shape of the post-war Middle East through a series of treaties following the Paris Peace Conference of 1919. These treaties, which swept away four centuries of Ottoman rule and replaced it with a series of international Mandates caused a wave of secondary effects whose negative impacts are still being felt today. It has long been argued, for example, that one outcome of post-war British and French imperial rule was to set back the development of Arab democratic institutions and thus stifle national political debate, effectively impeding the cause of Arab independence and national identity by failing to offer any significant mechanism through which the expression of popular opinion might be seen to result in positive change. Whilst it is true Britain carved out borders and introduced political structures after the War, it did so alongside a narrative that played up its own technological, administrative and military superiority and perpetuated the prevalent Orientalist doctrine that had framed its interventions in the region.

A line of investigation in the book is an analysis of how the West's information and propaganda front has developed since the First World War in tandem with a succession of advances in the theory and practice of persuasive communications. This has invariably involved some predictable but other more Machiavellian concepts such as perception management and psychological operations which bear further explanation or at least opening up to scrutiny. In the course of this analysis, highly contemporary themes such as the manufacture and distortion of news, the use of atrocity propaganda and the psychological and behavioural engineering associated with persuasive communications techniques are revealed as constructs that all have their roots in the first half of the 20th century and in specific cases have been linked to some of today's most extreme expressions of radical Islamism.

A further theme is concerned with tracing and articulating the rise and development of propaganda and information war in the Middle East through the lens of its individual theorists and practitioners, a trajectory which reflects the journey from generally amateur and experimental origins up to and during the First World War to their most contemporary incarnation as modern day information warriors, a critical dimension of the conflict and policy planning process itself. This development has in turn driven a secondary trend to outsource some aspects of the conduct of information war to those whose modus operandi most often remains shrouded and inaccessible. It is on this arc that the prevailing notion of strategic narratives as ways in which to make popular sense of the psychological and physical dimensions of conflict has paralleled the rise of individuals who are as much politicians and ideologues as they are communicators and propagandists, post-modern navigators of the treacherous currents that govern the manipulation of public opinion.

To those who make it their business to follow the ways in which Western military intervention and foreign policy in the countries of the Middle East have been sold, much of the content of these pages can already be located in the public domain. Yet it is only through the process of reflection that the more holistic perspective enabled by scrutiny over time reveals a pattern of striking similarity between the propagandist's manifesto a century ago, as the British marched into Jerusalem to declare their simultaneous liberation and occupation, and the mixed messages that currently offer equivocal support for a generation of modern Palestinians whose wheels are, as it were, spinning in the same sand of moral ambiguity disguised as solidarity.

It would be wrong though to depict the information war in the Middle East as an entirely one-sided affair. Over the decades since the outbreak of the Second World War, Arab nations intent on making the case for national identity and political sovereignty have developed their own expertise in the use and manipulation of regional and international media and have found a way to pull the levers of mass communication to suit their own aims. Notable examples include the masterful media projections of Egyptian President Gamal Abd Al Nasser in the 1950s and 1960s and Palestinian leader Yasser Arafat in the 1980s and 1990s. Latterly, however, the media planners and propagandists of Islamic State, drawn from disparate nations and professions, have shown themselves to be the new masters of the genre, developing organisational models, skill sets, multimedia content and distribution channels which have together ensured a global reach based on a simple existential message that connects directly with audience emotions. Evidence is even beginning to show that degrading of the physical Caliphate may have little impact on its ability to release stockpiled propaganda output for decades to come.

Information warriors in the West and Islamist 'media mujahidin' therefore represent two sides of the same coin and have developed in plain sight of each other, the latter an assiduous student of the former. The servant rising through the ranks to become the new master is an overused trope, but it nonetheless brings into focus the conundrum at the heart of the propaganda and information wars that have raged in the region. Through the past century's flashpoints of Western interventions – Palestine, Suez, Iraq, Libya – it seems that the propaganda and information endgame of the West has played its part in failure to deliver the predicted benefits of new style governments and relationships across the region, especially in the export of the vision of democracy sold by the ideologues within the US neo-con Republican class of the 1990s. Instead, variations of old alliances and ententes have survived amidst wholesale political confusion brought on through a series of disruptions and upheavals whose outcomes are not yet in sight. If a new order is to emerge, this situation still requires resolution; most importantly it needs a political and social manifesto that has yet to find solid form or expression.

Information war, as opposed to old style propaganda, is still a relatively modern term whose precise definition remains elusive, especially when one takes into account the growing phenomena of cyberwarfare and other state sanctioned technological intrusion. Nonetheless, its overarching effect is to promote a more general and corrosive conspiracy theory which makes it difficult to take any narrative accounts, or the facts on which they are based, at face value; it is becoming generically harder to know who or what to believe, often leaving suspicion in place of trust as the default response. The founder of modern public relations, Edward Bernays, was clear about his intentions to use communications to create credible renditions of reality in pursuit of his clients' self-interest. There is little reason to doubt today the clarity or foresight of his vision nearly a century ago but perhaps more urgent cause to examine its moral underpinning, an existential dilemma of the digital media age.

Acknowledgements

The realisation of 'Information Warriors' is the culmination of a project that had its genesis at the end of 2016, which now seems a lifetime ago. I suspect like all books, most especially in the field of non-fiction, it started out as one thing and slowly developed into rather more, gathering on the way fresh perspectives, scale and scope which had not formed part of the initial vision. As a general observation, I should record that I have tried throughout in good faith to verify facts and identify and acknowledge sources for the information I have used. I have not in every case according to best journalistic practice double sourced all information, neither am I a professional historian; thus, any resulting inaccuracies are mine and I take full responsibility for them. There are a number of people who have helped me greatly along the way. I would like to thank John McHugo, Dr Peter Barham, Jennie Metaxa-Barham and David Perkins for their comments and interest on the early ideas and outlines of the book's plan and for assessing selected chapters for accessibility. Most especially for his enduring encouragement and detailed editorial suggestions from the earliest stage I must thank Stephen Brough without whom the book would not in all probability have seen the light of day. For his generous and practical help I owe gratitude to James Barr who contributed some very valuable and entirely unsolicited detail on Britain's information war in the Middle East immediately prior to the Suez crisis and at the same time introduced me to the amazing world of British spy John Slade-Baker; and to Nick Hill, of the Palestine Veterans Association for contributing generously both information and images about an important and neglected group of British servicemen who did what they were asked and got a lot less in return than they deserved. Thanks too are due to Helen Upcraft at the Imperial War Museum Film Archive who organised the viewings of rare and fascinating films which had yet to be digitised as part of the Museum's ongoing programme of widening access to its treasure trove of material, among them 'The Anglo French Aggression Against Egypt.' I cannot recommend highly enough the experience of a visit there for anyone who wants to explore this important archive and its rich heritage at first hand. I want too to thank Chris Doyle and friends and colleagues at the Council for Arab British Understanding, an organisation I have been a member of since my student days and which has been consistently involved with some of the issues, initiatives and statistics which are represented in this book and which framed more than a few of my views, some of which I have recorded here. The transcript of Alastair Burt's speech at Caabu's 50th anniversary event and the results of the joint 'British Attitudes to the Arab World' survey with Arab News form just two of these many contributions. To my publisher Max Scott, editor Joe Worthington and designer Martin Humphries I also owe a debt of gratitude; it is an important moment when a writer can feel that someone shares their enthusiasm and belief in a project and will help it breathe its own oxygen. Lastly, I cannot thank my wife and children enough for being there and accompanying me through the obsession years; I can only guess at what they have had to put up with. Finally, I think it right to dedicate Information Warriors to my late father James Kinross who would most certainly have enjoyed this tangent to more mainstream military fare.

Vyvyan Kinross,
Chiswick, August 2019

On Information War . . .

'Indeed, there is no question, but that government management of opinion is an unescapable corollary of large-scale modern war. The only question is the degree to which the government should try to conduct its propaganda secretly and the degree to which it should conduct it openly.'

Harold Lasswell,
Propaganda Technique In the World War,
Propaganda Organisation, New York (1927), p15

'From being the most misunderstood nation, America became the most popular. A world that was either inimical, contemptuous or indifferent was changed into a world of friends and well-wishers.'

George Creel,
How We Advertised America, Harper & Brothers, 1920

'It may well be the secret of fascist propaganda that it simply takes men for what they are: the true children of today's standardised mass culture, largely robbed of autonomy and spontaneity instead of setting goals the realisation of which would transcend the psychological status quo no less than the social one.'

Theodor Adorno,
Freudian Theory and the Pattern of Fascist Propaganda,
Frankfurt Reader, (1951)

'There is a group of media operatives and companions of the pen that has a prominent and important role in steering the war, shattering the morale of the enemy and raising the spirits of the ummah.'

Osama bin Laden, 2002

'Interestingly, some compare propaganda to pornography: you can tell it when you see it, but you can't define it.'

John Brown,
Public Diplomacy & Propaganda, Their Differences,
American Diplomacy, Foreign Service Despatches and Periodic Reports on
US Foreign Policy (2008)

'We are in a battle and more than half of this battle is taking place in the media.'

Abu Musab Al Zarqawi,
Leader, Al Qaeda in Iraq

'Information could have served as a tourniquet in Iraq. With information, an informed Iraqi people could have slowed, if not stopped the societal and cultural violence in their world. There is a direct link between information operations and influencing opinion,'

Steven J Alvarez,
Selling War, A Critical Look at the Military's PR Machine,
Potomac Books (2016), Preface, p. xii

'The smart way to keep people passive and obedient is to strictly limit the spectrum of acceptable opinion but allow very lively debate within that spectrum— even encourage the more critical and dissident views. That gives people the sense that there's free thinking going on, while all the time the presuppositions of the system are being reinforced by the limits put on the range of the debate.'

Noam Chomsky
The Common Good, Odonian Press (1998) p. 43

Terminology:
The Language of Persuasion

Information Operations:
'The integrated employment of the core capabilities of electronic warfare, computer network operations, psychological operations, military deception, and operations security, in concert with specified supporting and related capabilities, to influence, disrupt, corrupt or usurp adversarial human and automated decision making while protecting our own. Also called IO.'

JP 3-13, US Department of Defense, militaryfactory.com

Information War:
'A war during which the reporting or manipulation of information is particularly important or notable; a conflict over the possession or distribution of information.'

Oxford English Dictionaries

Perception Management:
'A mix of actions to convey and/or deny selected information and indicators to foreign audiences to influence their emotions, motives, and objective reasoning; in various ways, perception management combines truth projection, operations security, cover and deception and psychological operations.'

US Airforce Intelligence & Security Doctrine,
Psychological Operations, Air Force Instruction 10-702,
Secretary of the Air Force, July 19, 1994

Propaganda:
'...is concerned with the management of opinions and attitudes by direct manipulation of social suggestion rather than altering other conditions in the environment or in the organism.'
Harold Lasswell, Propaganda Technique in the World War, 1927

Psychological Operations (PsyOP):
'Planned operations to convey selected information and indicators to foreign audiences to influence their emotions, motives, objective reasoning, and ultimately the behavior of foreign governments, organisations, groups and individuals. The purpose of Psychological Operations is to induce or reinforce foreign attitudes and behaviors favorable to the originator's objectives.'
PsyOp, Military Psychological Operations Manual, Field Manual 3-05.30, Department of the Army, Washington DC, April 2005

Public Relations:
'...is the discipline which looks after reputation, with the aim of earning understanding and support and influencing opinion and behaviour. It is the planned and sustained effort to establish and maintain goodwill and mutual understanding between an organisation and its publics.'
UK Chartered Institute of Public Relations

Public Diplomacy:
'The public, interactive dimension of diplomacy which is not only global in nature, but also involves a multitude of actors and networks. It is a key mechanism through which nations foster mutual trust and productive relationships and has become crucial to building a secure global environment.'
USC Center on Public Diplomacy

Social Architects:
Those individuals whose theories and actions have together been pivotal in developing the way in which mass communication is used by governing elites to influence the opinions of populations.

Soft Power:
'The ability to get desired outcomes because others want what you want ... the ability to achieve goals through attraction rather than coercion.'
Robert O. Keohane and Joseph S. Nye,
'Power and Interdependence in the Information Age'
Foreign Affairs, Vol. 77, No. 5, September/October 1998, p. 86

Strategic Narratives:

'...compelling story lines which can explain events convincingly and from which inferences can be drawn ... designed or nurtured with the intention of structuring the responses of others to developing events.'

Lawrence Freedman,
The Transformation of Strategic Affairs, Adelphi Books, 2006

CONTENTS

CHAPTER I

The Asymmetric Front: Information and Conflict in the Arab World

Freedom of the press can never be the licence to say anything one desires. Freedom of the press is not freedom to slander and attack and must never be used to fight other people's wars. It does not mean manipulating a story into speaking your views. One might think it common sense, but in the world of journalism a lot of what makes sense is lost to the lure of favouritism, greed and fame. Sadly, in this truth-telling business truth is hard to find.'

Aysha Taryam, Editor, *The Gulf Today*

Beyond the mere recording and selection of facts to achieve certain aims and agendas, the writing of history is about context and interpretation, a reflection of the way individual historians assemble the links between people and events that others may simply find disparate or unrelated. Seen through one lens, the history of the Middle East over the last century can be perceived predominantly as a series of conflicts. The first and most violent of these types of conflict is military, a genre which in the region accommodates two world wars, numerous independence struggles including for a Palestinian state, violent revolutions in countries such as Algeria and Egypt, civil wars in Syria and Yemen and insurgent wars, the most recent of which, the Western invasion of Iraq in 2003, is still framing the extreme Islamist narrative. Added to these military conflicts and their various ideological themes including imperialism, colonialism, Arab nationalism, communism, socialism, Nazism and jihadism, is the very particular sectarian war now fuelled by the schism between Sunni and Shi'a Islam and its increasing militarisation by the regional powers of Saudi Arabia and Iran, together with the proxy war fought in Syria by these and the United States, Russia, Turkey and others, all of whose motives and commitments are subtly differentiated.

Though easily the highest impact, military confrontation comprises just one branch of the conflict tree. In a somewhat parallel timeframe a second, economic war has also been waged by the West which has written its own story of calculated opportunism in trade and commerce, formalised by the opening of the Suez Canal by the British and French in 1869 and subsequent exploitation until 1956 as a means of connecting Britain with its extensive interests in the Levant and Mesopotamia and across the Arabian Gulf to India. The primarily British and French imperialist agenda in the modern Middle East was further enabled by Mandates granted at the Treaty of Sèvres in 1920 which largely determined the exploitation of the region's natural assets such as oil and gas, shaping commercial relationships that remained intact for 50 years and still retain elements of their form. It was not until October 1973 that this trading model was upended with the weaponising of oil production and supply that quadrupled the price within a matter of months. Since then, governments and the private sector have simultaneously sought to negotiate a solution that aligns the mutual economic interests of the West with Arab oil power, more finely calibrating the forces of supply and demand through regular, though sometimes vexed, intermediation.

There is a third class of conflict, about which less is consistently acknowledged or recorded, and which has in some respects underwritten the first two. The ongoing battle to shape and control public opinion in and about the Middle East has been a significant part of the backdrop to the military and economic narrative of the region and its design and management has taken up the attention of the world's superpowers, most predominantly Britain and the United States. It has also caused leaders of Arab political states and independence movements to exploit the levers of mass communication in order to construct a counter narrative with a message that connects to their own worldview and agenda of sovereignty and national identity. Getting to grips with the concept and reality of information war is therefore an important part of the Middle East puzzle that helps explain how the West, and latterly the Arabs themselves, have sold their vision to the world and sought to frame actions that have encompassed both the orthodox and extreme elements within their societies.

In deconstructing the role of propaganda in the First World War, the political scientist and communications theorist Harold Lasswell wrote in his 1927 book, Propaganda Technique in the World War, that propaganda 'is one of the three chief implements of operation against a belligerent enemy: military pressure (the coercive power of land, sea and air forces); economic pressure (interference with access to sources of material, markets, capital and labour power); and propaganda, the direct use of suggestion.'[1] One of the great analysts and visionaries behind the then new science of mass communication, Lasswell was amongst the first to state the importance of giving the propagandist a place not only in the execution of policy but in its formation, taking the view that policies are not safely formulated without expert information 'upon which they rely for success.'[2]

This book tells the story of how a century of Western propaganda and public diplomacy has played a controlling, though often hidden part, in shaping the Middle East from the start of the First World War until the present day, tracing a line from the first atrocity propaganda used by the Allies in 1914 to the global media jihad currently being fought by the information warriors of Islamic State. It shows how the information wars waged in the region have been every bit as potent and destructive as the military adventurism and why, after years of seeking to frame the image of the Arab world and control the narrative of its future, the old information and communications paradigm has shifted. Among the principal characters in this story are the theorists and practitioners of propaganda, the social architects who have provided its intellectual fuel and applied their minds to the practical task of campaigning, opening up between them this potent and under-reported asymmetric front of modern conflict. They include figures as seemingly disparate as British Prime Minister Sir Anthony Eden, Iraqi President Saddam Hussein and Sigmund Freud's nephew, Edward Bernays.

The Power of Public Opinion
The state of public opinion is an everyday obsession in the goldfish bowl inhabited by Western politicians used to the constant scrutiny of an often vitriolic democracy served up media style. For Western governments active in the Middle East, public opinion in the region itself has not always been a central concern. The focus has, in the main, been on their domestic audience and, in time of war especially, the tipping point between public support or opposition, a problem that Herbert Asquith encountered over Gallipoli in 1916, Sir Anthony Eden grappled with in 1956 at Suez, and Tony Blair confronted before and after the invasion of Iraq in 2003. Evolving evidence now points to public opinion becoming a new and powerful consideration for all political decision-makers in

the region since the 2011 Arab Spring. The growth of consistent and reliable opinion polling amongst Arab populations shows consensus that the reputation of the West and confidence in its policy agendas are at a consistently low point; the 2017 Arab Opinion Index, for example, found that only 12% of more than 18,000 respondents in 11 Arab countries across the region felt at all positive about US foreign policy; the number reflects a new low in what has been a steady decline over the last few years according to its author, the Arab Center for Research and Policy Studies.[3] This overall decline is striking, as Arab public opinion embraces over 400 million people and has implications that go well beyond the West's national security and counter-terrorism agendas. Research into British attitudes towards the Arab world, conducted in 2017, found that only around one in 10 of the population (13%) believe British foreign policy has been a stabilising force in the region; and a majority (57%) think that it has been largely ineffective in upholding either human rights or promoting global security. It showed that few people know very much about the Arab world and few are interested in finding out more.[4] This perceived failure in policy is intimately connected to a parallel failure in both communication and education about the Arab world, suggesting that an institutional lack of Arab perspective and inclusion in public debate has laid the groundwork for negative stereotyping and rising levels of Islamophobia. These findings, results from one of the largest public surveys undertaken of British attitudes to the Arab world, also tell us much about the failure in communication to effectively put across our foreign policy objectives or make a case for our former or current military interventions in the region. Without the basis of a broad understanding of our objectives and modus operandi, both at home and in the Middle East, how can we hope to secure the weight of favourable public opinion? The research also highlights our inability to make a case for our historical interventions that have left a toxic legacy that now seems difficult to shift.

As the old Western narrative characterising the Arab world has broken down, that of the whole region sharing a common culture, religion and identity, the opposite has been true of radical Islamist propaganda which has been conspicuously successful in crafting a clearer and more direct vision that pitches simplified albeit distorted ideological solutions to complex existential questions; it has packaged and sold these personal and emotional appeals to vulnerable and disenfranchised Muslim communities around the world, especially amongst young people. This matters particularly in the Middle East, as over a quarter (28%) of its population is aged between 15 and 29, representing 108 million young people, the largest number of young people to transition to adulthood at one time in the region's history.[5]

At the same time, as Western propaganda and public diplomacy have become more oblique, they have also proved less effective. The explanation of why this might be requires charting the progress of Western attempts to harness and shape public opinion in the region, from the early development of propaganda in the Great War through to its deployment as part of an integrated communications approach, drawing on abstract and sometimes secretive models that include psychological operations, information operations, perception management, public diplomacy and soft power. At the heart of the book are a set of questions the West needs to address in order to re-establish trust and thereby reset its relationships with the Arab world. Do we have a credible vision for our role in the region that we can communicate with conviction, one which is supported by a clear connection between what we say and what we do? Can we pull together and manage our national brand and information output to support this purpose and vision at a level that can make a difference? As Lasswell noted in his analysis in 1927, 'it is not necessary that the heads of the propaganda services should formally occupy ministerial or cabinet posts, but they should have ministerial or cabinet influence.'[6] These questions need answers, and in the process, we must give room to the idea that a change of approach can reverse this information deficit and shape an alternative vision for the region. Development of policy itself should focus on front line issues such as conflict resolution, the refugee crisis, Palestinian self-determination, radical Islamism, the role of civil society, human rights and a more inclusive dialogue that accommodates a range of Arab voices, especially young people. But policy is only one part of a much bigger picture. As former British Foreign Secretary David Miliband argued in 2009, we need to build broader coalitions and alliances of citizens that go beyond the interests and concerns of elites if we are to shift the weight of public opinion in the region more towards the West as a long term ally and equal partner.[7] It is only this kind of radical thinking that stands a realistic chance of breaking the patterns of failure and reaching out towards a more enduring peace and stability in the region.

The Rising Cost of Conflict
A century on from the end of the First World War, the most savage conflict the world has ever seen, and war is still bleeding nations and peoples

dry. International strategic power plays, regional tactical aggression, religious and civil wars, border incursions and land grabs, local territorial struggles, armed extremism, factional fighting, tribal unrest, gang wars, drug wars, children's armies; everyone is still at it. We do not seem to have learned anything. The attraction of war is as mystifying as it is enduring, given the glaringly obvious human and economic price that has to be paid by everyone, whether actively partaking in it or not.

Research by the World Economic Forum (WEF) shows that armed conflict is now more costly for societies than ever before, at a time when we are spending less on peace. In its 2015 Global Peace Index Report, the organisation found that there had been the highest number of global battle deaths, terrorist activity and displaced persons for 25 years. It put the cost of violence to the global economy in the same year at $13.6 trillion in terms of purchasing power parity (PPP). 'This is equivalent to $5 per day for every person on the planet, or 11 times the size of global foreign direct investment (FDI),' the report stated.[8] Yet, at the same time we are spending less and less on peace. Figures show that UN peacekeeping expenditure of $8.27 billion totalled only 1.1% of the estimated $742 billion of economic losses from armed conflict.[9] US expenditure for its wars in the Middle East and the war on terror now totals $4.79 trillion, according to figures from the US based Watson Institute of International Public Affairs. The United States has spent or taken on obligations to spend more than $3.6 trillion on the wars in Iraq, Afghanistan, Pakistan and Syria and by the Department of Homeland Security. These numbers, however, do not include all future interest on debt associated with the wars, which could climb to $7.9 trillion by 2053, according to the Institute's Cost of War Project. This is the most comprehensive analysis of the budgetary costs available and represents 'a staggering, human and social impact of the wars,' says Catherine Lutz, co-director of the project and the Thomas J. Watson Jr. Family Professor of International Studies and Professor of Anthropology at Brown University.[10] Even Britain's military operations since the end of the cold war have cost £34.7bn and a further £30bn may have to be spent on long-term veteran care, according to a study by the Royal United Services Institute (RUSI); its 'Wars In Peace' report, also argues that the bulk of the money has been spent on interventions in Iraq and Afghanistan, both judged to have been strategic failures.[11]

The costs of war can conceivably be sidestepped as an abstraction but the processes themselves are always more immediate. Acted out in variable settings and at differently calibrated intensities, they seem to deliver the same menu of modern apocalypse and nihilistic destruction, built around a steady diet of death, injury and dislocation. The machinery of war is designed with a set of moving parts that are instantly recognisable, a constant presence in the topography of our active imagination alongside the accompanying mental photo-library. When we visualise war, we tend to conjure up the same stock of images: khaki clad ranks going over the top on the first day of the Somme, bombers jettisoning their payloads over Dresden or Cambodia, a platoon of grunts wading knee-deep through rice paddies in the Mekong Delta, and latterly Iraqi special forces inching their way into a booby-trapped and toxic West Mosul.

We all harbour images of war, though most of us in the West are lucky enough not to have to experience its reality at close quarters. These images and what we think and feel about them come to us through a series of filters that involve layers of moral and pragmatic choice, often including censorship, fact selection, packaging and presentation by others, most of them unknown to us, unelected, unaccountable and driven by interests that in hindsight often prove not to have coincided with our own. What messages are we directed to take from our wars and by whom?

With an increasing degree of sophistication, propaganda stories have been used in tandem with some form of censorship to shape public opinion about war throughout the 20th century and into the 21st, along a trajectory that reaches from the first atrocity propaganda in 1914 depicting Belgian babies skewered on the points of German bayonets to the 1990 Gulf War fiction of Iraqi soldiers snatching babies from hospital incubators in Kuwait City and the allegations of Viagra fuelled mass rape in Ghaddafi's unravelling Libya in 2011.[12] The military management practice of Information Operations (IO) imposes a form of initial censorship by manipulating the communications process, variously restricting access, content or sources to media, a strategy which enables greater control of output and can lead to factual distortion or omission.

Whilst we might be aware that contemporaneous media coverage of our wars has not always been reflected in the facts on the ground, we need wider recognition that the practices of media manipulation, perception management and the growing role of the information warrior now hold comparable status in conflict design alongside action in the field, a strategic and operational view shared by US and Islamic State war planners alike. 'I am not a national security strategist or a military tactician; I am a politician and a person who uses communication to meet public policy or corporate policy objectives. In fact, I am an information warrior and a perception manager.' This now notorious statement was made by John Rendon, founder of the Washington PR firm, The Rendon Group, in his speech to cadets at the U.S. Air Force Academy in 1996, in relation to his part in the Gulf War of 1990.[13]

What did he mean when he talked about perception management? Aside from within a professional bubble, this is an abstract concept that largely resonates in the briefing rooms of strategic war planners and communications teams in the Pentagon and Whitehall or the upper echelons of the communications business; its labyrinthine definition decodes as a mix of actions to convey and/or deny selected information and indicators to foreign audiences to influence their emotions, motives, and objective reasoning; 'in various ways, perception management combines truth projection, operations security, cover and deception and psychological operations.'[14]

This smoke and mirrors definition, using a language deliberately exclusive to insiders, is designed to remove an area of legitimate public interest further from view, creating in the process a self-sustaining sub-culture, a cabal of professionals over whom we have little authority. In the same breath, the mandate and role of the information warrior became an equal theme and priority of the Islamic State mind-set for total war, an approach which in many respects has meant that contemporary Islamist jihadist propaganda has been able to match and overtake its Western opposite as a more effective communication tool. 'Media weapons can actually be more potent than atomic bombs...indeed, it is no exaggeration to say that the media operative is a martyrdom-seeker without a belt; this decoration is well-deserved.' This powerful and provocative pronouncement was part of an Islamic State Directive about its use of propaganda for jihad against the West first published online in April 2016.[15] The Directive encapsulates at length just how important media strategy is in the IS grand scheme for total war and suggests that certain kinds of propaganda will have the power to outlast the act of conventional war itself. In the analysis which accompanies the translation and presentation of the Directive, it is referred to as setting a benchmark for insurgent strategic communications the world over.

Strategic Information Warfare

The use of information as a method of warfare is causing Western strategists and planners to rethink their approach. Addressing the information dimension of the global war on terrorism, experts such as former chief strategist in the US State Department's Counterterrorism

Bureau, David Kilcullen, have called for the development of a capacity specifically for strategic information warfare and an integrating function 'that draws together all the components of what we say and what we do.' Kilcullen has noted that '.'.. for Al-Qa'eda the main effort is information; for us, information is a supporting effort.'[16] The emphasis on the relationship between the physical and psychological aspects of contemporary operations highlights the importance of the role of strategic narratives. These are compelling storylines 'which can explain events convincingly and from which inferences can be drawn ... designed or nurtured with the intention of structuring the responses of others to developing events.'[17]

A successful narrative can help achieve strategic aims and 'link certain events while disentangling others, distinguish good news from bad tidings, and explain who is winning and who is losing.'[18] Establishing and putting across a convincing narrative is a concept at the heart of all successful modern communications, and it is one of the defining elements conspicuously absent from the West's approach to framing its relationships in the Arab world, either at home or in the region.

It is the inability to articulate and communicate a consistent and credible narrative that has been at the heart of Britain's reputational crisis in its information wars in the Middle East, from its equivocal promise of Arab independence after the First World War, to its abandonment of Palestine and a two-state solution in 1948, the deceit and disaster of the Suez betrayal in 1956, the arguably illegal invasion of Iraq in 2003 and its chaotic aftermath and the 2011 intervention in Libya. A story of poorly thought through information strategy and subsequent crisis management, disaster recovery, damage limitation and finally reputational deficit. The narrative structure through which these events has been processed shows how Britain's record comes up short, revealing a consistent and dismaying disconnection between what we say and what we do; what's more, it offers convincing proof that the communications medium can never overtake the message, that authentic information output cannot be trumped by any amount of sophisticated wrapping. If this is to change, we have to construct a different kind of narrative that enables us to communicate on equal terms, on a basis that is integrated and centrally managed, powered by modern values of leadership, governance, civil rights, and a clear break with the time served models that have shaped our past world view of the region, defining a narrative that above all is accommodative and inclusive of mainstream Arab and Islamic thinking.

Social Architects and War

Whilst in no sense a linear or exhaustive history of propaganda in individual conflicts, the evidence supports the case that modern communications thinking and tactics have been progressively engaged as part of an ongoing struggle for hearts and minds in the Middle East alongside objectives on the battlefield and in boardrooms; and furthermore that their use has been planned, managed and organised at the highest national level to operate with maximum impact on the collective psyche of nations and individuals.

In this context, modern information war can be plotted from its origins prior to and during the First World War through to the development of more ideologically driven and closely curated propaganda in the 1930s and Second World War, and beyond that to the more fragmented and opaque practices of the present day. What does the term social architecture mean, and who qualifies as a social architect?

Though generally taken in its meaning to describe the conscious design of an environment that promotes particular types of social behaviour, I have interpreted the term in this case more narrowly as applying to those individuals whose theories and actions have together been pivotal in developing the way in which mass communication is used by governing elites to influence public opinion. The term sits alongside other more specialist phrases such as 'engineer of consent' to describe those innovators at the confluence of systems theory, organisational development, psychology, social psychology and communications theory.

Together with the intellectual explorers who have collectively enabled this new and often secretive mechanism for selling ideas on a mass scale, this analysis examines some of the more strikingly successful interpreters of those ideas, the politicians, propagandists and mythomanes with the means and opportunity to convert theory into campaigning and in the process change attitudes, behaviours and lives. These include the earliest theorists of crowd behaviour such as Gustave Le Bon and Wilfred Trotter alongside formative analysts and shapers of public opinion, among them the groundbreaking American journalist and liberal thinker of the 1920s, Walter Lippmann, whose book 'Public Opinion' (1922) was so instrumental in fueling the ways in which both liberal democracies and fledgeling European dictatorships alike sought to influence and harness the public mind in Europe during the 1920s and 1930s. Some of the major contributors to the propaganda front that developed in tandem with the Great War, both in the US and Britain, are names perhaps less well known these days, among them George Creel, head of the US Committee on Public Information and Sir Campbell Stuart, Deputy Director of the British government propaganda department from early 1918; both these men were instrumental in setting the dial for the future development of propaganda in wars to come and wrote compelling accounts of their work in the Great War years. Creel's 'How We Advertised America' and Stuart's 'The Secrets of Crewe House' are both worthy of fresh consideration in the light of later, more complex styles of propaganda.

The American journalist and publicist Lowell Thomas' account of his time in the Hejaz and Palestine with Colonel T. E. Lawrence, recalled in 'With Lawrence in Arabia,' offers a unique representation of perhaps the greatest icon of wartime propaganda. Never have these techniques been more cleverly or assiduously applied to promote the story of one individual in the national cause – Lawrence remaining a man whose time in harness in the service of the British Empire remains more mythologised than perhaps any individual in military history. The exploitation of Lawrence and the Arab Revolt to counter the narrative of military jihad propagated by Ottoman Turkey and its German ally was at the heart of the West's strategy to dominate the post First World War Middle East, and its impact has resonated through the subsequent century of political realignment in the region.

The major influencers on the Middle East's development in the second half of the 20th century include a clutch of Arab political leaders and consummate propagandists such as Egypt's Gamal Abd Al Nasser, Iraqi President Saddam Hussein and PLO leader Yasser Arafat in Palestine, alongside the lesser-known Haj Amin Al Husseini, the Palestinian Grand Mufti of Jerusalem who worked closely with the Nazis to unseat the British and saturate the Arab world with anti-Jewish propaganda throughout the Second World War. In turn, the British Prime Minister during the era-defining Suez crisis of 1956, Sir Anthony Eden, took a strong personal hand in the strategic direction and tactical roll out of British propaganda directed at Egypt and especially his direct adversary, Nasser.

Britain's secret wars in Yemen and Oman in the 1970s, and the subsequent outsourcing of propaganda and information war since Operation Desert Shield in 1990, has spawned its own growth industry around the world and brought with it niche suppliers of independent, conflict conversant communications expertise; specialist interventionists who are more pervasive and intrusive in their inherent model and game plan. Too little is still known about this new breed of social architect, men like the head of the US-based The Rendon Group,

John Rendon, or British firm Bell Pottinger, whose style and legacy of perception management came so badly unstuck during the summer of 2017 in the outing of its role in destabilising the South African government. These and others were highly influential in selling the tainted versions of freedom and democracy in the First Gulf War of 1990 and the 2003 Iraq War to the West, the Iraqis and their neighbours. Above all else, it is the switch in Western propaganda to this model, fragmented, un-coordinated and driven by private sector expedience which has in part created the deficit now being felt by the West in its battle to control hearts and minds in the region.

One illustration of this gap is afforded by current Salafi jihadist propaganda, and most overtly the precision tooled output of Islamic State under the supervision of its late Head of Media Operations, Syrian Ahmad Abousamra.[19] On this jagged front line of the information war, the West is losing territory to students of propaganda who have now moved beyond their Western teachers to become stylised 'media mujahidin,' in whose hands the camera is judged to be as important a weapon as the gun. What they have absorbed and refined in their information operations reproduces some of the traditional traits previously outlined but also marks a departure into the innovative and darkly imaginative, even capable of injecting a modernist twist by introducing the child friendly animated cartoon as a softer, lower impact propaganda tool.[20] With the merging of conventional and insurgent war in the melting pot of the modern day Middle East, especially in countries such as Syria and Iraq so recently under occupation by Islamic State and others, the technology-enabled digital and social media based propaganda campaigns that have taken the images associated with war atrocities and their appeals for recruits directly into the Western home through the mobile channels of the tablet and the smartphone require increased scrutiny.

A report by UK based think tank Policy Exchange in September 2017 found that online jihadist propaganda attracts more clicks in the UK than any other country in Europe.[21] Britain is the fifth-biggest audience in the world for extremist content after Turkey, the US, Saudi Arabia and Iraq, the report found. In the 21st century, it seems that propaganda must now occupy new spaces, bypassing traditional channels and opening up a direct dialogue with individuals, groups and tribes, a much more devolved and informal sort of communications model than in previous wars, one less inhibited by censorship and facilitated by the ubiquity and speed of mobile communications and the powerful concept of open and shared access.

Defining Propaganda

Propaganda is concerned with the management of opinions and attitudes 'by direct manipulation of social suggestion.' The concept of propaganda as an instrument of war and a means of achieving foreign policy aims can be seen in one sense as a management tool exercised by governments in their pursuit of power; the term is most often used in a pejorative context to give the sense of information that is one-sided and intrinsically corrupted and propagandists portrayed as hidden persuaders, puppet masters pulling the strings of the public consciousness. Even now, its methodology is little understood by outsiders even whilst its practice has leaked into almost every area of public life. The late Arthur Siegel (d. 2010), Professor of the Communications Studies Program at Canada's York University is credited with categorising propaganda into four basic varieties: the first, and one which he argues that Western Governments no longer engage in as untenable, he defined as 'The Big Lie,' for example the Nazi paranoid delusion that an international Jewish conspiracy planned to seize power in the US, Britain and the Soviet Union and then launch a war to destroy the Nazi regime and exterminate the German people. The second variety relies on the precept that something doesn't have to be true, but simply plausible. The third variety requires the truth but a withholding of the other side's point of view, generally meaning censorship or at least self-censorship; and the fourth and most productive according to Siegel is to tell the truth, warts and all.[22]

Whichever model propagandists might use, they tend to mine the same rich seam of practical campaigning tools; highly selective stories are presented as comprehensive, stories are underpinned by partial facts, planted 'experts' supply informed opinion, insight and thought leadership when in reality they are peddling an officially approved version of events, and often the focus on a narrow range of discourse in which the boundaries are limited gives the illusion of free debate where in reality none exists. One example of this latter approach can be found in Kuwait's parliamentary elections in 2013, which offered an approximation of democracy (sometimes described as a 'semi-democracy') but denied voters a full version due to the absolute nature of the monarchy, a model that is replicated in the island state of Bahrain.

Understanding propaganda means getting inside its language. This language can be deliberately obscure, partly reflecting its technical basis and partly its trajectory over the last century from a relatively simple construct into progressive specialisms, sub-cultures and a heavily nuanced set of hybrids. These include a bewildering confusion of fundamentally abstract concepts, from perception management to psychological operations, and from Information Operations to public diplomacy.

Modern propaganda is perhaps best rationalised in three distinct phases, the first 'systematic' of these broadly incorporating First World War practices; the second 'scientific' phase emerging into use through the early 1920s and 1930s and into the post-war period; and a third phase of 'specialist' propaganda which, from the Second World War onwards has accommodated a range of different interpretations of the traditional form including psychological operations, perception management and public diplomacy. Sir Campbell Stuart, head of the British propaganda effort at Crewe House from early 1918, could be seen as one of the first along with his US counterpart, George Creel, to systematise the formal practice of propaganda, building it into a recognisable management discipline with a set of structures and processes which made it accountable and its impact, by the standards of the time, measurable. Whilst he personally believed that all propaganda needed to be true, unlike some of his predecessors, he equally prescribed that before any propaganda could be produced a clear information policy should be defined based on rigorous analysis of the military, economic and social facts and any outstanding counter arguments identified and eliminated. Only then could the tactical dimension of propaganda be deployed effectively. In his book, 'The Secrets of Crewe House,' Stuart, like Creel, was especially anxious to stress these formalising aspects of his approach, seeing himself as someone whose department's wartime success was at least in part due to his ability to bring some sort of order from chaos.

The emergence and rise after the First World War of public relations (PR) as a more scientifically centred and complex discipline driven by the principles of systems theory, organisational development and group psychology, brought a fresh strategic dimension to the possibilities of propaganda and infused its second post-World War One phase. Defining itself as a discipline that looks after reputation with the aim of earning understanding and support and influencing opinion and behaviour, PR now describes its modus operandi as 'the planned and sustained effort to establish and maintain goodwill and mutual understanding between an organisation and its publics.'[23] The milestone that marks the formal advent of this more psychological approach is the publication in 1923 of 'Crystallising Public Opinion,' the manifesto written by Edward Bernays about the new pseudoscience of public relations which was to change the way in which communications was both perceived and used.[24]

Persuasive PR is now a growing and legitimate part of the organisational management process, a global business in its own right worth over £13 billion annually in the UK alone.[25] PR and propaganda, though ethically distinct from each other, share many of the same genealogical features and are part of the same intellectual tradition designed to bring systematic force to bear on shaping the public mind. In war it is inevitably realpolitik that trumps ethics and this, after all, was the reality of the hidden government information machine that manufactured the first fake news and created atrocity propaganda so effectively in the Great War, and which as a matter of founding principle, was designed to leave no trace of ownership. It is a reality that has resonated in successive interventions in the Middle East, as part of the information landscape prior to Suez, in the case for pre-emptive action put to the British Parliament to support the invasion of Saddam Hussein's Iraq in 2003 (the so-called 'dodgy dossier') and in the subsequent campaign of perception management and distortion rolled out by the US and its allies to subvert the post-invasion information environment in Iraq.

All About Perception

Since the 1930s, when this more psychological style of propaganda was taken up as the predominant model by all sides waging information war, successive specialisms have fragmented the field so that deeper layers of knowledge and skills have been added to the propagandist's toolkit. The post 1945 decades of colonial and insurgent wars introduced more comprehensively the practice of psychological operations (PsyOps) as a narrower, more targeted construct using advanced ideas and techniques of persuasion and employing deliberately opaque operational terminology (for example, the PsyOps lexicon uses the terms 'black,' 'grey' and 'white' to grade degrees of disinformation). This more modernistic reinterpretation of propaganda has been applied in wars from Vietnam and Kenya to Malaya and Korea and was part of Britain's military response to the insurgent wars in Oman and Yemen during the 1960s and 1970s.

The military ownership and deployment of PsyOps in war theatres has served to make propaganda more mysterious and to remove it further from public view. An example of 'Black' PsyOps, taken from post-invasion Iraq in February 2003, tells the story of Radio Tikrit, a reportedly CIA established radio station which built its credibility on the basis that it was being run by loyal Saddam supporters in the Tikrit area but which, within weeks, changed its tone to become overtly critical of Saddam, a ruse which the CIA hoped the audience would not detect.[26]

To this highly specialised branch of conflict centric propaganda can be added 'perception management,' a further extension of the practice. This concept, a hybrid of a modern communications model but with a conflict zone focus, has grown into maturity since the first Gulf War of 1990, the invasion of Afghanistan in 2001 and the Iraq War of 2003; it has become the predominant, most powerful and pervasive propaganda tool at work in the service of the West in the conflict zones of the Middle East.

The concept was pioneered in the 1980s under the Reagan administration in order to avoid the public opposition to future wars that was seen during the Vietnam War, according to journalist Kenneth G. Eade.[27] At the onset of the Iraq war in 2003, journalists were embedded with US troops as combat cameramen. The reason for this was not to show what was happening in the war, but to present the American view of it. 'Perception management was used to promote the belief that weapons of mass destruction (WMD) were being manufactured in Iraq to promote its military intervention, even though the real purpose behind the war was regime change,'[28] he wrote.

The idea driving perception management is to change attitudes and behaviours by creating a pseudo environment, controlling critical elements of information (including disinformation) central to decision-making by the targeted audience. This methodology allows the propagandist to overlay a constructed version of reality upon the existing facts, the equivalent of an existential conjuring trick.

One of the most quoted examples of perception management at work concerned the story spread after the Iraqi invasion of Kuwait in August 1990, when a variation of 'bayonet baby effect' atrocity propaganda caught the news agenda. This infamous incident, later to be challenged, promoted a supposed eye witness account of Iraqi soldiers breaking into the Al-Adan hospital in Kuwait City and throwing babies out of intensive care incubators in order to take the expensive machines back to Iraq, leaving up to 300 premature babies to die on the floor. The story travelled around the globe and was held up time and again as an example of Iraqi barbarism; in the public discourse about the wrongs or rights of the war it achieved in time an iconic, emblematic status. Only when its originator was revealed as the 15-year-old daughter of the Kuwaiti ambassador to the United States, Saud Nasir Al-Sabah, and her testimony at the Congressional Human Rights Caucus on 10th October

1990 was shown to have been prepared for her by a senior executive of the global PR firm Hill & Knowlton, did the truth emerge. Her account was exposed by investigative journalists as fictitious and part of Hill & Knowlton's campaign of perception management undertaken for the Kuwaiti Government in exile.[29]

Public Diplomacy and Soft Power

Public diplomacy, a term only coined in the mid-1960s by the Dean of the Fletcher School of Law and Diplomacy, Edmund Gullion, is now ubiquitous though it remains little understood. It has morphed over the decades to embrace conceptual shifts in both meaning and application. These days, the term tends to be applied to the multiple ways in which governments can bypass traditional mechanisms and channels of communication in favour of direct interaction between groups, peoples and cultures beyond national borders; it has been defined as 'a key mechanism through which nations foster mutual trust and productive relationships.'[30] The idea is that organisations which are representative of a nation's values and reflective in the broad sense of its policies and civil and human rights profiles, should act as primary influencers in shaping the views of people in other countries, thereby impacting indirectly on their own governments and affecting policy accordingly.

The travelling companion of public diplomacy is soft power. Harvard University Professor Joseph Nye coined this phrase to describe a nation's power of attraction as opposed to the hard power of coercion; soft power most typically derives from culture, political values and foreign policy.[31] Soft power, itself an opaque concept to many, has been defined as the ability to get desired outcomes because 'others want what you want ... the ability to achieve goals through attraction rather than coercion.'[32]

But where does propaganda finish and public diplomacy start? Edmund Gullion admits they are basically the same thing:

> 'to connote this activity, we tried to find a name. I would have liked to call it 'propaganda.' It seemed like the nearest thing in the pure interpretation of the word to what we were doing. However, 'propaganda' has always had a pejorative connotation ... to describe the whole range of communications, information and propaganda, we hit upon 'public diplomacy.'[33]

It is hard to escape the echoes of Edward Bernays 45 years earlier, minting the phrase 'public relations counsel' to explain how he too arrived at a more palliative way of describing propaganda in a peacetime, private sector context.

In the Middle East, both the West and Arab states have been practising public diplomacy for years, though it was not always necessarily travelling under that name. A year before the Suez crisis of 1956, the British government had noticed with growing concern that the Egyptians were seeking to spread their influence by gaining cultural leadership of the Arab world using Egyptian press, radio and the teaching profession to gain a beachhead amongst Arabic speaking audiences. To counter this insidious threat to their oil interests, the British committed more money and resources to beefing up their capacity to influence opinion in the region indirectly, by committing more cash to initiatives including the British Council, which they identified as 'perhaps the most effective instrument for spreading our power.'[34] Accordingly, the British Council was awarded in 1956 a special budget of £150,000 (equal to about £3.5 million today) to fund expansion in the region. This, says the Council today, was the 'result of Government reviews into its activities, reinforcing the importance of the region to future British interests, and our unique role in developing relationships between the UK and countries in the region.'[35] The organisation has remained amongst the most visible and enduring examples of soft power in action, providing language skills and broader cultural opportunities to students from across the region. However, the Council is regularly accused of cultural imperialism or worse; Russia has closed its offices in Moscow and St Petersburg on more than one occasion in recent decades amidst accusations of spying for the state.

It is the emphasis put on spreading influence via the power of attraction that retains the essence of the meaning of public diplomacy and which is generally considered as the most appropriate to its modern usage. In other words, if one interprets hard power as the ability to change another's position by force or inducement, soft power implies the ability to shape the preferences of others by attraction, an idea that becomes more fraught with complexity the more it is scrutinised.

CHAPTER II

The Machinery of Public Opinion, Propaganda and Persuasion

Yet democracies, if we are to judge by the oldest and most powerful of them, have made a mystery out of public opinion. There have been skilled organisers of opinion who understood the mystery well enough to create majorities on Election Day. But these organisers have been regarded by political science as low fellows...'

Walter Lippmann,
Public Opinion (1922)

For both historical and political reasons, the testing and measurement of public opinion in the Arab world has been infrequent and hard to achieve; indeed the term 'public opinion' in the Arabic political vocabulary (Arr'ai Al 'amm) exists only as a direct translation from the English meaning. This anomaly, which is finally correcting itself, created a mask through which it has been difficult to perceive the attitudes, opinions and behaviours that together have characterised either any national or distinctly 'Arab' point of view towards the West. More recently, regular consumer polling by the Arab Opinion Index, Arab Barometer, Zogby Research, Arab News and others has started to provide a much more consistent and statistically valid picture of public opinion on a range of national and regional issues across the Arab world. It has become possible, for example, to quantify the widespread lack of belief in US foreign policy and the worry about its exercise of power in the region. Similarly, the testing of British and US domestic opinion about events in the Arab world has also been infrequent, generally being considered only at critical points when political and military crises such as Palestine, Suez or the Iraq war overrode commercial or political agendas. Most Western publics then as now did not know very much about the Middle East or Arab people, having traditionally seen them as distant and disconnected; propaganda and misinformation were thus perfectly placed to play a major role in establishing and perpetuating negative images of an Arab stereotype. Some of this thinking has had an enduring legacy in the West.

A UK public opinion poll, commissioned in August 2017 by the newspaper Arab News to measure British attitudes to the Arab world, put a spotlight on the extent of this issue. The poll revealed that the levels of stereotyping of Arab people remains worryingly high, especially amongst a section of the British population who are against immigration and the large minority (41%) who do not feel that Arab immigrants make a contribution to society. The tendency to be concerned about Islamophobia whilst at the same time holding Islamophobic views comes as no surprise to some commentators. Scott Lucas, Professor of International Politics at the University of Birmingham in the UK says of the apparent disparity, 'our society is not immune to government rhetoric; everyone is being influenced by it, even if they are not aware of it.'[1] Miqdaad Versi, assistant secretary-general of the Muslim Council of Britain (MCB) goes further. He claims that 'Islamophobia is now socially acceptable within society. The government needs to take real action…a direct link between government rhetoric and Islamophobia is difficult to prove but the atmosphere of hostility that has been created by certain politicians is clear and dangerous.'[2]

Cracking the Orientalist Code

Some of the roots of this negative stereotyping lie in the near distant past. The occupation of Egypt by Napoleon Bonaparte's France between 1798 and 1801, accepted by historians as the starting point of the modern Middle East, offers the best snapshot of the state of public opinion in the Arab world at the start of the 19th century. This powerful, though brief, episode in history was to reveal that the relationship between Europeans and Arabs was, in essence, one of colonial master and subject, scientist and specimen. It is here where the curious might most productively seek the first systematic evidence of 'otherness' that in time was to develop into racial stereotyping and eventually the more modern phenomenon of Islamophobia. Napoleon's invasion force arrived with a commission of over 100 scholars and scientists (known as 'savants') tasked with observing and recording every aspect of life in Egypt, including its administration, social organisation, religious practices, cultural mores and even cuisine. One of the lasting impacts of this vast French 'hothouse' study, the *Déscription de l'Egypte*, was to reveal the major strategic and tactical significance of the Middle East to Europeans, and it acted as a trigger for the French and British to play out their ambitions of colonial domination in the eastern Mediterranean, becoming in time 'the foundation of modern research into the history, society, and economics of Egypt.'[3]

The eventual codification of this phenomenon as 'Orientalism' has now entered the lexicon as a distinct way of describing the overall dynamics of the relationship between the European West and the Arab world as the 19th century progressed. Orientalism, according to the American Palestinian academic Edward Said, had three interconnected designations: as a set of ongoing academic doctrines and theses, a style of thought based upon epistemological and ontological distinction made between 'Orient' and 'Occident' and as a Western style for dominating, restructuring and having authority over the Orient.[4] Said referred to Orientalism as a primarily British and French cultural enterprise, 'a project whose dimensions take in such disparate realms as the imagination itself, the whole of India and the Levant, the Biblical texts and the Biblical lands, the spice trade, colonial armies and a long tradition of colonial administrators, a formidable scholarly corpus, innumerable Oriental "experts" and "hands..." ' [5]

The logical conclusion of Orientalist thought and effort is to be found in the conception and construction by the French visionary Ferdinand de Lesseps of the Suez Canal in November 1869. De Lesseps, at a stroke, had managed to 'melt away' the Orient's geographical identity by almost literally dragging the Orient into the West and finally dispelling the threat of Islam. It was especially telling that, to trigger the Suez crisis in November 1956, Egyptian leader Gamal Abd Al Nasser used the code word 'De Lesseps' to signal the nationalisation of the Suez Canal Company whilst at the same time Egyptian nationalists tore down his statue.[6]

Edward Said sparked an ideological war upon the publication of his seminal and provocative work in 1978, most notably with the late Middle East historian and influential conservative ideologue Bernard Lewis (1916-2018). Said's iconoclastic analysis has struck an enduring if controversial chord. 'Since the Oriental was a member of a subject race, he had to be subjected: it was that simple,' he wrote.

Egypt's importance to Britain increased dramatically with the construction of the Suez Canal, and the subsequent Anglo-Egyptian War of 1882 marked the start of a new era of foreign policy in the Middle East based on active intervention in the political and economic trajectory of the region. With a continuous presence in Egypt that was to last in some form until the withdrawal of its military garrison from the Suez Canal in 1956, Britain never stopped to ask too many questions about the legitimacy of the occupation. Public opinion within the country was monitored as a doctor would a patient, with a view to treating cases of political inconvenience by surgical removal. For example, Egyptian nationalist Ahmad Al 'Urabi was exiled to Ceylon in 1882, the leader of the Wafd Party, Saad Zaghloul, to Malta and then the Seychelles in 1919 and Muslim Brotherhood founder Hasan Al Banna exiled to Qena in Upper Egypt in 1948. The Anglo-Egyptian War proved a turning point in Egypt's growing political consciousness, nationalist ambition and desire to move public opinion towards political action.

In some respects, this treatment was consistent. At the time of Gustave Le Bon's writing of 'The Crowd: A Study of the Popular Mind' in 1895,[7] public opinion as an independent force in the Arab countries of the Middle East had been repressed by nearly four centuries of occupation and political and intellectual domination by Ottoman Turkey. All the countries of the modern Middle East had been progressively incorporated into the expanding Ottoman Empire, Egypt in 1517, Algeria in 1529, much of Persia by 1638 and the entire region including the Hejaz by 1683. Still largely intact at the start of the First World War, the Ottoman Empire was only finally dismantled by a series of international treaties in 1920 when the impact of its defining decisions up to and during the war was finally reflected in pariah status and near bankruptcy. Whilst the Ottoman occupation of the Levant, Hejaz and Mesopotamia had continued uninterrupted until the start of the First World War, it had been forced to deal with setbacks elsewhere in its territories; progressively Algeria, Libya and Egypt had slipped from its control, starting a process of irreversible erosion of its power and reach in North Africa.

Manipulation of Public Opinion
To frame modern propaganda in the context of the geopolitics and historical trajectory of the Middle East, it is necessary to have an overarching view of the political, social and psychological currents that were sweeping across Europe as the 20th century progressed. For it is amongst this confluence of ideas and tensions that propaganda came to knit itself into the narrative of the region and this process which in turn enabled a more codified and scientific style of communications

to emerge from the propaganda successes of the First World War. This advance took the possibilities associated with the manipulation of public opinion into a new dimension, in contrast to the 'craft' publicity model typically practised until then by the hucksters and press agents who successfully exploited newspapers as vehicles for their clients. In seeking to explain the mechanisms driving propaganda, the American journalist Walter Lippmann wrote, 'the creation of consent is not a new art. It is a very old one which was supposed to have died out with the appearance of democracy. But it has not died out. It has, in fact, improved enormously in technique, because it is now based on analysis rather than on rule of thumb.'[8]

Influence and control over crowd behaviour, a critical issue for the British in Egypt and other colonial territories, was of serious interest to Western political leaders in the late 19th and early 20th centuries as the age of mass movements started to both enfranchise and destabilise populations fired up by popular revolution in Russia in 1917, the birth of European socialism and the rise of trade unionism as the industrial revolution matured. Until then, the ruling classes had lived on the basis of comfortable assumptions of superiority, propped up by centuries of inherited wealth derived from land ownership, tax raising power and profitable trade. It became a matter of greater urgency not only to understand the motivations but also to be able to control the behaviour of these increasingly empowered masses as they grew in strength and confidence in pursuit of civil and human rights, living wages and better working conditions. A select group of thinkers became instrumental in trying to unlock this dilemma and were, in turn, to become highly influential in shaping the way in which the elites thought about containing and managing the masses and, in turn, exerting some control over public opinion as an existential threat.

A towering figure in this intellectual debate, whose work was to be studied by US Presidents and Fascist dictators alike, was the French social psychologist and theorist, Gustave Le Bon (1841-1931). Le Bon set out his ideas in a number of important works, the most widely circulated and best known at the time being 'The Crowd: A Study of the Popular Mind.' This radical, analytical tour de force became arguably the most influential treatise of its time. The book sought to isolate the central characteristics of crowd psychology, claiming that 'an individual immersed for some length of time in a crowd soon finds himself...in a special state, which much resembles the state of fascination in which the hypnotised individual finds himself in the hands of the hypnotiser.'[9]

At the heart of Le Bon's thesis was the assertion that crowds are the enemy of civilisations, which themselves are only ever constructed by a small intellectual aristocracy. Left to the mercy of the crowd, civilisations were inevitably brought down. 'History tells us that from the moment when the moral forces in which a civilisation rested have lost their strength, its final dissolution is brought about by those unconscious and brutal crowds known, justifiably enough, as barbarians,'[10] he wrote, comparing the destructive nature of crowds to microbes that hasten the dissolution of enfeebled or dead bodies.

Amongst Le Bon's conclusions was the notion that the crowd did not have the wit to adopt ideas that were complex; to be accessible they must be simplified and, having been simplified, they then needed to become 'a sentiment,' as it were to be felt. Only at this point could an idea then enter the unconscious and become influential. Le Bon's idea of the simplification of a message to an essential core, and its packaging as a powerful image to inspire emotion that could transcend rational response, has been one of the most potent and enduring insights underpinning the modern practice of communications.

The Quality of Prestige
A contemporary and critic of Le Bon was the Austrian psychoanalyst Sigmund Freud. Referring to Le Bon's book as 'deservedly famous,' Freud concluded that the book presented 'a brilliantly executed picture of the group mind,' though he did not accept all of the book's findings and did not believe that it brought forward much that was new.[11] One area of disagreement was in Le Bon's analysis of the qualities required for leadership and their relation to individual leaders, who he saw as needing to be imbued with prestige, regarding this quality as a form of domination which paralyses the critical faculties of the individual much in the same way as hypnosis. Prestige, according to Le Bon, ebbs and flows with success and is lost in the event of failure. Freud's own crowd behaviour theory suggested the formation of any group automatically allowed the possibility of the revival of what he called 'the primal horde' and that human groups therefore exhibit the familiar picture of an individual of superior strength ('the primal father') among a troop of similar companions. 'The psychology of such a group... corresponds to a state of regression to a primitive mental activity, of just such a sort as we would be inclined to ascribe to the primal horde,'[12] he wrote.

The role of leadership as a gatekeeper to authority and thus also control of the crowd was an obsession that came to pervade British thinking about the shaping and preservation of its interests in the Middle East, and they were quick to identify and sideline nationalists, religious leaders and others who they thought might pose a threat to order. Subsequent analysis of the leadership style commonly ascribed to the authoritarian Arab political state reveals a type somewhere on the axis of prestige and strength, usually but not exclusively associated with the officer class of the armed forces, nurtured by a power base built on small, receptive closed groups who in turn are beneficiaries of a pervasive culture of patronage.

This association is recognisable in Egypt's leadership succession since 1952 that includes General Muhammad Neguib, Colonel Gamal Abd Al Nasser, Colonel Anwar Sadat, Air Chief Marshal Hosni Mubarak and General Abd Al Fattah Al Sisi, excluding the brief aberration of the democratically elected Muslim Brotherhood member President Muhammad Morsi following the Arab Spring. The attendant iconography of this style of leadership is thus heavily imbued with military regalia and symbols and invariably fuelled by psychological principles including idealisation and projection, a template that could be said to also embrace the profiles of Libya's Colonel Muammar Ghaddafi and Iraq's Saddam Hussein. Both of these could be retrofitted into the leadership thesis proposed by Gustave Le Bon that the groups they control, suffused with an extreme passion for authority, naturally 'thirst for obedience.'[13] In perhaps the supreme example of this archetype, a detailed psychological analysis of PLO leader Yasser Arafat cast him as a living symbol of the Palestinian revolution, his perception of himself as a revolutionary leader reinforced by every detail of his external appearance, from his unshaven face and the kufiyah on his head to his military uniform and his ever present pistol, thereby reinforcing the myth surrounding his image as the father of the revolution and the very creator of its symbols.[14]

Freud also turned his attention to the work of British neurosurgeon and social psychologist Wilfred Trotter (1872-1939), whose 'Instincts of the Herd in Peace and War' published in 1916 became an influential and much studied source of expert diagnosis of crowd behaviour and group instinct. His thesis, which Freud referred to as 'thoughtful,'[15] offered an alternative explanation of crowd behaviour which Freud regarded as simpler but flawed. Trotter believed that gregariousness, like self-preservation, nutrition, or sex was a primary instinct of all individuals. Leaning on his observations of the behaviour of animals, Trotter claimed that herd instinct was manifested in three distinct types, 'the aggressive, the protective and the socialised, which are exemplified in Nature by the wolf, the sheep and the bee respectively.'[16] As part of his analysis, he pointed out the paradox of Germany being a state consciously directed towards a series of ideals and ambitions but also a state in which there exists 'a primitive type of the gregarious instinct – the aggressive – a type which shows the closest resemblance in its needs, its ideals and its reactions to the society of the wolf pack.'[17] This kind of comparison and analysis was highly influential in shaping British public opinion as to the character and ethos of the German military and was helpful in enabling the focus and direction of British propaganda in World War One, including laying the groundwork for the plausibility of some of the atrocity propaganda which was to become a feature of the information war on both sides. The psychology underpinning the manifesto of Islamic State and its leadership as exemplars of the aggressive and humourless type might have played neatly into Trotter's eccentric analogy of the wolf pack.

From Caricature to Character Assassination

Walter Lippmann suggested that the opportunities and means to manipulate public opinion were open to anyone who understood the process of influence. In his 1922 book 'Public Opinion,' he floated the notion that the knowledge of how to create consent would alter every political calculation and modify every political premise: 'under the impact of propaganda, not necessarily in the sinister meaning of the word alone, the old constants of our thinking have become variables.'

One of the most striking aspects of propaganda is its chameleon-like properties. Some propaganda strategies are underpinned by a reliance on the truth, others by the judicious use of falsehoods and yet others may deploy both these options and more besides. The difficulty tends to lie in determining which is which. Propaganda, though, is invariably motivated and organised so that it proves a particular point or showcases a certain value which can be either positive or negative. Its purpose is to inform, influence and persuade with a particular set of attitudinal or behavioural objectives in mind, for example, in war, the bolstering of civilian morale or the demonisation of an enemy. The trick of the propagandist is to deploy arguments and supporting facts on a selective basis to produce an emotional rather than rational response. The desired result is a change of the cognitive narrative of the subject in the target audience.

The use of psychological principles, including association and suggestion as means of shaping public opinion, is to be found threaded throughout Western communication strategy in the Middle East. The systematic personal stereotyping by Western media and politicians of a succession of uncompliant Arab political leaders from the 1950s onwards ranges from caricature to character assassination, both effective strategies in undercutting personal and political reputation. British Prime Minister Sir Anthony Eden unjustly characterised Egyptian President Gamal Abd Al Nasser as a fanatic and 'the new Mussolini' or 'Hitler of the Nile' up to and during the Suez crisis, and throughout the course of his leadership of the Palestinian political movement, the PLO leader Yasser Arafat was relentlessly lampooned and caricatured by Western media.[18] Naji Al Ali, the Palestinian cartoonist for the Kuwaiti newspaper Al Kubs, was even to lose his life in London because of a caricature that ridiculed Yasser Arafat and his supposed concealment of an unnamed lover. In turn, Saddam Hussein, for many years a convenient if not entirely trusted ally of the West, was latterly typecast as an uncontrolled psychopath as part of the PsyOps and perception management based information war waged against Iraq from Desert Shield in 1990 onwards, and Libya's President Muammar Ghaddafi made it all too easy for cartoonists to ridicule his posturing, public grandstanding and explosive, unpredictable narcissism.

Like Lippmann, the political scientist Harold Lasswell's contribution to the theory that underpins mass communications goes both wide and deep. Responsible for the first process-based model of propaganda in the 1920s, he expressed it as a simple progression through the communicator (who), the message (says what), the medium (in which channel), the receiver (to whom) and the effect (with what effect). During and beyond the First World War, Lasswell's model underpinned most government propaganda. He believed that the average person could quickly become vulnerable to the impact of political confrontation or economic depression, leaving them susceptible and open to persuasion by propaganda which had the innate power to offer them reassurance. Democracy, he thought, was fatally flawed in that openly conducted argument and debate led to psychosis and trauma amongst onlookers, requiring some control to be found over all forms of political communication that might lead to conflict. His solution was to use social research to find a way of replacing public discourse with democratic propaganda. 'The problem of the propagandist is to multiply all the suggestions favourable to the attitudes which he wishes to produce and strengthen, and to restrict all suggestions which are unfavourable to them,'[19] he wrote. In time, people would come to associate certain simple emotions, such as love or hate, with symbols and, in the longer term a systematic architecture of collective or 'master symbols' built on these individual symbols would in turn have the power to generate mass action in the targeted audience, for example in the emotional and patriotic response afforded by sustained exposure to a flag and national anthem. The adoption of this architecture of symbols was in due course to be manifested in the rituals and paraphernalia of the Green Shirts, Egypt's version of the Fascist Party that sprung up in the 1930s in parallel with the rise of European Fascism in Italy and National Socialist Germany; Lebanon's Christian Phalanges party, which originated at the same time, adopted the brown shirt as a graphic marker of political affiliation. This grand and all-encompassing vision of propaganda, its organisation and its use became the prevailing model for decades and itself became recognised in the minting of the new term 'scientific democracy' to describe its constitution, purpose and manipulation by groups of carefully selected social scientists chosen to propagate the use of 'good' propaganda in the cause of democracy.

The Father of Public Relations
As the most conspicuous individual to straddle the bridge between the ages of systematic and scientific propaganda, Edward Bernays (1891-1995) remains a figure of enduring importance and relevance and one whose impact on the narratives characterising the modern Middle East has been profound. His Olympian views, many of them based on the principles of group psychology studied through his uncle Sigmund Freud, were set out in a series of books spanning the inter-war years. Among them are works still widely acknowledged to be seminal, among them 'Crystallising Public Opinion' (1923) and 'Propaganda' (1928).

A nephew of the Austrian psychoanalyst Sigmund Freud on his mother's side of the family, Bernays was never slow to lean on the great man's ideas and reputation for a sense of direction and legitimisation of his own downstream theories on the role of human behaviour in shaping public opinions and attitudes. In 'Manipulating Public Opinion' (1928) he wrote, 'This is an age of mass production. In the mass production of materials, a broad technique has been developed and applied to their distribution. In this age, too, there must be a technique for the mass distribution of ideas.'

Bernays returned to the United States after his attendance at the Paris Peace Conference of 1919, greatly impressed by the success of US wartime propaganda in changing American public opinion in favour of entry into the War, and at the same time influencing European thinking. In a moment of profound insight, he realised that propaganda presented possibilities far beyond the government agenda, 'when I came back to the United States, I decided that if you could use propaganda for war you could certainly use it for peace. Propaganda got a bad reputation because of the Germans using it during the Second World War. So, what I did was try and find some other words, so we found the words 'counsel on public relations,'[20] he recalled.

What set Bernays' approach to propaganda apart from its wartime antecedent, though, was its use of psychological principles to engender human behaviours alongside perceptions so that the propagandists could 'engineer the consent' of the public without them knowing they were the subject of a subtle and pervasive manipulation. After the war, Bernays began to apply these principles successfully on behalf of a growing clientèle which embraced individuals, corporations and even nations all attracted by his powers of alchemy.

But his ideas were being noticed outside America too, and not just by corporates. In his own story, 'Biography of an Idea,' Bernays recounted how a famous foreign correspondent of the Hearst newspaper empire, Karl Von Wiegand (1874-1961), went to dinner with him at his home in 1933. During dinner, Wiegand talked about the Nazi Information Minister, Josef Goebbels, and his propaganda plan to consolidate Nazi power. 'Goebbels had shown Wiegand his propaganda library, the best Wiegand had ever seen. Goebbels, said Wiegand, was using my book 'Crystallising Public Opinion' as a basis for his destructive campaign against the Jews in Germany. This shocked me... obviously the attack on the Jews of Germany was no emotional outburst of the Nazis but a deliberate, planned campaign,'[21] he wrote. The academic and PR historian Stuart Ewen, who went to see Edward Bernays late in his life, reported being dazzled by the old man's ability to stage manage the presentation of his PR manifesto with masterful authority and yet come across as somewhat self-deluded in the process. 'Throughout our conversation, Bernays conveyed his hallucination of democracy, where a highly educated class of opinion moulding tacticians are continuously at work, analysing the social terrain and adjusting the mental scenery from which the public mind, with its limited intellect, derives its opinions,' he wrote in his introduction to 'Crystallising Public Opinion.'[22]

News, Images and the Truth
The role of truth in selling ideas in democracies is a perennial line of enquiry, ever more so now that we find ourselves in a post-truth world of alternative facts and fake news, and with traditional media ownership

and control more narrowly based than ever alongside a social media ecosystem that can successfully bypass conventional news distribution channels. But since the first press release was issued in the United States by Ivy Leadbetter Lee in 1906, the news process has been open to manipulation, often by journalists themselves.

Between government media departments, corporate press offices, military Information Operations and outsourced experts, it is little wonder that many people remain baffled by the authenticity of news and that there is a widespread and growing lack of trust in the quality of news content. The news sources that have traditionally been trusted as qualified, professional curators of impartial and independently verified facts, are themselves under growing pressure to produce more for less. Wherever the premium for professional journalistic intermediation is lowered, reliable public decision-making and the sources on which it depends are commensurately rendered more vulnerable.

A decade ago, research for the book 'Flat Earth News' by the Guardian newspaper chief investigative reporter Nick Davies revealed the extent of this declining news balance by showing that only 12% of the typical news content of quality UK daily newspapers is written by reporters, and only 12% of their facts are checked; the bulk is either entirely or partially sourced from PR and news wire sources.[23] The nature of the relationship between the news and the facts had also been a major source of investigation for Walter Lippmann; he was first to deconstruct the process of news gathering and dissemination, breaking it down from the point at which journalists identify news opportunities to the gathering and selection of facts and the random choices that are made in news editing, demonstrating that the final product may have little to do with the truth of anything but more to do with the 'shape' of events that can be reported.[24]

He took as his example the outbreak of the Great War, at which he believed American newspapers were caught at a major disadvantage, without any knowledge or experience of the subject. As London was the global news and cable centre and English was their native language, American newspapers with enough money to pay cable tolls imported their news from the British press, in the process developing a predetermined technical approach to reporting the war.[25] Lippmann came to conclude that the integrity of news was only really protected when there was a good machinery of record, otherwise the reporter would be simply overwhelmed with unrelated possibilities. The random nature of news prospecting made it all the more important for people to have press agents to introduce some control over news management, according to Lippmann.

Having hired a press agent, the temptation to then exploit his strategic position became very great. This process included fact selection and the introduction of opinion posing as news, together creating a filter through which the public were not allowed to see. Lippmann's analysis has clear resonances in the contemporary and pervasive epidemic of fake news and alternative facts that dominates today's news and current affairs debate. The impact of Lippmann's analysis of how to unlock the door of public opinion cleared the runway for propagandists to take off to a vast array of destinations they had not considered in any meaningful way, in directions not confined to national interests alone but across business, society and organisations.

From still photography and posters to cartoon and film, images were to become the consistent currency of successive iterations of propaganda over the ensuing decades, the connection that was most conspicuously able to evoke recall, response and action in audiences of all classes and persuasions. The power of images over words has also turned out to be a function of the highest impact journalism and has led in modern warfare to a new generation of digitally derived, image based propaganda that has become a highly effective weapon.

Early in the Great War, it became clear to British, then German, propagandists that still images and subsequently moving images, were more powerful than written reports in influencing the views of people on the Home Front. One British innovation that was remarkably effective was the idea of making films to support the war effort; a total of 240 feature length films were made in all, together with numerous shorts, among them a clutch of films explicitly produced to promote the British world view and its military campaigns in the Middle East, both in Palestine and Mesopotamia, in an effort to glamorise the war in the desert and portray clear British victories to audiences on the Home Front.[26] Whilst making relatively few official long films itself, the government deployed for the time the imaginative process of franchising these to voluntary organisations such as the British Topical Committee for War Films, which made a number of films from which the profits went to war-related causes, together with countless short films, many of which people accessed through newsreels influenced by the Ministry of Information (MOI). Most film output was overtly nationalistic and patriotic, with titles like 'Being Prepared' (1915) or 'For the Empire' (1916). As the war progressed, films became much harder hitting, forerunners of the new art of documentary. One classic, 'The Battle of the Somme,' directed by Geoffrey Malins and released in 1916 (now granted UNESCO Memory of the World status) was deeply controversial because of the shocking battle scenes, some of which it transpired had been re-created. Some 20 million people saw 'The Battle of the Somme,' which was shown in almost every cinema in Britain.

Many government documents show what an impact film had on the propaganda makers.[27] The follow-up to 'Battle of the Somme,' the more cinematically ground-breaking 'Battle of the Ancre,' shot live for the War Office by four different cameramen between September and November 1916, offered a new kind of personal and more holistic account of war seen from the ground up. 'The Battle of the Somme changed the attitude of the State to film and use of it. The film was widely regarded by elites as trashy and plebeian,'[28] says Dr Toby Haggith, Senior Curator at the Imperial War Museum and the man who re-mastered the film. "People who went to the cinema were starved of images, there were no scenes of infantry fighting so people would go and see the films in order to try and see their loved ones. The Battle of the Ancre was very successful in its aim of getting people behind the war effort. The benchmark of quality in documentary is truth and the cinematic elements of the film are very fine. Documentary comes of age with this film; this is an unimpeachable historical record, considered as gospel."

This documentary style was to be further pursued in 1917 and 1918 by the American film maker Lowell Thomas in his compelling account of T. E. Lawrence and the Arab Revolt, destined to become a post-war public sensation. Some of the grandiose, cinematic Islamic State propaganda set pieces, such as the mass execution of Syrian soldiers in the amphitheatre of the ancient Greco-Roman city of Palmyra in 2015, have borrowed from this dramatic style and tradition, in the process marking the arrival of atrocity propaganda films on an epic, movie theatre scale for the first time. In the years after the Great War, Lippmann, wrote, 'pictures have always been the surest way of conveying an idea and, next in order, words that call up pictures to memory.'

Information Culture and the Middle East

Propaganda in war thrives most easily when there is an overt or tacit agreement between government, the judiciary, the military and the media, using a combination of propaganda models coupled with self-censorship and/or formal censorship to manage a methodical and effective propaganda operation. This process has been successfully used multiple times by western democracies which have to eventually, under Freedom of Information Acts, account for their output of official information. This approach was first understood and mastered most conspicuously by British propaganda chief Sir Campbell Stuart from March 1918, as it was by George Creel, the architect of the US Committee on Public Information (CPI). Creel struck a voluntary deal with the media when the US intervened in the Great War, but German wartime propaganda, conversely, was initially less systematic and less reliant on a voluntary code, as a result, its output suffered early on from being perceived as inauthentic and lacking credibility.

Propaganda can be a difficult and delicate construct to manage in democracies where a high nominal value is placed on the integrity and authenticity of official information, however, in some other political environments propaganda values simply provide the prevailing standard of information and the ground is consequently more fertile for both domestic and foreign propagandists to exploit.

For the four centuries leading to the Great War, Ottoman rule in the Middle East was characterised by a close managerial style combined with the ever present threat of military force. Until the conclusion of the First World War and the partitioning of the Levant and Iraq into a series of Mandates, the role and status of public opinion and cultural expression in the Arab world was therefore typically marginalised, in some measure driven by the Ottoman ban on the Arabic printing press that endured from the 15th to 19th century. The political decision-making process did not commoditise the idea of public opinion to the extent that it was quantified, measured or taken into account in any systematic way. There were few mechanisms or channels via which people could make their views felt or receive information which they could independently validate; the information monopoly extended its grip through government, civil society and religious life and the mosque was as important a source of political and social exchange, as were the newspapers that existed. Thus, the Arab countries of the Middle East have traditionally found it difficult to balance a generally authoritarian model of government and clientelist culture with the parallel environment and demands of a free press, notwithstanding any faux liberal institutional reforms. From the late 19th century onwards, despite the regional literary and cultural revival known as the Nahda, which included the founding of the Egyptian daily newspaper Al Ahram in 1875, Arab journalists have generally been required to enter into an often dangerous struggle in order to investigate the facts and report the news that impacts their own populations and those across the region more widely, especially where it is critical of the political status quo.

Muhammad Heikal, arguably still the Arab world's most famous journalist was editor in chief of Al Ahram, Egypt's flagship state newspaper and the Arab world's most influential publication, from 1957 to 1974. His relationship with Egyptian President Gamal Abd Al Nasser was very close and the journalistic role he carved out included one as Nasser's speech writer and spokesman. Through years of on-off censorship of Egypt's media (at one stage every newspaper had its own individual censor) Heikal himself fell foul of the system and was arrested and temporarily jailed in 1978 by Nasser's successor Anwar Sadat, accused of both atheism and plotting to establish an alternative centre of power. Being a journalist in the Arab world often means walking the same high wire.

Most governments of Arabic speaking countries operate a system of full-time or occasional censorship to ensure control over newspaper and broadcast content and distribution, including recently the Internet. This system goes back a long way but contemporary examples are numerous: in May 2017, Egypt banned 21 websites, including the main website of Qatar-based Al Jazeera television and prominent local independent news site Mada Masr, accusing them of supporting terrorism and spreading false news,[29] in December 2016 Doha News, an independent news site based in Qatar, accused the Gulf states of blocking access to its website[30] and in reporting the seizure of the Arabic language newspaper Al-Sudani in Sudan in 2013, the organisation Reporters Without Borders (RWB) stressed the dire state of media censorship in Sudan after the Arab Spring, recording in 2012 the seizures of 20-plus newspapers by the intelligence and security services.

A further telling example is present in the West Bank, in the Occupied Palestinian Territory (OPT), currently under the shared control of the Palestinian Authority (PA) and the Israeli military. The introduction by the PA in summer 2017 of the Electronic Crimes Law made it simpler for the PA to crack down on any kind of dissent posted on web sites like Facebook, a major communication channel for journalists, civil society and consumer groups in the West Bank and Gaza. The arrest of the Al Aqsa TV reporter Tariq Abu Zaid, shortly after five other journalists were arrested on a single day in August, highlighted the PA's strategy of using the new law to close down up to 30 web sites used by independent journalists for news distribution in the West Bank. More sinisterly, a report by the human rights NGO Amnesty International says that the initial campaign has gone on to use the same law to widen its attack on journalists and activists, subjecting them to 'arbitrary arrests, violent interrogation, physical assaults and reporting bans.'

Amnesty has gone on to accuse the PA of stifling freedom of expression in Palestine, using police state tactics to silence critical media and arbitrarily block people's access to information. The scale of discrimination faced by journalists and independent media operations is daunting. In its 2017 Press Freedom Index, Reporters Without Borders (RWB), the world's leading NGO in the defence and promotion of freedom of information and support of independent journalism, ranked North Korea at 180, at the foot of all the countries included in the index, yet of those nearest the bottom, in the 12% worst ranked countries overall, were Syria (177), Sudan (174), Yemen (166), Bahrain (164), Libya (163) and Egypt (161).

The Palestinian West Bank and Gaza Strip, Oman, Egypt, Syria, and Saudi Arabia were picked out as five examples of Middle Eastern countries notorious for tight control over freedom of expression and information in print and online media. The Index serves to highlight the distance that still remains to be travelled in much of the region to achieve unhindered reporting of the facts and, at the same time, reinforces the notion that much of the information in public circulation is subject to censorship and the propagandist's scrutiny and control.

But alternative views are slowly finding expression, mainly due to the increasing democratisation of social media. The Egypt-based British freelance newspaper and television journalist Hugh Miles believes that the Qatari news organisation Al Jazeera has played a major role in opening up and democratising the media space in the Arab world. Speaking at the Fourth Annual Gulf Studies Forum in February 2018, he addressed the topic of regional and international dynamics and the role of the media, telling the audience that today the Gulf tops the world indexes for social media. 'These days, developments in new communications technology have dramatically levelled the playing field between the people and their regimes,' he said. Social media is toxic for totalitarian regimes, says Miles, who believes that a 'brutal process of defrocking and de-iconising' is a necessary psychological step before scaling the wall of fear, mentioning mass outings of individuals by WikiLeaks, the Panama Papers and investigative newspaper reporting. Miles believes too that Arab regimes 'have lost control of the Islamic message.'[31]

The news that British Government spin doctors have been dispatched to countries across the Middle East and North Africa (MENA) to help them improve the image of their own governments has come as proof, if it were needed, of the increased mainstreaming of information culture and policy in many Arabic speaking countries.[32] The report confirmed that a special unit in the UK Prime Minister's office now offers consultancy services in areas including crisis communications and 'establishing political clarity'; clients already include Jordan and Tunisia. Introductory meetings have taken place with the governments of Egypt and Algeria alongside a £2 million budget that is set to increase. Human rights groups have questioned whether British civil servants should be assisting countries with repressive censorship and little press freedom to improve their communications, the report concludes. The story is a powerful reminder that this generally closed information culture and media environment has played a major role in creating accommodative conditions for propaganda, both domestic and foreign originated. It flags up the need to move past the prevailing model of state control, censorship and proscribed media ownership to a more open culture which accommodates the realities of the digital and social media age.

Unfortunately, contemporary evidence has been generally conclusive that the Arab Spring has not only done little to improve the status quo but has actually exacerbated the position and speeded up the process of censorship and persecution of editors, journalists and photographers. Since the uprisings, there has been a sweeping movement to repress journalists and the press in the region in almost all Arab countries, except Tunisia, which currently persists with moving towards allowing broader freedoms. Many other countries, Turkey, Syria and Egypt among them, have fallen into political and social disarray as leaders have tightened media control and censorship in a bid to promote official lines. Turkey, in particular, under the increasingly interventionist government of Recep Tayyip Erdogan has mounted a systematic campaign against the country's free press, attacking journalism as a profession and targeting individual journalists, photographers and even cartoonists, making it more ironic that he turned the murder of Saudi dissident journalist Jamal Khashoggi in the Saudi consulate in Istanbul in October 2018 into an international cause celebre. 'The freedom of the press in the countries of the Arab Spring – Egypt, Libya, Syria, Iraq, Tunisia and Yemen – became more restricted than before,"[33] Mahasen al Emam, director of the Arab Women Media Center in Jordan, told The Media Line (TML), one of the first American non-profit news agencies created to address the need for full unbiased reporting from the Middle East. Whilst the Arab Spring called for overall reform, stability, and democracy, the outcome has been anything but. 'The real result of the Arab Spring is more political turbulence and instability,' Al Emam said. 'We have seen a global decline in freedom of information in the region because of the unstable regimes and unstable political and security environments.'[34]

But not all journalists working in the region are pessimistic. "It is very interesting to be working in a country that is transforming. I didn't think I would live to see the day when live entertainment is being imported, such as the Cirque Du Soleil, or even break dancing and when the power of the religious police is being curbed," says Faisal Abbas, Editor-In-Chief of Arab News, the English language daily based in Jeddah on Saudi Arabia's more cosmopolitan west coast. "We are living in a cryptic part of the world; are journalists still relevant when people can get access to content on social media that is convincing?"[35] he asks.

The brutal and premeditated murder of dissident Saudi journalist Jamal Khashoggi in October 2018 in the Saudi Consulate in Istanbul by a hit squad equipped with paraphernalia including syringes, bone saws and even a body double, may yet prove a game changer. The threat of a critical, independent voice such as Khashoggi's with his global audience reach was clearly deemed an existential threat but, even in the context of a closed and repressive information culture, the means and circumstances of his disposal sparked universal outrage. Perversely, the Khashoggi murder and its leverage by Turkey in its public fallout with Saudi Arabia has simply served as a further reminder that information war and the battle to control public opinion is now centre stage in the region, putting yet more reforming pressure on traditional closed information structures that have defined the media environment.

CHAPTER III

Military Jihad: Images and Themes of the Great War

'What is propaganda? It is the presentation of a case in such a way that others may be influenced. In so far as its use against an enemy is concerned, the subject matter employed must not be self-evidently propagandist. Except in special circumstances, its origin should be completely concealed. As a general rule, too, it is desirable to hide the channels of communication.'

Sir Campbell Stuart,
Secrets of Crewe House, The Story of a Campaign,
Hodder & Stoughton, September (1920)

For the most part, the First World War is still thought of as a European conflict, its seeds sown in the Balkans, its geopolitical interests and military battle lines drawn by the imperial powers of Germany, Britain, France, Italy and Russia, with armies from their colonial outposts progressively sucked into the conflict. Later, in 1917 when America entered the war, an international dimension was added to the fresh regiments of khaki-clad young men marching along the lanes of northern France. Statistically, the records do indeed show that the principal threads of the war were woven into the tapestry of the old imperial Europe, the political, economic and military effort between these great European powers focused on a struggle for control of the continent. In contemplating the scale and scope of the war itself and the campaigns in which it was fought and won, the mind is inevitably drawn to the Western Front, the jagged line that between 1914 and 1918 stretched from the English Channel down through Belgium, France, the borders of Germany and the disputed land of Alsace Lorraine as far as

Switzerland in the south, a 440 mile trenchscape marked by fields of torn metal, barbed wire and mine craters.

And yet, there was another war taking place in parallel with the European conflict, one which, as a relative sideshow, attracted far less publicity. The facts of this other war were more distant and thus its conduct never held the same immediacy as events on the Somme or at Verdun in the café and drawing room chatter that regulated the public mood. Though it did not generate the same headlines, its geographic reach made it intrinsic to the global perspective of the First World War, one in which Ottoman Turkey, Russia, Britain, Germany, France and a nascent Arab nation engaged in a long and bitter struggle for control of the lands that comprise the modern day Middle East, none of which existed politically in 1914 and all of which had been uninterruptedly part of the Ottoman Empire for over four centuries. These predominantly Muslim lands comprised much of what had been categorised by the British as the Orient, a still largely mysterious and exotic space that lay between Egypt and India, linked by the Suez Canal and entered generally by negotiation rather than accident.

They included little travelled areas of the region such as the Hejaz in the Arabian Peninsula, Baghdad in what was then Mesopotamia and a plethora of ancient cities and towns, many of which, for Westerners, were of biblical significance, part of the Christian heritage central to Western identity. Iconic names like Bethlehem, Jerusalem, Nazareth, Damascus and Aleppo sparked enduring images and emotions that had populated Christian consciousness since the Crusades were launched to retake the Holy Land between 1095 and 1291. These crusading years, in which Jerusalem provided a focal interest and physical goal, were spent in combat with the Sunni Arab dynasty of Saladin Al Ayyubi, leader of the Muslim resistance to the invading Crusaders. Saladin's greatest triumph came at the Battle of Hattin in 1187, which paved the way for the Islamic re-conquest of Jerusalem and other Holy Land cities in the Near East. Modern historians debate Saladin's motivation but for those contemporaries close to him, 'there was no question, Saladin had embarked on a holy war to eliminate Latin political and military control in the Middle East, particularly Christian control over Jerusalem.'[1]

Unlike the European war on the Western Front, the war fought in the Middle East always had a sectarian dimension to it, a sub-text that was riven with theological complexities, issues of historical ownership, and blurred distinctions between political and religious rights and authority. The military dimension of this confrontation between ideologies and beliefs bled into the nature and act of war itself, and in some respects the story of the Great War in the Middle East is the story of religious wars fought in the modern age, its echoes picked up a century later in the propaganda of Islamic State and other Islamist jihadists seeking to reclaim the concept and the language of battle against an invading Crusader army. In November 1914, the Ottomans were to declare a military jihad against Britain and its allies; Germany too saw the advantages of a close association with the jihadist idea and prepared their own version in the region. Forced to respond with a strategy that might carry the predominantly Muslim population, Britain in turn organised its own 'counter-jihad' in alliance with the Arab-led forces of Sharif Hussein of Mecca. Jihad came with its own fertile propaganda dimension. Thus, the core motivating force driving the military narrative and counter-narrative across the contested Middle East during the war years was centred, by default, on the imperative of military jihadism. It could never be simply a war fought between Christians but invariably one entered into between Christian and Muslim, with all the incendiary potential for sectarian division. To that extent it was a war that presented a set of sensitivities, whether downplayed or not, which needed to be accommodated by war planners both through their strategic response and in the associated propaganda to which a domestic audience increasingly looked for inspiration and affirmation.

Advent of Systematic Propaganda
Until the outbreak of the First World War, public awareness of propaganda was relatively low; the word itself and its later almost exclusively negative connotation did not have much of a place in the public mind. This was to change as the war progressed and the Allies were increasingly successful in using the word itself as a synonym for large-scale lies deployed by the Germans to deceive the British and American publics. It was only when centrally managed efforts were made to demonise German barbarism that the word and the idea behind it gained wider purchase, in effect heralding the first great wave of systematic propaganda in the modern age. Thus, the business of propaganda and the reputation of propagandists both became sullied and unwholesome, defined by their association with the enemy. In his 2005 introduction to the modern edition of 'Propaganda' by Edward Bernays, first published in 1928, New York University Professor Mark Crispin Miller expressed the view that it was the propaganda on the Allied side that first made the word so opprobrious. Fouled by its association

with 'the Hun,' the word never regained its neutrality or innocence, even when the Allied propaganda itself had been belatedly exposed to the British and American people. 'Indeed, as they learned more and more about the outright lies, exaggerations and half-truths used on them by their own governments, both populations came, understandably, to see propaganda as a weapon even more perfidious than they thought when they had not perceived themselves as its real target,'[2] he wrote.

At the time, newspapers were open to the idea of working closely with the government to help put across the official line, and they were by far the most common means for people to access news and thus central to shaping public opinion. Readership of newspapers had grown as a result of greater literacy, social mobility and the need for information sharing across all layers of an increasingly educated and connected post-Victorian society. British newspaper proprietors such as Lord Northcliffe (his best-selling Daily Mail accounted for half the circulation of all newspapers in London by 1914) and the Canadian Max Aitken, later the first Baron Beaverbrook, along with their editors and journalists, enjoyed a disproportionate degree of power, considered to be dispassionate, authoritative sources of news and analysis, driven by ethical standards that entrenched their status, as Edmund Burke's Fourth Estate claimed, the balancing mechanism between the other three major forces of the realm: clergy, nobility, and commoners.

According to the British historian Niall Ferguson, the Great War was the first true media war. Wars had, of course, been reported in newspapers before 'but never before 1914 had a war been covered so extensively for such a huge readership. Never before had newspapers been so deliberately used to misrepresent events. And never before had the press itself been a weapon of warfare in its own right,'[3] he wrote. This hitherto unquestioned status of newspapers and newspapermen was to come under much greater scrutiny and criticism after the Great War, particularly for their monopolistic practices and the unbridled influence of a few proprietors over the shaping of public opinion.

In 1914, Britain had no recognisable propaganda capability and at first the propaganda effort seemed both random and patchy. Posters, newspaper proclamations and claims of German atrocities, along with army recruitment drives, were the result of a mix of decisions by individuals, politicians and business. Only as the war continued did the government start to extend its grip on propaganda output as on many other aspects of society.[4] Firstly, it invoked the new Official Secrets Act and Defence of the Realm Act (DORA) to impose press censorship and ban all war reporting. As a stopgap measure, a serving officer, Lieutenant-Colonel Ernest Swinton (who later became celebrated more widely as the inventor of the tank), was designated as its official reporter, writing under the by-line 'Eye Witness.' Lord Kitchener, the War Minister, appointed Swinton to the job as journalists were barred from the battlefield and Swinton's neutral accounts of the conduct of the war were personally vetted and censored by Kitchener himself prior to release to the press.[5] Everyone else had to make the best they could out of a situation that offered them no access and no official status, reliant on press briefings where they could get them and off-the-record conversations when they couldn't.

The government also set up a secret propaganda bureau under Charles Masterman in London's Wellington House, using the offices of the National Insurance Department as a front. At first, the principal role of the bureau was to control information, which meant a strict enforcement of censorship; a guiding principle of the bureau was that it ensured there was no visible link between the government and the information that was compiled and distributed. At the same time, the government carefully chose the facts that it gave to the newspapers. The end result was that government propaganda was all factual but it was the facts themselves that were very carefully chosen – especially the facts that were left out, a practice that the late Conservative politician and government minister Alan Clark would some eight decades later during the 1992 Arms-to-Iraq trial of British firm Matrix Churchill infamously describe as being 'economical with the actualité.'

Protector of Islam

In pursuit of its imperial ambitions in the Middle East, Germany was both opportunistic and imaginative, adding a dimension to its propaganda effort which it would develop with typical organisational flair in partnership with Ottoman Turkey, its Muslim ally in the region. Already on the back foot by the outbreak of war due to its losses in the Balkans, and in order to preserve its remaining territories, Ottoman Turkey needed support, especially in Europe, and swiftly concluded an alliance with Germany on 2nd August 1914. In the Turkish capital of Constantinople on 14th November, an announcement was made which was to have major consequences for the future of the Middle East for the duration of the war and the following century. The religious leader, Shaikh-ul-Islam, declared an Islamic holy war on behalf of the Ottoman government, urging his Muslim followers to take up arms against

Britain, France, Russia and all its allies. The announcement of military jihad, as opposed to personal or societal jihad, is permitted within Islam only under a strict set of guidelines: its rationale must be based on self-defence or direct threat, it must involve no gaining of territory, provide justice for enemy wounded, and it rules out damage to property or any abuse of non-combatants, including women and children.

The Shaikh's declaration called on Muslims around the world to rise up and defend the Ottoman Empire, as a protector of Islam, against its enemies. The declaration read in part, 'Of those who go to the jihad for the sake of happiness and salvation of the believers in God's victory, the lot of those who remain alive is felicity, while the rank of those who depart to the next world is martyrdom. In accordance with God's beautiful promise, those who sacrifice their lives to give life to the truth will have honour in this world, and their latter end is paradise.'[6] Germany's planners and its officer corps, already embedded within the Ottoman army, had in fact already understood the significance of the strategic advantage this offered them in its direct relevance to military operations across the region, including in Turkey, Palestine, the Hejaz and Mesopotamia.

The effect of this declaration was to radically change British strategy in the region by flagging up the urgent need to find a counter narrative which might reassert their moral authority and establish a legitimacy to their own military ambitions. By 1915, the British and Indian armies were already engaged in a number of theatres in the region, including the invasion of Mesopotamia through Abadan and Basra, the planning for the fateful Dardanelles campaign at Gallipoli, and the exploration of possible alliances with the rulers of the Hejaz, Sharif Hussein of Mecca and his family. This was all jeopardised by the wider political and military ramifications of a Holy War. Whilst the immediate effect was to undercut the legitimacy of the British military agenda in the region, its impact was echoed and amplified on the ground at community level, where local Arab populations were suddenly less inclined to feel sympathy with the British cause and more liable to succumb to pressure from their Ottoman masters. The tactical implications went further though and were potentially more worrying.

Significant numbers of the British Indian 6th Army, for example, who were part of the invading force in Mesopotamia, were themselves Muslims. As the invasion campaign progressed, the Turks began to use propaganda leaflets, inflammatory speeches by local Imams and public meetings for the local populations to point out to serving Muslim soldiers in the British army the anomalies of their position and, later in the campaign at the disastrous siege of Kut Al Amara in November 1915, they even sought to persuade some Indian soldiers to desert and change sides. This conflict was felt no less keenly within the ranks of the French army on the Western Front, where some of its elite North African regiments, mustered in Algeria and Morocco, were Arab or Berber Muslims whose primary allegiance to colonial France was now also threatened. The Germans and Turks were quick to turn the call to jihad to their advantage by fostering a propaganda subculture designed exclusively to target and exploit the divided loyalties now felt by serving Muslim soldiers in the French and British armies. The Germans recruited Islamic activists like Tunisian Shaikh Salih Al-Sharif to the cause. In 1914, Al-Sharif even moved to Berlin, where he joined a new propaganda unit under the German Foreign Ministry, the *Nachrichtenstelle fur den Orient* (Intelligence Office for the East). Al Sharif drafted 'a number of pamphlets, published in both Arabic and Berber which were dropped over enemy lines in areas held by North African soldiers along with news of the Ottoman Sultan's declaration of jihad.'[7] This German opportunism was to be repeated by the Nazis in 1941 with the arrival of the Grand Mufti of Jerusalem, Haj Amin Al Husseini, and a group of Arab nationalists in Berlin, from where they could plan and manage their information war in the region against the British and their allies.

The German Jihad
The principal German advocate for the benefits of jihad as a propaganda tool was the unconventional aristocrat and member of the banking dynasty Max von Oppenheim (1860-1946), an archaeologist and renowned expert on the Near East, who had been extolling its virtues to the German Kaiser for some time before the war. He was a strong believer in Islam's potential to upend Imperial Germany's enemies if its forces could be harnessed and put to work. To do this, Oppenheim believed that a well organised and targeted propaganda campaign would stir up a mass Muslim uprising against Britain and France from within colonial territories such as India, Indo-China and north and West Africa.[8] He persuaded Kaiser Wilhelm to back his judgement and, in due course, set up two camps specifically to house Allied Muslim Prisoners of War (POWs), Halbmondlager (Half Moon Camp) primarily for Indian, British and French POWs at Wunsdorf, 50 kilometres south of Berlin and Weinbergslager, for Asian and Russian Muslims, at nearby Zossen.

Here, up to 10,000 detainees could be housed as 'guests' of the Kaiser with their own mosque, the first on German soil, set within a structure that was modelled closely and deliberately to mimic the design of the sacred Dome of the Rock. The camp provided Qur'ans, resident imams preached sermons, religious observances were kept, and even halal dietary requirements catered for.

The camps, now largely forgotten other than as curiosities in German history books, were designed as the physical manifestation of its propaganda for jihad, the purpose to create a cadre of jihadis whose primary loyalty was to Germany and thus who might be fit to prosecute its case across the Muslim world. The strategy was at best only partly successful, the camps' rationale increasingly snarled up in a managerial tussle between German army and foreign office tensions between the demand for secrecy and thirst for publicity. However, between February 1916 and April 1917, several units of graduate jihadists from the camps were sent to Turkey and over 1,000 of them enlisted in the Ottoman army as evangelists for the cause.

Oppenheim's views were instrumental in laying the groundwork for the alliance between Germany and Ottoman Turkey which was signed in August 1914. The declaration of jihad, with all its complexities, was a cathartic and enduring factor in the development of British strategy in the Middle East in 1914 and its lasting effects have a resonance on contemporary events in the region. Though this was still the early 20th century, the British intelligentsia viewed Islamic jihad as a 'very important issue,' inspiring policy makers to exploit it in order to encourage jihad against Britain's adversaries, according to the historian Ahmad Al-Rawi.[9] In time, the ingenuity of British planners, driven by the paramount need to safeguard Britain's imperial interests, assured a solution to the problem. Via the British administration in Egypt, a conversation was developed with Sharif Hussein of Mecca, head of the predominant family in the Arabian Hejaz (now in Saudi Arabia), and he was persuaded to raise an Arab revolt which might, with financial and military support from the British, rise up and banish the Ottomans from these long subjugated Arab lands. The outstanding issue was the question of what Sharif Hussein might want in return for his support. In the now famous and pivotal ensuing correspondence between Sharif Hussein and Sir Henry McMahon, British High Commissioner in Egypt, the price of independence for the Arab people in the post-war realignment of the region was directly discussed. The question of precisely what was agreed has been subject to constant debate over the ensuing century and still provides a root cause for accusations of British deception and moral ambiguity in the region. There can be little doubt that Britain has been on the losing side of this battle in the propaganda war and that the perceived betrayal of its obligation for the lands of Palestine west of the Jordan River to be included in the post-war Arab settlement has had a festering and debilitating effect on its reputation.

The role of military jihad as part of the Muslim Arab response to imperialist ambition and occupation in the region, and as a weaponised propaganda tool in politicised Islam has formed a consistent thread over the last century. From the safety of Berlin, where he had established a base alongside fellow Arab nationalist exiles sympathetic to Nazi Germany, the Grand Mufti of Jerusalem, Haj Amin Al-Husseini, was to formally declare jihad against the Allied Powers on November 25th 1941, almost precisely 27 years after the 1914 announcement in Istanbul. A century after the entry of Turkey into the First World War, jihad was again a central part of the vision shared by Islamic State leader Abu Bakr Al Baghdadi when he announced the formation of his caliphate in July 2014 from the minbar of the Great An Nuri Mosque in Mosul. In the imperialist struggle for ascendancy in the region, it was Germany who was first to use its Muslim alliances and the potency of military jihad as a highly effective lever to place right at the centre of its propaganda strategy and as a major weapon in its information war.

A Case of Mythopoeia: Lowell Thomas and PR Gold

The black and white film is silent, grainy and at times the central narrative is somewhat opaque. But the content is unmistakeably authentic and the story it tells has endured and even now still lies at the heart of a very British legend that continues to grow in fascination and psychological complexity with the passing decades. 'With Lawrence In Arabia,' assembled in 1927 from footage shot by US filmmaker Lowell Thomas in the Hejaz and in Palestine between Autumn 1917 and Spring 1918, records the progress of the British-backed Arab Revolt as part of the strategic initiative to drive the Ottomans from the Arabian peninsula and the lands of the Levant, the area comprising modern day Palestine, Lebanon, Syria and Israel.[10] This relative sideshow to the war on the blood soaked and deadlocked Western Front was generally, apart from those directly involved, little known about, however, its strategic importance made it highly significant. In the Allied war planners' grand scheme to establish a counter narrative, or counter-jihad as it has been alternatively described,[11] the Arab population of the Hejaz had a central role. As guardians of the most holy sites in Islam, the cities of Mecca and Medina along the Red Sea coast, they too had been living under Ottoman Turkish rule for four centuries. If they could coalesce and rise as a military force, break out and drive the occupying Ottoman army from the Hejaz, would they not have a corresponding moral authority and mandate to claim the loyalty of Arab Muslims and even those Muslims further afield in the region? Furthermore, in the planners' minds, would the pressure on the British caused by the declaration of jihad by the Ottomans not be dissipated if they were seen to be in alliance with a second great Muslim force, this time Arab rather than Turk and legitimate their claim as inheritors of the holy places?

The task of just how to establish and promote this new narrative was the subject of discussion amongst British war planners at the same time as government propagandists were casting around desperately to find success stories with which to inspire a public on the Home Front, increasingly disillusioned with the bloody and decidedly unheroic attrition of the trenches of Flanders. They looked to the under-reported British military campaign in Palestine as a source of both a rare military success and positive, inspiring news. With the major British military effort in the region finally moving forward under the command of General Sir Edmund Allenby, the irregular campaign was now being waged from the mountains and deserts of the Hejaz, with the help of just a few British officers and some very limited resources of arms and money. One of these young British soldiers, the intelligence officer Major T. E. Lawrence, was a close advisor to Faisal and his father Hussein, Sharif of Mecca, whose support the British had secured in return for the promise of self-rule for the Arabs when the war against the Turks had been won.

When Lawrence carried out his most effective and remarkable part in the Arab Revolt, these promises, as history records, had already been broken by the secret collaboration of the British and French governments in the drawing up of the Sykes-Picot Agreement of 1916, dividing up the Mandates for the countries of the Levant between the British and French colonial powers at the expense of Arab self-determination. But Lawrence's role, combined with his publicly self-effacing character and eye-catching exploits behind the Turkish lines, made him an attractive symbol and potential figurehead for the counter narrative they were trying to establish. This shy, physically unimpressive Englishman, who provided the model for Sandy Arbuthnot, a principal character in John Buchan's 1916 novel of Ottoman decline 'Greenmantle,' was in time to emerge as perhaps the most famous individual of the entire First World War era.

In due course, initially in 1922 with a manuscript that he lost on Reading Station, Lawrence was to write about his own exploits in the Arab Revolt in 'The Seven Pillars Of Wisdom' (Doubleday, 1935), a vast work which he used partly to set down a historical record of events and his part in them but equally as a vehicle for his literary ambitions, which were considerable. The book remains a masterpiece, containing a remarkably accurate record of events given that they were largely written by Lawrence direct from memory rather than archive, and a high literary style which is dramatic and evocative, though at times reverting to excessive rhetorical flourishes. At the time, the book generated an enthusiastic response, its only detractors coming from those who believed it was guilty of factual omissions, especially relating to the work of the French whose ambitions in the Middle East Lawrence abominated.[12] According to novelist E. M. Forster, however, 'round this tent-pole of a military chronicle, Lawrence has hung an unexampled fabric of portraits, descriptions, philosophies, emotions, adventures.'[13]

Premium PR Currency
The prodigious efforts of George Creel's Committee on Public Information had played a major part in securing the entry of America into the First World War on 6th April 1917. But, as American troops headed for the Western Front, the decision to participate was still being questioned domestically. President Woodrow Wilson and US propagandists were also looking for narrative vehicles which might persuade public opinion further of the glory of the enterprise. Publicist and film maker Lowell Thomas was asked by Wilson to be part of an official delegation to the war theatre to compile a history of the conflict. Thomas, an iconoclastic figure in the fast developing world of publicity, realised that film was the only medium that could remotely fulfill his brief and, without the necessary funding from the US government to pay the costs involved with producing a documentary film (around $75,000 at that time), he raised the finances from a group of private backers in Chicago's meat packing industry.

The bet was to pay off handsomely, and in time set Thomas up for the rest of his life on the back of the remarkable films that he and cameraman Harry Chase were able to shoot with Lawrence and his Arab army. Propelled by an injection of cash, Thomas and Chase made their way to France, although Thomas could not find a suitable focus for his intended heroic narrative in the trenches. Ending up in Jerusalem in November 1917, courtesy of John Buchan at the British Ministry of Information, Thomas planned to film the entry of the victorious British occupying army into the city. In the course of his visit, however, he was introduced to Lawrence, who agreed to embed him and Chase on location with Lawrence's irregular Arab forces. Thomas and Chase subsequently spent some weeks with Lawrence and Faisal making the films which offer, to this day, the best record of military events unfolding in Palestine and the Hejaz in late 1917 and early 1918. From the moment he met Lawrence, Thomas recognised that he was in the presence of a potential PR powerhouse, a subject that, given the right access, he would have little trouble selling to the public as a modern day hero, an Achilles of his age. Thus, the first and most accessible window into the world of Lawrence, and therefore Thomas as the filmmaker, lies in the film of the actual events that he was part of and the places and people in the Middle East that he engaged with. In the raw footage produced in 1917, there is a steady progression in the story of the Arab Revolt on film that runs across five separate reels.[14] The collection groups the films into episodes, progressing from Thomas' departure from Salonika and his voyage to Egypt to footage of the Imperial Camel Corps on the move in Palestine.

The seminal characteristics and associations of the Lawrence legend can best be summarised in Reel Three. Here, we find the cast-iron evidence of the principal projection of the Lawrence of Arabia persona shaped by Thomas, stirring and romantic wide shots of Arab horsemen during a cavalry charge towards the camera, Lawrence and Faisal careering across the desert in a Model T Ford, a column of Lawrence's armoured cars throwing up billowing dust clouds, Faisal and Lawrence with their advisers, Lawrence in full Arab dress standing and then seated in conference. In the second, more polished version produced in 1927, 'With Lawrence in Arabia: A Lowell Thomas Adventure Film,'[15] the film opens up with a still portrait of Lawrence and then proceeds to stitch together the majority of the contents of the reel from the initial version, maintaining a similar narrative.

The Lawrence of Arabia Industry
Echoes of this original documentary footage can still be found much later in the development of Lawrence's legend, especially in the feature film epic 'Lawrence of Arabia,' produced in 1962 and starring Peter O'Toole as a tall, blond and blue eyed version of Lawrence, serving only to propagate further his myth.[16] The film reimagines some of the shots from Thomas' and Chase's original documentary, including the irregular Arab cavalry charge, Lawrence in traditional Arab robes set against a spectacular

canvas of desert and mountain scenery and a somewhat mannered and self-conscious depiction of Faisal by the actor Sir Alec Guinness along with a moodier version of Faisal's brother by the late Egyptian matinée idol Omar Sharif. Even the film's trailer is a classic example of the powerful and persuasive role that Hollywood and the medium of film would go on to play in ensuing wartime propaganda. The mobilisation of Lawrence as a propaganda instrument and precursor of the cult of personality offers a textbook case study of how propaganda techniques can be applied to promote ideas through a subject of human interest in order to spin the most compelling type of narrative, one whose messages and images connect with the public on a visceral, personal level as well as conforming to the public conception of what, at that time, constituted heroic activity – the loner who can take on armies, the cross-cultural polymath who excavates Hittite remains yet also blows up trains, a poet by temperament yet a soldier through necessity, a modern day Crusader following in the footsteps of another great English hero, Richard the Lionheart. Above all, Thomas understood the combination of romance and enigma offered by Lawrence and his story's ability to rise above the dreary inevitability of unheroic death in the mud of Flanders, inspiring the public with an altogether more compelling vision of war, weaving glamour and intrigue into success on the battlefield. In realising these possibilities, Thomas revealed himself as a social architect of enduring vision, a consummate storyteller and genius of populist publicity who, above all else, understood the full power of the moving image and its place in the new propaganda style increasingly demanded by the Allied war machine. It was ironic that, by the time Thomas went public with his captivating global lecture tour in March 1919, the war in Europe was over and thus the original propaganda purpose had been superseded, however, the peace had yet to be settled and it was this greater prize that Lawrence had in mind in return for his participation.

An Orchestra Pit Filled with Palms

When he returned to America after the war, Thomas needed to start using his films and first-hand account of events in the desert to generate money with which to repay his investors. Initially, he created a series of six lectures out of the film archive he had generated, but only two of these, Allenby's Palestine campaign and 'Lawrence of Arabia' generated any consistent interest, or takings on the door for that matter. He quickly combined these later in March 1919 at New York's Madison Square Gardens to create a presentation which he called 'With Allenby in Palestine and Lawrence in Arabia.'[17] The showman in Thomas emerged and he started to wrap this extended lecture up in an exotic Eastern tinged packaging, including moving images of veiled women, Arabs in their traditional dress and dashing Arab cavalry on camels and horses. Together with cameraman Chase, he built the show into much more than a conventional lecture, pioneering between them the world's first multimedia entertainment, with Chase using three separate projectors to show films and slides in full colour alongside sound effects. Alongside Thomas' inspirational narration, the show created a sensation, its impact was massive and audiences flocked to see this imaginative and informative evocation of the war in the Middle East and the enigmatic legend at its heart. Thomas relocated his show to London's Covent Garden, at the invitation of the King, in the summer of 1919. It attracted the interest of a British impresario, Percy Burton, who added further to the visual impact by having the orchestra pit filled with palms and the set decorated as a Nile scene, lit by a backdrop of moonlit pyramids. An additional air of the exotic was added by the entrance of a belly dancer and the fragrance of heavy incense being introduced into the hall. 'It was Mr Percy Burton, the impresario formerly associated with Sir Henry Irving, who came to me in New York and inveigled me into agreeing to appear for a season at Covent Garden Royal Opera House, London with my production,'[18] he wrote.

Lawrence himself saw the show a number of times, even posing in London for further portraits in Arab dress by Chase in order to strengthen the story line which focused on him, but perhaps also to use the publicity for his own purposes. He was, though, at this time more ambivalent towards Thomas' project and his role in it and their relationship entered a more vexed phase. It was around this time that Thomas recorded his now famously undermining remark about the duality of Lawrence's nature, remarking that 'he had a genius for backing into the limelight.' Their relationship steadily deteriorated thereafter, with Lawrence referring to Thomas as a 'vulgar man' but the impact of the publicity was telling. Politicians including Winston Churchill sought Lawrence's views and advice on the Middle East and he received many offers of important work, but from this point onwards, Lawrence was in a lifelong losing struggle with his increasingly fragile and masochistic psyche, enjoying the trappings of fame and celebrity yet constantly overridden by a sense of unworthiness and the need for anonymity and obscurity.

It is estimated that some four million people saw the Thomas film around the world, and it made him the vast sum for that time of $1.5

million, the equivalent of $22 million in today's money. He later wrote the book 'With Lawrence in Arabia,' an account of his time in the desert with Lawrence and of the role that Lawrence had played in the ultimately unsuccessful Arab Revolt. In the introduction to the book, Thomas admits that he may have gone too far in his eulogistic praise for 'the uncrowned king of the Arabs, who usually dressed in robes of spotless white.' He wrote, somewhat defensively, 'there are those who say that Lawrence has received altogether too much publicity through me. They piously declare that this is not in accordance with military ethics. There may be something in this, though I doubt it. But, if there is, the blame should all be mine.'[19] How successful was Thomas's work as a propagandist? In some respects, it was less successful than originally envisaged by Thomas and his bosses, principally because he was overtaken by events on the Western Front which drew the Great War to a conclusion before the impact of the publicity and its inherent messages could meaningfully bolster US public opinion in favour of the war commitment, however, the effects of the publicity were felt up to and during the ensuing peace process which started in January 1919 at Versailles. Though ultimately unsuccessful in bolstering the cause of Arab independence, this finally resulted in some advancement of British supported Hashemite Arab ascendancy in the region through the creation of the kingdoms of Jordan and Iraq. The belief in the nobility, sacrifice and heroism of war and its demands on the individual was, through the narrative of Lawrence, restored to the public imagination, taking their minds away from the grim despair of the trenches to an altogether more Homeric, exotic landscape in which the myth of the solo adventurer, soldier, poet, shaper of worlds so ingrained in the British love of myth and legend, could be successfully constructed.

Entry into the Holy City
The First World War in the Middle East was to wholly capture the West's imagination, as Britain's conventional army of empire eventually started to win back territory from the Ottomans, presenting in the process opportunities with which to raise morale at home and reassert authority on the ground. But by the middle of the war, the course of the Allies' campaigning across the region was far from smooth, expected victories turned out to be crushing, even humiliating defeats, in particular the 1916 disasters of Gallipoli, where Allied Forces lost many thousands of soldiers, surrounded and trapped on an indefensible Turkish peninsula, and the surrender of the British Indian 6th Army at Kut El Amara, the

Mesopotamian city situated in a loop of the river Tigris 100 miles south of Baghdad. The capitulation and surrender of Kut amidst widespread starvation and disease amongst the garrison followed a five-month siege under the leadership of General Charles Townshend, one that a relieving British force had been unable to break in time to rescue over 13,000 British and Indian troops.

These unprecedented failures in Mesopotamia and western Turkey were supplemented by a fierce Turkish defence of Palestine and the Hejaz, where Ottoman forces put up stubborn and unexpected resistance to thwart Allied ambitions. The picture changed, however, with the arrival on the scene from France in June 1917 of General Sir Edmund Allenby as commander of the Egyptian Expeditionary Force (EEF). Known as 'the bull,' his powers of organisation, strategic thinking and tactical execution that were first exercised on the Western Front were slowly to turn the tide and change the fortunes of the British in the region. In the successes that were to follow, until final victory at the Battle of Megiddo (Biblical Armageddon) in Syria in September 1918, British propagandists were to find the images and stories they were searching for, ones that painted an altogether more glamorous and reassuring picture of war, a story they could sell at home and abroad with conviction as an embodiment of imperial imposition of will and military achievement against the odds.

In Allenby, and his defeat of the Turks in Palestine, they found the consummate opportunity of the entire war. The carefully orchestrated entry of the British Army into the city of Jerusalem on 11th December 1917, after Allenby's defeat of the Ottoman defenders, is one of the finest wartime examples of transcendent propaganda, a moment that rises above its immediate purpose to reach for an altogether greater, more symbolic prize. The sensitivities of a Christian army occupying the Holy City for the first time in over 700 years, a city moreover of such religious and historical significance and in which so many interests were at stake, was not lost on the British war planners in Whitehall. They did not want to make a blunder in misreading these sensitivities, but they also realised they could turn the event to their advantage if they crafted it as a piece of theatre.

The manner of Allenby's entry into Jerusalem and exactly what he was to announce once inside had been considered at the highest levels of government, and London had sent him precise instructions on 21st November before the battle for the city began. Sir William Robertson (1860-1933), the Chief of Imperial General Staff, had advised Allenby of the need to enter the city on foot and cited the example of Kaiser Wilhelm

II, who had entered the city on horseback in 1898; 'the saying went round: a better man than he walked.'[20] The Prime Minister had demanded in the House of Commons a checklist of nine items to be covered prior to Allenby's announcement, among them he needed to know how Allenby had been received, that he had entered the city on foot, and that suitable precautions had been taken to guard the Holy Places.

The proceedings in Jerusalem were captured on film by Harold Jeapes, a cameraman working for the War Office Cinematograph Committee (WOCC) in Palestine and Egypt. Thus, when Allenby made his formal entry into the city, the WOCC filmed the carefully staged event to ensure the widest possible audience for the greatest victory of the war to date. 'General Allenby's Entry Into Jerusalem,' the 12 minute film made to commemorate and promote the event, was released on 23rd February 1918 and seen widely by the British public, its focal scene records the reading of Allenby's proclamation to the citizens of Jerusalem (later to be officially disowned by the British government), in which he makes the point that the British troops have not come as invaders, unlike the Ottoman Turks, but will occupy the city only for as long as martial law dictates, and will furthermore ensure that everyone, of whatever religion, will be able to continue to pursue their 'lawful business.' Upon entering, he also reportedly made the remark 'only now have the Crusades ended.'[21]

The imagery and associations of the Crusades were used extensively by the British press and the Ministry of Information (MOI) to describe the campaign, and Lowell Thomas also made it fashionable to think of Allenby as the modern 'Coeur De Lion,' repeatedly reinforcing the redolent image of Allenby on horseback at the head of his cavalry units. The MOI released a film about the Allenby-led British attacks against the Ottomans in Gaza early in 1917 called 'The New Crusaders – with the British Forces on the Palestine Front.' Shot by cameraman Frank Hurley, the film follows the British forces' advance from Al Arish to Beersheba in the First Battle of Gaza.[22] A second film, 'The Advance of the Crusaders into Mesopotamia,' was made in September 1917 by Jury's Imperial Pictures. Directed by William Jury, it charted the advance of British forces up the Tigris River beyond Kut Al Amara and Ctesiphon to Baghdad itself, reinforcing the merely temporary nature of any earlier, and costlier, defeats.[23] Thematically, these films might be seen as continuations in a tradition started in the 19th century by the novels of Sir Walter Scott, both Ivanhoe (1819) and The Talisman (1825) narrating the Crusades through the romanticised character of Richard the Lionheart. In 1916, John Buchan's novel Greenmantle was to present an updated and reimagined version of the Crusades, in which British military and intelligence superiority was to triumph over Ottoman plots to control the Muslim world.

Allenby himself, though, was more thoughtful. Mindful of the Pan-Islamic propaganda used by the Ottomans and their military jihad, he personally discouraged the use of the Crusader imagery, banned his press officers from using the terms Crusade and Crusader in their press releases, and always went out of his way to insist that he was fighting merely the Ottoman Empire, not Islam.[24]

The association with the Crusades, along with its imagery and layered sub-texts, has since become a recurring propaganda trope which has been integral to the successful negative stereotyping by Islamist extremists of Western military intervention in the region and can be linked to this cataclysmic event. Replete with symbolism and significance that permeated the consciousness of the entire Christian world, the entry into Jerusalem caused every church bell in Rome to be rung continuously for an hour.[25] The WOCC film records a pivotal moment in 20th century history, 'a carefully stage managed sham,' which initiated the British occupation of Palestine for the following 30 years before it walked away from both the country and its people. As such it was also evidence of the seamless blending of Imperial and military agendas 'in a moment of fluid and opportunistic expansion, where the advancing front effectively claimed for the Empire the self-same territory it officially maintained was being liberated.'[26] The public relations exercise took only 15 minutes of Allenby's time before he left the city via the Jaffa Gate. The betrayal of Britain's Arab allies was to start almost immediately thereafter.

CHAPTER IV

Legacies of Atrocity:
The Aftermath and Settlement

'In my humble opinion, propaganda is one of the most evil tools humans have used against humans throughout history to justify wars, justify atrocities, justify evil. ISIS has taken it to a new extreme.'

Matthew Heineman,
Director, *City of Ghosts*

Versailles and the New Middle East

The close of the war and the negotiation of the peace brought with it a period of appraisal and reflection, encompassing all the aspects of what had turned out to be a technical victory for the Allies on the battlefield, disguising a wider catastrophe, the real cost of which took years to be properly counted. However, if Britain and its allies had made the highest national sacrifice, that of Germany had been even higher, in political influence, economic clout and an insupportable bill for reparations. Only the Ottoman Turks had fared worse, losing what territory or rights remained over their empire and with a leadership branded as war criminals scattered and hunted down across the globe in retaliation for the Armenian genocide of 1915.

In January 1919, as the victorious Allies assembled in Versailles for the Paris Peace Conference, British Prime Minister David Lloyd George was focused on protecting British interests in the Middle East, key to the security of India but since the Ottoman surrender now in a state of political and economic drift. US President Woodrow Wilson's 'Fourteen Point' settlement plan, seen as idealistic, proposed that the principles of national self-determination and autonomy should guide the division of national boundaries and recommended the founding of the League of Nations to manage the international sphere.[1] The victors ultimately negotiated a total of five treaties at Versailles, encompassing the resetting of national boundaries, allocation of Ottoman territories, German reparations and the formation of the League of Nations. The Treaty of Sèvres marked the beginning of the partitioning and dismemberment of the Ottoman Empire. The Treaty's terms included the renunciation of all non-Turkish territory and its cession to the Allied administration; this in turn enabled the thinking that would create new forms of government, including Mandatory Palestine and the French Mandate for Syria and Lebanon. Within this thinking lay the germ of the PR and perception problem that was to infect Britain's ability to sell its post-war vision of the region with conviction.

In a detailed, secret Memorandum prepared by the Political Intelligence Department of the British Foreign Office on 21st November 1918, the British Government set out the principles for its formal negotiating position at Versailles. The 'Memorandum respecting settlement of Turkey and the Arabian Peninsula'[2] reveals the core case, analysis and justification subsequently used by the British to redraw the post-war map of the region and, in the process, shows a flexible approach to previous public undertakings. In a volte face, the Memorandum states that the draft proclamation prepared for General Allenby's entry into Jerusalem, a major cornerstone of its central message and PR projection in the region, had not been issued officially 'either on that occasion or subsequently,' conceding only that it had been published in the English press, and was referred to in the statement of British policy issued by the Foreign Office on the 11th June 1918 'in reply to a memorial from Syrians resident in Egypt.'[3]

Point Six of the Memorandum reaffirms British pledges made to Sharif Hussein of Mecca that the whole mainland of the Arabian Peninsula with the exception of the Aden Protectorate shall be independent and Arab. It also reaffirms its commitment to statements made on 11th June 1918 that, 'in regard to areas in Arabia which were free and independent before the outbreak of war, and areas emancipated from Turkish control by the action of the Arabs themselves during the present war, His Majesty's Government recognise the complete and sovereign independence of the Arabs inhabiting these areas, and support them in their struggle for freedom.'[4] However, the planners are unequivocal about the strategic case for Britain's occupation of Palestine, saying it 'adjoins the Sinai Peninsula, the Suez Canal, and Akaba, and a British

The Middle East Before and After World War I Settlements, 1914 - 1922

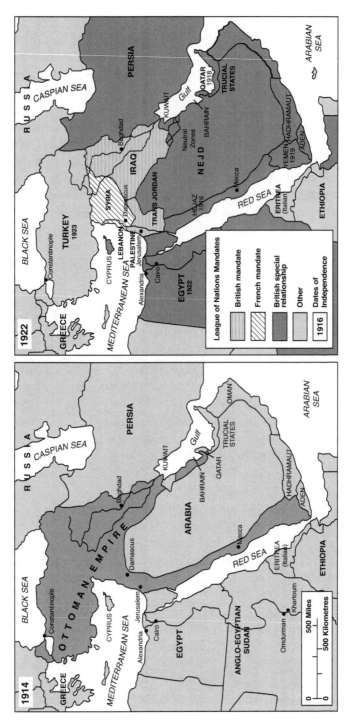

railway from Akka-Haifa to Irak (sic) would traverse Palestine in its first section. It is therefore a British desideratum that if the effective government of Palestine demands the intervention of a single outside Power in its administration, that power should be either Great Britain or, failing that, the United States.'

British policy, it emerged, was behind an administration capable of conciliating religious interests, both to ensure orderly government in a country where disorder would impact neighbouring countries in which Great Britain was interested, and to prevent the possibility of any of the international bodies interested in Palestine feeling resentment against Great Britain as a party to an arrangement there which they might consider unfair to themselves.[5] The document, and its implied narrative, articulates the British government's desire to ensure reasonable facilities in Palestine for Jewish colonisation without giving Arab or general Muslim opinion an opportunity for considering that Great Britain has been instrumental in handing over free Arab or Muslim soil to aliens. It reveals British policy to be flexible on the question of self-determination, making a direct comparison with circumstances relating to the mixed population of Armenia, suggesting that the Jewish colonists will for special reasons be entitled to a position 'more than mathematically proportionate to its numbers at the start.' The policy in turn sets out the downstream difficulties that would have to be confronted by any conflict of interest and the attendant need for any Mandatory power to be impartial and effective, rather than an international administration in the literal sense of mixed executive bodies, 'which would be the very worst regime which could be devised to meet the special Palestinian conditions, and should be decidedly ruled out. The practical choice lies between a Mandate to the United States or a Mandate to Great Britain.'[6]

The Memorandum is the blueprint that largely determined the eventual shape of much of the post-war Middle East and set out British interests alongside the solutions to the practical challenges of reconciling an Arab agenda with international opinion, and imperial interests. The issues of an Arab Federation, the future of the Caliphate ('we should abstain from all direct action'), and the rule of Iraq, Jordan, Syria and Lebanon are all addressed by the document. Alongside this sweeping and comprehensive analysis can be found the seeds of the institutional and leadership crisis that went on to afflict the Arab political will. Along the way, it explains too why Britain struggled to establish a narrative that it could package and sell when some of these issues, fueled by Arab Nationalism, assumed a new urgency in the decades between the wars.

The Role of Atrocity Propaganda

When the bloodiest war in the history of human conflict came to an end in 1918, much of the British propaganda machinery was gradually dismantled. In the extensive examination that took place of the wartime propaganda of both sides, one British pacifist concentrated on exposing the extent of the lies that had underpinned much of the strongest and most lurid output. Arthur Ponsonby MP, 1st Baron Ponsonby of Shulbrede (1871-1946), is perhaps best remembered for the statement 'when war is declared, truth is the first casualty,' although subsequent accounts have linked the original coining of the phrase to US Senator Hiram Warren Johnson in 1918. But Ponsonby, nevertheless, had a keen and detailed understanding of the nature and purpose of propaganda and had profound doubts about its use as a legitimate weapon of war. Acknowledging that the psychological factors in war were as important as the military, and that the maintenance of civilian morale was critical, Ponsonby cut to the chase of what he saw as the morally flawed argument of the propagandists, 'departments have to be created to see to the psychological side. People must never be allowed to become despondent, so victories must be exaggerated and defeats, if not concealed, at any rate minimised and the stimulus of indignation, horror, and hatred must be assiduously and continuously pumped into the public mind by means of 'propaganda,'[7] he wrote.

In researching and writing 'Falsehood In Wartime, Propaganda Lies of the First World War,' published in 1928, Ponsonby revealed much to the discomfort of the government and the military that some of the most famous Allied atrocity propaganda comprised gross distortion and even fabrication. He was the first figure of authority, later to be challenged, to expose the government's role in stoking up fear and hatred as a mechanism for maintaining civilian focus on the war effort. Of the many examples that Ponsonby used to populate his book, some are remarkable for their resonance with contemporary atrocity propaganda and the theatre of the grotesque style and setting we have come to associate with modern day Islamist insurgent output in the wars of the Middle East. Perhaps the highest impact of these stories, and one whose echoes still resonate in the killing fields of the Caliphate today, emanated on the Western Front and became known in the British press as 'the crucified Canadian.'

The story started life as an eye witness testimony by Canadian soldiers caught in fierce fighting around Ypres, who arrived at a base hospital in Versculles with an account of how one of their officers had been crucified by the Germans. 'He had been pinned to a wall with bayonets thrust through his hands and feet, another bayonet had then been driven through his throat, and, finally, he was riddled with bullets. The wounded Canadians said that the Dublin Fusiliers had seen this done with their own eyes, and they had heard the officers of the Dublin Fusiliers talking about it,'[8] wrote the Paris correspondent of the Times on 10th May 1915. Though reporting it and elaborating on the detail (the officer had by then mysteriously become a sergeant), the Times newspaper was subsequently unable to corroborate this story, the correspondent reporting that he had not heard that 'any of our men actually saw the crime committed.' By that time, the story had been embellished to such an extent that the Germans were said to have removed the figure of Christ from a large village crucifix and fastened the sergeant, whilst alive, to the cross. The story surfaced again after the war in 1919 when a supposed eye witness, Private E. Loader, 2nd Royal West Kent Regiment, declared that he had seen the crucified Canadian. The 'Nation' was informed in a subsequent letter from Captain E. N. Bennett that there was no such private on the rolls of the Royal West Kents, and that the 2nd Battalion was in India during the whole war.[9]

It is hard to overstate the impact on the public consciousness at the time of this alleged crucifixion. For Christians, the act is steeped in Biblical and religious symbolism and its iconography lies at the heart of the Christian ethos of self-sacrifice and suffering for others, part of the very psychological fabric of the Crusades themselves. The subsequent reworking of crucifixion that has travelled across the ensuing century from the Western Front to Raqqa and other cities in the Caliphate, to become a recurring trope of Islamist atrocity propaganda, owes everything in its mode of execution and projection to the conscious and direct emotional power of image as a propaganda tool.

Under the heading 'Manufacture of News,' Ponsonby used the fall of the city of Antwerp to German troops in 1914 as one example of how distortion in the reporting of the sacking had gradually ramped up real events into fictitious ones. He tracked the progression of the story from newspaper to newspaper across Europe by exposing the fanciful hype of successive headlines as it moved in ever widening circles. What started out in the Kölnischer Zeitung as 'When the fall of Antwerp got known, the church bells were rung' (meaning in Germany), ended up in the French newspaper Le Matin as 'According to the "Corriere della Sera", it is confirmed that the barbaric conquerors of Antwerp punished the unfortunate Belgian priests for their heroic refusal to ring the church bells by tying them as living clappers to the bells with their heads down.'[10]

The list of German brutalities which Allied propagandists chose to highlight was long and included the destruction of Louvain during the invasion of Belgium, the execution of British nurse Edith Cavell and the sinking of the passenger liner the Lusitania in May 1915, with the subsequent loss of 1,200 innocent civilian lives. Atrocity propaganda became in many respects the focus of the British and French national effort to turn opinion against the enemy. It offered a clear and simple message about the nature of the 'Hun' and the barbarity with which the German military conducted its war effort. The attack on the Lusitania provoked its own backlash against the U-Boat, depicted as a silent killer lurking in the depths ready to strike, like a shark, ready to take innocent civilian lives. In a pamphlet put together to recruit women for Britain's Land Army in 1915, 'a woman writer' described the U-Boat scourge: 'the U-boats are out for murder, not for honest war, and they do their work in stealth and calculated secrecy as a poisoner commits his crime.' The sinking of the Lusitania coincided with the release of the Bryce report of 1915, an official British government account of German atrocities compiled by a former UK ambassador to America. It played an important role in legitimising a clutch of atrocity stories emanating from Belgium, using eyewitness accounts to substantiate rumour and provide all-important detail. These first-hand accounts made the atrocities all the more real and their style of reportage became much used in propaganda. The French went even further, setting out in 'Le Livre Rouge des atrocités allemandes,' popularly known as The Red Book, immensely powerful graphic images of violence and rape amongst the civilian population.

The nadir in atrocity propaganda, subsequently shown to be a fake news masterpiece, was reached with the rumours which started to circulate in the British press in the Spring of 1917 about a corpse factory, where the bodies of dead soldiers were allegedly being transported from the trenches by the Germans to be rendered down to produce glycerine in a special, hidden facility. The rumour of this *Kadaververwertungsanstalt* was reported in both the Times and Daily Mail in April of 1917, based on the supposed eye-witness account of a Belgian who had seen the facility and reported on the grim details of the processing itself. Over the ensuing century, the story spawned its own niche literature, covered by numerous academics and researchers anxious to prove or discount the accuracy of the contemporary press reports. Only in 2017 did a British academic, Dr David Clarke of Sheffield Hallam University, track down the original source of this rumour to a British Intelligence officer and Conservative MP, John Charteris, who revealed in 1925 that he had fabricated the story in order to help support the effort to bring China into the war on the allied side,[12] seeding the first account of this ghoulish facility in the South China Morning Post and setting off a chain reaction which culminated in China's entry into the war in support of the Allies in August 1917.

Atrocity propaganda has become a consistent feature of subsequent wars over the past century, sometimes as in the case with genocides and mass exterminations on a scale that human conscience and the justice system have between them found hard to process. This is true, from the Armenian genocide of 1915 onwards, in the conflict zones of the Middle East and this ultimate expression of the transgressive act has gone on to play an increasingly significant role in the manipulation of public opinion to influence and justify the direction of war and policy in the region. From the First World War to the First Gulf War and beyond, there are myriad examples of its use as a means of influencing public sentiment, from the exposure of the Ottoman Turks' treatment of British and Indian prisoners of war captured at the siege of Kut Al Amara in Mesopotamia in April 1916,[13] through to the use of lethal gas in the ethnic cleansing by Saddam Hussein's forces of Iraq's Kurdish population at Halabjeh in 1988. It is also possible to discern recurring themes in atrocity propaganda in the region, amongst them lineages of extremist anti-Jewish Arabic language Nazi propaganda of the Second World War traceable to the manifestos of today's radical Islamism. The terrible road of atrocity propaganda is marked by regular milestones that encompass both the grotesque and absurd, the fake and the authentic, limited only by the twin forces of imagination and credulity. In 2011, as Libya collapsed under the weight of Coalition bombs and Muammar Ghaddafi's imploding regime, his reputation as an out of control monster was reinforced by the news that he was supplying troops with industrial quantities of Viagra which they were alleged to be using to subjugate dissidents through the systematic mass rape of Libyan women. This piece of consummate fake news, seeded by regime opponents, was taken seriously and widely circulated in the world's media until, in time, it was successfully challenged by international human rights organisations such as Amnesty International and Human Rights Watch.

As with most other fields of human endeavour, the atrocity propaganda business has evolved with the introduction of new ideas, new methods and more extreme players. Since Operation Iraqi Freedom in 2003, a fresh generation of Islamist extremist propaganda pornography has hijacked the world's attention, a genre and style yet unseen and one which has seemed to finally burst the dam of moral order, showcasing an altogether dystopian vision that manifests itself through the fusion of extreme images and content with cinematic scale production values. This sensationalist output, which has gained the world's attention on an unprecedented scale, includes a succession of fetishised and psychologically deviant films and images, some involving children, and all now banned by mainstream conventional Western media. Some of these films, however, in their highly choreographed and ritualised style stand out as iconic and masterful examples of atrocity propaganda, their aims to project overwhelming power, to idealise the Caliphate and attract recruits to its cause.

The capture, confession and execution of Jordanian fighter pilot Lieutenant Muath Al Kasasbeh by Islamic State in January 2015 was turned by the Caliphate's propaganda department into a 22 minute Arabic language video, 'Healing The Believers Chests,' containing a detailed account of the 'Crusader' assault on the Islamic countries of Iraq and Afghanistan and focusing on the air campaign waged against Islamic State in Syria by the combined air forces of Jordan, Saudi Arabia and the United Arab Emirates. On this cinematic journey, the viewer is invited to witness the injury and horrors suffered by women and children as a direct result of the air campaign. The video ends in the south of Raqqa, near the Euphrates River, with a highly ritualised immolation of the pilot who, having confessed to camera, is filmed taking a respectful and newly enlightened look around him at massed silent ranks of uniformed and masked jihadis before he enters a metal cage. Featuring a range of imagery, graphics, stills, archive film, news reports, commentary and interviews, the work is a showcase for the prominence of propaganda in Islamic State's asymmetric approach to war. It is powerful evidence of a strategy which projects overwhelming moral and physical force by employing cathartic images and simplified yet powerful messages to reach out to global audiences, simultaneously repelling and attracting, generating an overpowering emotional response with its vision, purpose and sense of destiny. Now a Jordanian national hero and symbol of universal courage, Kasasbeh's terrible legacy is to remain frozen in digital time, the coerced and convenient protagonist of a propaganda blockbuster.

The power and impact of films like 'Healing the Believers Chests' is such that its methodology has been closely studied for wider clues it might offer to the technical capabilities and psychological approach of the authors. One Hollywood filmmaker, the highly respected Matthew Heineman, who made the film 'City of Ghosts' about the organisation RBSS – 'Raqqa Is Being Silently Slaughtered' (City of Ghosts, Dir Matthew Heineman, 2017) – says that IS has in its films weaponised 'the tics and rhythms' of the modern blockbuster, presenting a highly stylised vision of militant life. Researchers at the University of Chicago found that some of these films utilise the 12-step 'hero's journey' plot structure found in Star Wars or Titanic, according to Heineman. They can be appealing to disaffected, disenfranchised or lost people, he believes. 'It looks exciting. It makes people think, 'Oh wow, I can become part of a movement, I can walk around with guns, all in the name of doing something important.'

In the battle to control hearts and minds in the Middle East, atrocity propaganda and its transgressive role as a crime that offends against the shared collective consciousness, has carved for itself a central position in the narrative of conflict, successfully adapting its content, style and impact to cater for the ever more extreme, voyeuristic tastes and image centric attention profiles of the modern consumer. To do this successfully has also meant mastering the new science of digital logistics and connection, accessing a global audience through the worldwide web and using both its own and third-party news networks to generate coverage and win endorsement.

National Perspectives on World War I Propaganda

German consensus on their own propaganda effort during the war was that it had been both conceptually weak and unfocused, entirely eclipsed by US and British visions, effort and resources. The German military commander, General Erich Von Ludendorff, claimed that German propaganda was only kept going with difficulty. 'In spite of all our efforts, its achievements, in comparison to the magnitude of the task, were inadequate. We produced no real effect on the enemy peoples,'[14] he wrote in his memoir. Ludendorff went so far as to attribute the collapse of the German army and of civilian morale to 'mischievous and lying propaganda,' concluding that 'we were hypnotised... as a rabbit is by a snake.' As evidence of Allied success, British propaganda chief Sir Campbell Stuart (1885-1972) in his own book, the Secrets of Crewe House, cited Ludendorff's 'pathetic.... apologia' drawn from his War memories.[15] The book was part of the detailed post-war inspection and analysis of Britain's own role as propagandists; this new and potent weapon of total war had at first been deployed as something of an afterthought, its organisation, content and funding somewhat random and improvised, its management written off as 'cranks.' Initially under the leadership of Charles Masterman, the propaganda function had subsequently come under the management of Government Minister Edward Carson and his 'mysterious high priest' John Buchan and, at the start of 1918, it had switched to the leadership of newspaper baron Lord Northcliffe. Northcliffe, in turn, had appointed fellow Canadian Campbell Stuart as Deputy Director of Propaganda in Enemy Countries.[16] Stuart's sensationalist book about the campaign revealed startling amounts of detail about the doings of the propaganda factory, although it coyly held back on the parts that he considered might have unforeseen consequences, either of reprisal or moral judgement.[17]

Stuart agreed with Ludendorff that propaganda had played a major role in the Allied victory, in effect opening up a third, asymmetric front alongside the military and economic efforts. The most insightful aspect of his analysis lies in its exposure of his strategic approach, which rested on establishing a clear information policy to shape the management of propaganda. According to Stuart, the issue of primary importance in propaganda or information war was first to create an atmosphere of receptivity and susceptibility. 'To do this, continuity of propaganda policy is indispensable....when a line of policy has been laid down, actual propaganda operations may be begun, but not before,' [18] he wrote. Stuart confirmed that after 1917, the British had adopted a propaganda model reliant on telling the truth and providing factual evidence, at the same time limiting the discourse to approved lines to ensure that there was no deviation from the official version of the truth. 'First of all axioms of propaganda are that only truthful statements to be made. Secondly, there must be no conflicting arguments, and this can only be ensured by close co-operation of all propagandists and by strict adherence to the policy defined. A false step may possibly be irretrievable,' he stated. This was something of a departure from the earlier more random versions of propaganda pursued by the British, when the manufacture and distortion of news had been commonplace, but it presaged a maturing approach to the propaganda business highlighted by the staging of a propaganda policy conference in London on 14th August 1918, attended by all the Allies and presided over by Lord Northcliffe himself.

The agenda was forward looking and sought to set out an agreed approach to policy on the major outstanding questions of the post-war settlement. Amongst the attendees in the US delegation was a certain Captain Walter Lippmann who was working in tandem with the US Committee on Public Information (CPI), indisputably the world's best financed and most advanced propaganda and publicity machine ever assembled in one nation's cause. President Woodrow Wilson, who formally took the United States to war on 6th April 1917, had discussed with advisors the need for a vehicle to co-ordinate censorship and publicity and the formal request for the creation of the CPI, with journalist and Presidential insider George Creel as its head, came in a letter of 13th April to Wilson from Secretary of State Robert Lansing: 'it is our opinion that the two functions – censorship and publicity – can be joined in honesty and with profit, and we recommend the creation of a Committee on Public Information.'[19] Wilson authorised the creation of the CPI, in effect a propaganda ministry, that same day in Executive Order 2594. Quickly, Creel recruited many of the finest minds in the country including Carl Byoir, Edward Bernays and trade unionist Samuel Gompers, founder of the American Federation of Labour.

Such was the detail in the communications plan overseen by Creel that bilingual speakers were hired to take the message to specific immigrant communities, farmers recruited to sell the war to America's farming community and children to sell it to other children.[20] The CPI succeeded in turning the tide of public opinion in the US against Germany and the German people, and even against works of literature by German authors, many of which were soon banned from public libraries, cast out as contaminated. Creel set out his own verdict of the US propaganda effort in his book 'How We Advertised America – The First Telling of the Amazing Story of the Committee on Public Information that carried the Gospel of Americanism to every Corner of the Globe,' published by Harper & Brothers of New York in 1920. He contextualised the CPI's creation thus, 'it was in this recognition of public opinion as a major force that the Great War differed most essentially from all other conflicts. Other wars went no deeper than the physical aspects, but German Kultur raised issues that had to be fought out in the hearts and minds of people as well as on the actual firing line.'[21] He went on to make the case for the CPI as a plain publicity proposition, 'a vast enterprise in salesmanship, the world's greatest adventure in advertising' as opposed to an agency of censorship or 'a machinery of concealment.' Approval for his vision was not universal, but proof of the CPI's effectiveness, at the time, lay in the results it achieved. By 5th June1917, the date on which eligible US males were required to register for the draft, ten million signed up. By the end of the year 516,000 draftees were in training camps across the country. Millions more were to sign up in later drafts.[22]

In 'Propaganda Technique in the World War,' Harold Lasswell observed that 'the modern world is busy developing a core of men who do nothing but study the ways and means of changing minds or binding minds to their convictions. Propaganda...is developing its practitioners, its professors, its teachers and its theories. It is expected that governments will rely increasingly upon the professional propagandists for advice and aid.'[23] It was becoming clear that the clock could not be turned back; the magic formula for propaganda seemed to combine the powers of science with the mystery of magic, producing like a rabbit from a hat the alchemy to turn the hearts and minds of the masses towards a common purpose and to mould their behaviour into predictable and desired outcomes. In any event, Allied propaganda had convincingly demonstrated German war guilt, and the nation would now face the consequences. Ludendorff lamented that the Versailles Treaty of 1919 'sent the German people into bondage, into an absolutely crushing one. All delusions have vanished,' he wrote. 'We look into nothingness. Something else is needed.'[24] Ludendorff recorded his efforts to induce the Imperial Chancellor to create a great organisation, as it had become 'undeniably essential to establish an Imperial Ministry of Propaganda,' and he was convinced that no adequate counter- campaign to Allied propaganda could be organised except by an Imperial department possessing special powers. This advice was not to go unheeded by the ensuing generation of National Socialist propagandists in Nazi Germany.

CHAPTER V

'Long Live the Arabs!'
The Nationalist Message in the Age of
Dictatorships

'False rumours and lies are not put down by replying to them or spreading similar counter-rumours, they are put down by positive and beneficial works that attract attention and cause people to speak, so that new rumours, this time true, will take the place of the false old rumours.'

Imam Hassan Al-Banna,
Founder of the Muslim Brotherhood

In 1928, with the publication of Arthur Ponsonby's 'Falsehood In Wartime,' the reputation of British propaganda deployed in the Great War came under intense scrutiny and was partially discredited as details of the lies and distortion used in some of its creation and dissemination were exposed for the first time. This, in turn, stoked the debate about the wider compatibility of propaganda with liberal democracy; propaganda inevitably involved a degree of censorship and control that sat uneasily alongside perceptions of democratic societies as free and open.[1] One of the most damaging consequences of this suspicion about the integrity of propaganda was to surface in the scepticism with which future Nazi atrocity stories were to be met, including the scale and scope of the Nazis' 'Final Solution of the Jewish Question.' The challenges to the established liberal democracies of the West from the Fascist ideology of the 1920s were to precipitate the second great wave of scientific propaganda that concluded in the Second World War. With the maturing of communications as a profession, propagandists on both sides were to show they had learned lessons, not simply about how they might better understand the motivation of the unpredictable crowd in order to shape their opinions but how the more tightly defined psychological principles underpinning propaganda might be exploited through more persuasive mediums of mass communications such as radio and film and increasingly through the cult of personality, in order to induce the public to move from perception and acceptance to direct action and behaviour change. These lessons were to have profound implications for the pursuit of the ambitions of both the Allies and the Axis powers in the countries of the Middle East, and were to be reflected in the content and style of a new generation of wartime propaganda, some of it characterised by race hate and driven by Fascist ideology later to find its way into the profile and expressions of extreme Islamism.

The liberal democratic experiment in Italy was amongst the first casualties of the new peace, and its collapse opened the door to a fresh era of triumphalist, censorship driven propaganda which enabled and nurtured the one-party state that was to follow. Defeat against the Austrians at the Battle of Caporetto, wholesale loss of military and civilian lives, and what was seen as a national humiliation, meant that the domestic political landscape was now open to being shaped by different forces. The Italian Fascist Party was established by Benito Mussolini in 1921 on the ideological foundation of extreme nationalism, setting strong leadership and the primacy of state interests above those of the individual.

Mussolini, a former socialist and powerful, persuasive speaker, displayed all of the fire and brimstone of the preacher seeking converts as he cleverly rebranded his Fascist movement as a political party; 'like Lenin, Mussolini believed that liberal democracy was a relic of the past; parliamentary politics produced only corruption and paralysis.'[2] Mussolini was highly aware of the need to manage the image and brand of the newly Fascist Italy, and immediately sought to tightly choreograph the production and distribution of information to the Italian people in order to control and communicate the Fascist narrative of strength, discipline, national effort and personal sacrifice for the state. In constructing his information and communications model, it was significant that Mussolini himself had been both a political journalist and propagandist, producing trade union literature which proposed strike action and advocating violence as a means of enforcing labour demands.[3] Mussolini's attempts to persuade Italians to commit to the Nation State focused on censorship and propaganda travelling hand in hand in the old style, but the early application of this twin track approach was largely random without real method to his effort. However, this was to change dramatically with the accession of Hitler to power in Nazi Germany in 1933. Just as Mussolini's example had inspired Hitler and the young National Socialist movement, the Nazis' Reich Ministry for Popular Enlightenment and Propaganda, established in 1933, seems to have motivated Mussolini to adopt a newly invigorated approach to censorship.[4]

In 1934, after his first meeting with Hitler, Mussolini set about constructing a more formal propaganda organisation through which to manage state control. His son-in-law Count Galeazzo Ciano (married to his daughter Edda) had been appointed Head of the Government Press Office in 1933, but the following year he was elevated to Under-Secretary of Press and Propaganda, seizing on the opportunity to expand the influence, power and prestige of the Press Office, and then in June 1935 became Italy's first Minister of Press and Propaganda; 'It was no coincidence that Goebbels's design for an organised and integrated propaganda bureau became the template for Ciano and Italy.'[5] Ciano, who in 1936 was elevated yet further to be Italy's Foreign Minister, was to play a major role in the development of Italy's relationship with Arab nationalists and their propaganda drive to unseat the British in Palestine and more widely in the region.

From Black Shirts to Green Shirts

The ideas driving Fascism found some resonance in other parts of Europe. Spain's civil war resulted in the ascent to power of the Fascist General Francisco Franco and even in Britain, Sir Oswald Moseley's parades of his Black Shirts in East London caused an unwelcome, albeit more subdued ripple on the public consciousness. But across the Mediterranean in the Arabic speaking Maghreb, nationalists were struggling to establish sovereignty and identity whilst under the colonial yoke – of the Italians in Libya, the British in Egypt and the French in Morocco, Algeria and Tunisia. In these geopolitically important and volatile countries, political activists had been long exposed to the practical realities of dictatorship or occupation, the idea of an exclusively Arab nationalist party gained a foothold in the public consciousness by the time of Hitler's accession to power as German Chancellor in 1933. In British held Egypt, The Young Egypt Party was formed by Ahmad Hussein in October 1933 as a radical nationalist party with a religious dimension, its aim to create an empire initially comprising Egypt and Sudan but with a vision of reaching out and drawing in other Arab member states, combining to serve as the leader of Islam. In addition to its facsimile political creed, the party leaned heavily on the visual fetishes of Mussolini and Hitler's fascist propaganda, using distinctive green shirts and paramilitary style formations and parades to carve out a dominating presence on the physical landscape. The Green Shirts made no secret of their admiration for Nazi Germany, and after 1933, the party's tone grew more strident and violent. During the 1930s, Gamal Abd Al Nasser, the future leader of Egypt who was to go on to nationalise the Suez Canal in 1956, was a member of the party. The ideas behind this more extreme nationalism caught on elsewhere in the Middle East, notably in the formation of Lebanon's Phalanges Party, founded by Maronite Pierre Gemayel in 1936. Disbanded in 1938, the Green Shirts were to become a footnote in Egyptian history, but the forces which had nurtured the ideas that characterised the Party – the potent mix of nationalism and Islam – were to surface again in future political incarnations such as the Socialist Party of Egypt and later still in other manifestations of extremist Islamism.

Between themselves, Ciano and Mussolini were to take a direct hand in the planning and management of the concerted propaganda campaign by the Axis powers in the Middle East up to and during the war. Germany's ties with Italy were not always convenient, Italian aggression in Ethiopia in 1936 having left a toxic legacy in North Africa, added to which Mussolini was more intent on advancing Italian interests in the eastern Mediterranean than actively supporting any Arab independence agenda. For Italy, the defining moment of its intervention in the region came with the arrival of the Grand Mufti of Jerusalem, Haj Amin Al Husseini in Rome on 13th October 1941. In a tripartite meeting in the Italian capital, Husseini, Mussolini and Ciano agreed on a joint Axis declaration regarding the Arab fight against British domination and oppression.

The draft stated that Arab independence and full sovereignty should be given to all countries of the Near East occupied or controlled by the British and further that they gave their consent to 'the elimination of the Jewish national homeland in Palestine.'[6] The Italians used short wave radio broadcasts in Arabic, through Radio Bari, to reach audiences in the region with their message, reporting extensively on Axis victories, uprisings against the British and support for the Grand Mufti as the leader of the Arabs in their quest for independence.

In cases of both military strategy and propaganda, the Nazis had in the early part of the war deferred to Italy in North Africa but, with the arrival of General Rommel's forces there in February 1941 to help prevent the loss of Italy's colonies, the Germans started to take more of an active role. This included walking a more delicate line between propping Italy up as a colonial power in the region, advancing their own interests and launching a more direct propaganda offensive with the Arabs to oppose the interests of the British and their allies in the region.

Whilst the Italians had the benefit of more direct, and certainly more contemporary experience of the Arab political and nationalist agenda through their occupation of much of North Africa up to and during the start of the war, it was the Nazis, who in many respects, cultivated the more telling alliances with Arab collaborators and nationalists, prepared to work with them closely to construct a propaganda front against the British and their allies, particularly the Jews who were already laying advanced foundations for the post-war Zionist political state in Palestine. The stealthy Orientalist stereotyping of the 19th and early 20th centuries had in time led to a more fundamental but connected racial problem for the Nazis in the 1930s as they planned the propaganda campaign to achieve their own imperialist ambitions in the Middle East at the start of the Second World War. Needing to secure the co-operation of the Arab population in the blitzkrieg of race-fuelled vitriol they planned against the Jews and the British in Palestine and elsewhere in the region, they were forced to contemplate ways in which to overcome two racial barriers their own eliminationist ideology had erected: the innate superiority of the Aryan master race and the fact that Arabs, like the Jews, were also Semites and in addition Muslims. In the Grand Mufti of Jerusalem, Haj Amin Husseini (1897-1974), they found a collaborator and partner in constructing their anti-Zionist, anti-Jewish narrative in the region, an initiative that had to run hand in hand with a scramble to clarify the Nuremberg race laws in the context of what being Semitic legally meant. In time, they were able to reassure concerned potential allies such as Turkey and Egypt that anti-Aryan laws did not apply to them and their citizens, only to Jews.

Despite eventual military defeat for Germany in the Middle East, Nazism left traces behind, especially traces of hatred of the Jews that drew on the distinctly European traditions of radical anti-Semitism, according to the historian Jeffrey Herf. 'The evidence of the immediate post-war years in the Middle East...lends plausibility to the thesis of continuity and lineages between Nazism's Arabic-language propaganda, on the one hand, and radical Islam in the subsequent decades, on the other,'[7] he wrote. Herf makes the further point that the thesis of continuity does not mean that Islamism is identical to Nazism, but it suggests that one chapter of its history was written in Nazi-dominated Europe and, in particular in wartime Berlin. To this extent, his theory gives some traction to the view also held by Islamic State, that its own propaganda may in some cases have a longer shelf life than the act of war itself.

Al Husseini was amongst the most significant and influential political figures in the Arab world at the time. Much has been written about his role in the propaganda front, including what have been described as gross exaggerations of his importance, for example in the accusation that he was personally responsible for triggering the Jewish genocide.[8] His direct intervention in the cause of Arab nationalism and his support for the elimination of the proposed Jewish state in Palestine are, however, widely evidenced in both written and cinematic records. Able to trace his genealogy directly to the Prophet Muhammad, Husseini was a wealthy native of Jerusalem who became in time an Arab nationalist bitterly opposed to Zionism, ironically in hindsight appointed Grand Mufti of Jerusalem (and later Palestine) by the Liberal Jewish politician Herbert Samuel who saw him as a potential ally during the operation of the British Mandate in Palestine between 1922 and 1948. Husseini's role in the revolt against the British in 1936 led him to flee Palestine, from where he proceeded to find a home first in Fascist Italy and subsequently Berlin. Principally resident in Berlin through the war years, Husseini sought refuge in Cairo when the war ended, aiming to escape the jurisdiction of any allied war crimes tribunals that might be intending to prosecute him; one of his activities had been to help recruit Bosnian Muslims for the 'Handzar' Waffen SS Bosnian Division.[9] During his time in Fascist Italy and Nazi Germany, Husseini carved out a role for himself as the principal social architect behind the vision of a post-war Middle East freed from the domination of the British and French, with an independent and empowered Arab state of Palestine uncoupled from both Jewish and Zionist ambitions and free from the building pressures of immigration.

His Arabic language propaganda campaign was directed at achieving these ends alongside the accommodation of Nazi Germany's colonial ambitions in the region and its racially motivated objective of annihilation of the Jewish people. To add weight to the acceptance of his strategy in the Arab world, on May 10th 1941, Husseini announced in a formal Fatwa a military jihad against the British and French, in theory binding all Muslims to his cause although in reality it created a moral dilemma for some who felt unable to ally themselves with extreme Nazi sentiment.[10]

The Nazi Arabic language propaganda campaign conducted in the region was highly productive, a 'political and ideological synthesis' between the Nazi Foreign Ministry's Orient Office, under the direction of William Melchers, and a group of Arab exiles in Berlin led by Husseini, producing and distributing between them a deluge of leaflets and radio broadcasts. In thinking through the strategy to drive Arab directed propaganda, the Nazis mainly adapted the anti-Semitic content they had already developed, bolting on the idea that the creation of a Jewish state in Palestine was an unacceptable threat both to Islam and Arab populations of the Middle East, urging Arabs to take matters into their own hands and kill the Jews. The international Jewish conspiracy theory which was at the centre of Nazi propaganda became self-fulfilling after the end of the Second World War and on the establishment of a Jewish state in 1948 and beyond, when some Palestinians were looking for reasons they could attribute for their national catastrophe (the 'Nakba'). Nazi propagandists used a mix of communication tools including extensive leaflets but relied heavily, as did the Italians, on short wave radio to reach large audiences with a mix of ideological and factual material, much of it railing against the 'shameful crime' that would be committed by the creation of a Jewish state but also targeting Communism, categorising Bolsheviks as enemies of religion generally and of Islam specifically. Whilst Fascist Italy broadcast Arabic programmes from 1934 to 1943, Nazi shortwave programmes began in 1939 and continued until March 1945. Radio stations in Berlin, such as the Arab Nation, Voice of Free Arabism and Berlin In Arabic broadcast a stream of announcements assembled by Husseini and his fellow exiles who included ex Iraqi Prime Minister Rashid Ali Al-Gaylani (1892-1965), who had staged a short-lived coup against the British in Iraq in 1941, and the prominent Arabic language announcer Younis Bahri ('This is Berlin! Long live the Arabs!'), in tandem with a large team of Nazi officials working closely on strategy and content. Programming included an eclectic mix of music, news and commentary seven days and nights a week and the content was perfect for café culture, thousands of which possessed and played short wave radio to entertain their clientèle.

The subject of Palestine and the sacred status of its Omar mosque opposite Jerusalem's Holy Sepulchre was the focus of a broadcast made by Husseini via Berlin in Arabic in July 1943. Referring to the day when Saladin had 'thrown the Crusaders out of Holy Jerusalem,' he conflated the fight for Islam with the fight for Palestine, 'the Muslims fight for Palestine because it is a sacred piece of Islam. At the same time the Jews plot against the Arabs and Palestine and claim that the Omar mosque is on the site of their ancient temple. In this they depend on the support of foreign powers. Their actions do not weaken the determination of Muslims but give them more confidence in their struggle.'

Just as they had done in the First World War on the Western Front, during the subsequent fighting in Italy, the Germans dropped leaflets aimed specifically at Arab soldiers fighting alongside the Allied forces. The leaflets included messages such as, 'Arabs!...the allies and the Jews are the people responsible for all the catastrophes that were inflicted on the Arab countries and on Arabism. Germany is fighting to prevent the menace of Jewry from harming her, and this is the common interest of both Arabs and Germans.'

Ahmad and Johnny

As German propagandists had been back footed at the start of the First World War, unable to sidestep their pre-emptive and illegal invasion of Belgium, the British Ministry of Information (MOI), by 1942 under the management of Churchill's ex-fixer Brendan Bracken, had to try and minimise the impacts of a plethora of deep rooted and inherent problems defining Britain's relationships with the Arab world by the start of the Second World War.

Firstly, it could not ignore the fact that since 1922 formal League of Nations Mandates had placed Britain as colonial masters over the Arab populations in Palestine (including Trans Jordan) and Iraq, even though the terms of the Mandates technically required them to leave once they had facilitated the conditions for home rule, and second, from the Balfour Declaration in 1917 onwards Britain had been actively contriving to create the conditions through which a Jewish homeland in Palestine could be established and developed into a political state, along with facilitating immigration of European and other Jews to the country at the expense of Palestinian civil rights and to the disapproval of the Palestinian authorities. By 1936, this position had become unsustainable and an Arab uprising in Palestine against the British, led by Haj Amin al Husseini and other nationalists such as Fawzi Al Qawaqji, had to be put down with military force. Arab nationalists and their propagandists thus found natural allies in the Nazis and a powerful and convincing narrative for their propaganda strategy. It was relatively easy to portray the interests of the British as being obstructive to those of the Arabs and consequently simple to develop swathes of propaganda material which could be driven by issues of territorial invasion, economic exploitation and race hate.

What was a little more complex, however, was sidestepping the issue of who might replace the British and the French if their ambitions in the region were thwarted. The obvious, and unwelcome answer was the Nazis, whose views on Aryanism and the inferiority of the Semitic race, whilst in regards to the Arab peoples moderated to some degree, remained fundamentally problematic. In framing their propaganda response to these prevailing issues, the British chose to exploit the dangers that anti-Semitic sentiment and Nazi values would pose for Islam, focusing on the common ground shared with Islam by Christianity and using a combination of pamphlets, posters and radio broadcasts to emphasise the solidarity which would be needed to defeat Nazism.

The RAF dropped one of the first of these leaflets over the Middle East just after the German invasion of the Soviet Union. Written by Palestinian intellectual and activist Najati Sidki (1905-1979), it quoted extensive passages from the Qur'an in response to Nazi propaganda and pushed the message, 'the peoples of the East and Muslims in general are all united in supporting the cause of democracy in both word and deed.' The pamphlet 'God Defend the Right' started out, 'Islam and Christianity, both, reject the godless world of Hitler's imagining...' and went on to appeal to Muslims and Christians around the world to come together to destroy Hitlerism.[11]

Under the leadership of Professor Laurence Rushbrook Williams (1890-1978), Director of Middle East Propaganda at the MOI, the British went on to develop a range of Arabic language propaganda, some of it in poster form ('The downfall of the dictators is assured') and others using the more extended leaflet or pamphlet style, such as 'Alphabet of the War' which used the Arabic alphabet as way of flagging up differing aspects of the Nazi threat. Under the 'H' for Hitler letter, the Nazi leader is described as the arch-enemy of God. 'The entry for corruption' shows German soldiers drinking alcohol and dancing with semi-naked women, an image which is clearly intended to offend the religious sensibilities of its Muslim audience. Focusing its propaganda on the religious dimension allowed Britain to play its only trump card in what was in reality an uneven contest. In his approach to the task of managing the propaganda campaign, Williams had to walk a fine line, vilifying Nazism but at the same time glossing over the fact that Britain itself was an occupying force in the Middle East, having used military assets to crush insurrections in Palestine in 1936 and Iraq in 1941, holding the Mandates for much of the Levant and Iraq and deeply implicated in enabling the first Zionist State. These inconvenient truths lent a certain hypocrisy to its claims of partnership and solidarity with its Arab 'allies.'

But there was a subtlety to some of the British Arabic propaganda output which reflected the more psychological underpinning of persuasive public relations. A series of illustrated children's books, each with a moral tale at the core of the message, were subversive and original in their approach to influencing Arab views across the Middle East and North Africa. 'Ahmad and Johnny,' told the fanciful and episodic tale of two young boys, one British and one Sudanese, who were thrown together by the circumstances of the war and who shared childish, though trenchant, views about its causes, horrors and injustices. Illustrated by W Lindsay Cable, who was also the illustrator of Enid Blyton's books, Ahmad and Johnny are portrayed as close friends. Ahmad, who in a nod to the tradition of British Orientalist stereotyping is always depicted wearing a Fez, is an exile from Sudan, possibly an orphan. Johnny, whose father is away at the war in Sudan, is a cypher for patriotic and deeply reassuring messages about the enlightenment of the British and righteousness of their cause. The series was later also adapted into Farsi and used to target Iranian families.[12]

British propaganda, in time, found a way of influencing events on the ground in the region, rather than indirectly. It was given three-dimensional life by one of Britain's most accomplished and extraordinary Arabists, a woman who put her considerable first-hand experience and knowledge at the service of the Ministry of Information in order to promote the British agenda. Freya Stark (1893-1993), best known as a traveller and writer in the Arab world, became a prime mover in the development of the Arab Brotherhood of Freedom, an organisation she founded in Cairo aimed at convincing the Egyptian people that they were better off being actively engaged in the Allied cause.[13] Whilst encouraged by British military commander General Wavell, Stark found the High Commissioner (later Ambassador, 1934) in Egypt, Miles Lampson, less supportive; he worried that the Brotherhood's commitment to democracy could backfire against British interests.

However, Stark's movement found its greatest success in Egypt where it grew to a membership of 75,000 before being suppressed in 1952 prior to the revolution of the Free Officers under General Neguib. It never really gained much momentum in Iraq, a 'more intractable society further removed from Axis danger.' Stark's efforts were assessed by the British government as generally successful and she ended up being deployed in the US to help counter the strength of Zionist propaganda against British rule in Palestine. In paraphrasing her career, Stark's obituarist speculated that it was her faith in humankind more than anything else which made her such an effective propagandist. Stark made her own defence of propaganda in a leaflet, 'Apology for Propaganda' produced with her husband, diplomat Stewart Perone, and now held with her archive at the University of Texas in Austin.[14]

In July 1944, the public relations section of the British Consulate in the southern Iraqi city of Basra showed a mix of ambition and imagination by hiring a river steamer to travel up the river Euphrates from Basra to take to the Marsh Arabs the latest in propaganda films and recordings promoting the British position and agenda in Iraq. The boat, which stopped at watering holes along the river bank, attracted huge audiences who came and watched a selection of movies, among them an account of the Regent of Iraq's visit to Britain and listened to recordings via a loudspeaker and radiogram. At Chibaish, 'Showboat' gave its third performance to as many as 2,500 spectators gathered on the quay to get as near to the big screen as possible. The Ministry of Information took extensive photographic records of 'Showboat' in action, which it judged to be 'a great success.'[15] This roadshow approach to propaganda in Iraq, pioneered by the British, was being mirrored at the same time in Palestine where public showings of propaganda movies proved equally popular with large audiences, in which men appeared to be welcomed in front of the screen whilst women were relegated to the gloom and frustration of the reverse side.

In 1938, in response to German and Italian Arabic radio broadcasts, Britain established the BBC Arabic Service, its first and long overdue foreign-language station and one which was to become an enduring means of influence across the region. The service quickly gained traction amongst Arab audiences as a trusted and reliable source of news, with brand values that gave it a distinct edge over its rivals and which it built in time into a major instrument of soft power. In the leaflet 'This Is London,' the MOI promoted the new station and its output, and the pamphlet contained details of the official opening of a mosque in Butetown, Cardiff in 1943, an event that was attended by Hafiz Wahba, Saudi Arabia's representative in London.[16] As part of its attempt to use religious sentiment to its benefit, Britain was keen to stress that the country's Islamic community were free to practise their faith and to open places of worship.[17]

At All Costs Avoid Being Boring
The Ministry of Public Enlightenment and Propaganda, set up in Nazi Germany in 1933 by the new Reich Minister Josef Goebbels, became in its time a model for the organisation, processing and distribution of state propaganda, its remit covering the press, radio, film, art, music and literature. Admired and replicated by contemporaries including Mussolini, its establishment was described by Goebbels himself as 'a revolutionary act.' To explain his intentions and to make clear to the German people what he had in mind with its creation, he made two important public speeches setting out the direction and elements of the detail. In the first, to members of the German Press on 15th March 1933, he characterised his aim as a national revolution through the spiritual mobilisation of the general population and stressed that he no longer intended to leave the people to their own devices.

'In the new Ministry of Public Enlightenment and Propaganda I envisage the link between regime and people, the living contact between national government, as the expression of the people's will and the people themselves.'[18] To put radio in the service of the regime, Goebbels explained that he would dissolve the independent broadcasting corporations that had existed up until then, replace them with a Reich station and arrange for the mass production of the 'People's Receiver' (Volksempfänger), a cheap radio that would allow even the poorest strata of the population to be included in his propaganda revolution. Goebbels, who began to take an interest in the use of propaganda to promote the party and its programme after his appointment as Gauleiter of Berlin in 1926, stressed that it was not enough for people to be more or less reconciled to the Nazi regime or to be persuaded to adopt a neutral attitude towards it, 'rather we want to work on people until they have capitulated to us, until they grasp ideologically that what is happening in Germany today not only must be accepted but also can be accepted.'

In his second major speech, to the staff of Berlin's Radio Corporation on 25th March 1933, he equated the Ministry's task as being to achieve a mobilisation of mind and spirit in Germany equal to that of the Ministry of Defence in the sphere of defence, a task which would require and receive appropriate finance. 'In 1914, we had been mobilised in material terms as no other nation had, what we lacked was the mobilisation of the mind within the country and in other countries which provided the basis for the material mobilisation. We did not lose the war because our artillery gave out but because the weapons of our minds did not fire.

Because people who knew nothing about it were employed to explain Germany to the world.'[19]

In his analysis of radio as the propagandist's paramount weapon in the moulding of public opinion, Goebbels displayed his mastery as a propagandist, communicator and social architect, showing both how much he had absorbed of the new theories and ideas that were driving modern, persuasive communications, and at the same time how much further ahead of other Fascist propaganda strategy that he had moved. 'The first principle: at all costs avoid being boring. I put that before everything,' he emphasised to his audience.

'So do not think that you have the task of creating the correct attitudes, of indulging in patriotism, of blasting out military music and declaiming patriotic verse—no, that is not what this new orientation is all about. Rather, you must help to bring forth a nationalist art and culture which is truly appropriate to the pace of modern life and to the mood of the times. The correct attitudes must be conveyed but that does not mean they must be boring.'[20] Goebbels went on to encourage staff to use their imaginations to bring material to the ears of the masses in a way which is 'modern, up to date, interesting, and appealing; interesting, instructive but not schoolmasterish.'[21]

Taking directly from the experience of their British counterparts, the Nazis were to focus in this new era of more scientific propaganda on both radio and film as mediums which they could exploit to a much greater degree and with much more effect. To carry this idea forward, the Reich Film Chamber was formed in June 1933 and all members of the film industry were required to join, a measure that in effect both centralised and censored film production at a stroke. The malign intent of much of the ensuing output is nowhere better expressed than in the 1940 film 'The Eternal Jew' (Der Ewige Jude), which was created to prepare the psychological ground amongst the German people for the Holocaust. The film, made after the occupation of Poland and lasting one hour and five minutes, uses the psychological principles of association, projection and spurious scientific suggestion to frame the narrative and the commentary in the laboratory setting of the ghetto, equating the Jews with a public health hazard, juxtaposing shots of Jewish families at home and in the streets with flies and rats, branding the Jewish nation 'a plague that threatens the health of the Aryan people.'

A consummate extrapolation of extreme race hate, it also suggests that the Jews 'whose dwellings are filthy and neglected, aren't poor,' playing into the racist theme of a Jewish banking conspiracy at the root of Germany's post-war economic crash; the film casts the Jews as chameleons who pollute modern European society by controlling finance, crime and the professions because they supposedly cannot produce goods for themselves.[22]

Hitler himself was always clear about the role that propaganda would play in the trajectory of the Third Reich, determined to act on Ludendorff's analysis of the way in which failure to manage public opinion at home had sold the German people short. 'The experience of 1914-1918 spurred me to take up the question of propaganda even more deeply than before. What we failed to do, the enemy did with amazing skill and really brilliant calculation. I myself learned enormously from this enemy war propaganda,'[23] he wrote in Mein Kampf. In his assessment of Allied propaganda, Hitler praised the manipulation of atrocity stories, concluding that Allied propaganda was regarded as 'a weapon of the first order, while in our country it was the last resort of unemployed politicians and a haven for slackers.' In his analysis and recipe for successful propaganda set out in Mein Kampf, Hitler is specific about the general approach he believes will work best, emphasising that it must be in popular form, addressed to the masses and within their intellectual comfort zone, dumbed down and simplified and designed, in line with the views of Gustave Le Bon, to elicit an overtly emotional rather than intellectual response. 'The art of propaganda consists precisely in being able to awaken the imagination of the public through an appeal to their feelings, in finding the appropriate psychological form that will arrest the attention and appeal to the hearts of the national masses,'[24] he wrote. His condescending take on the inability of the German people to think for themselves is reminiscent in its own paternalistic way of both Lasswell's theory of scientific democracy and elements of the thinking behind Bernays' new profession of public relations counsel, adopted and set out in his two manifestos, Crystallising Public Opinion published in 1923 and Propaganda published two years later in 1925. This vision provided the psychic backdrop to George Orwell's 'Ministry of Truth' and the reviled 'Big Brother' in his fictionalised world of '1984,' a nightmare regimentation of thought that obliterated individualism and disallowed every shred of human imagination. 'Every change that is made in the subject of a propagandist message must always emphasize the same conclusion. The leading slogan must of course be illustrated in many ways and from several angles, but in the end, one must always return to the assertion of the same formula,'[25] he wrote.

Crystallising Public Opinion

The relationship between Nazi and Arab nationalist propagandists was developed in order to stitch together a narrative in the Middle East that would satisfy distinctly mutual interests; if the end game of the alliance was geopolitical and territorial, the rationale for the propaganda content was largely driven by race hate of the Jews and the injustice of the denial of self-rule for Arab countries in the region by the imperial powers of Britain and France. To help construct their narrative, Nazi propagandists actively looked for clues and lessons that they might learn from both the success of Allied propaganda in the First World War and the new 'pseudoscience' of public relations developed as a consequence of it.

Both Hitler and Goebbels were aware of the new alchemists of public relations who were taking the corporations of America by storm in the late 1920s and early 1930s; they were generically interested in how the business worked but also open to actively exploring relationships at first-hand with some of this new profession's wunderkinds in order to get a hands-on idea of what advantage modernising techniques of persuasion might have to offer the National Socialist agenda. These possibilities were explored in time through contracts set up by the industrial conglomerate IG Farben with Ivy Leadbetter Lee and the German Tourist Authority with Carl Byoir, both of whom were destined to be formally investigated in senate hearings accused of propagating Germany's National Socialist message in the United States. From the personal evidence of the German-born American journalist Karl von Wiegand (1874-1961), it was clear that Goebbels, in the early 1930s, had closely studied the general theory and advice offered by Edward Bernays in his book 'Crystallising Public Opinion' in order to frame an approach to his campaign to deal with the Nazis' campaign against the Jews of Germany and Europe. According to Bernays himself, whilst the Nazis were interested in his written work, they also approached him to act for them personally, as did Spain's Fascist leader General Francisco Franco, but he turned them both down.[26] There can be no doubt that in their collective study of the new wave of scientific propaganda, whilst neither may have been fully aware of the most advanced findings of modern depth psychology, both Hitler and Goebbels accepted and embraced the theories which set out the connections between the psychology of groups and individuals and the influence of leaders over the crowds they seek to dominate.

Gustave Le Bon's defining of the requisite attributes for leadership, including the mercurial quality of prestige, was reinforced by Goebbels' admiration for the leadership skills of Mussolini, whose overwrought oratorical and presentational approach he viewed as a model for his own public persona. There can be no doubt too, after the chaotic disorganisation of Germany's own failed wartime propaganda effort, that they had learned lessons from George Creel's Olympian organisational feat in planning and managing the national publicity effort of the CPI and from the tightly managed British propaganda efforts overseen by the strategic mastery of Sir Campbell Stuart after March 1918. They had absorbed and could now follow a proven process to construct their own communications model, defining the parameters of organisation, structure and content.

In consequence, National Socialist propaganda, powered by its twin ideological pistons of race hate and paranoid conspiracy theory, was highly advanced in the thinking and means it applied to influence the psychology and opinions of both its own people and its enemies. Goebbels deemed British dominance in propaganda during the First World War an 'easy victory,' but times had changed, 'we have become political psychologists, whereas Churchill and Chamberlain are still employing methods from 25 years ago and think they are still dealing with the Germans of 1918,'[27] he wrote in the Nazi house newspaper Der Angriff in March 1940.

Palestine and 'The Jewish War'

The significance of Nazi propagandists casting a wide net to seek both evidence and professional input to bolster the theoretical and practical substance of their wartime propaganda campaign is considerable. Together with the structural architecture they put in place to centralise their propaganda resource and capability, it shows just how thoroughly Hitler and Goebbels delivered on their promise to place propaganda at the heart of the Nazi vision and execution of their war effort. Unlike other Fascist regimes, they were conspicuously willing to learn, interpret and adapt the lessons of the more nuanced version of propaganda that had opened up between the wars. Through the new Ministry of Public Enlightenment and Propaganda, they were able to define an entirely original model to tightly manage the processes and operational complexities of the Nazi propaganda effort; their output took significant account of the new orthodoxy defined by a generation of theorists and practitioners who had together shaped a conceptual revolution in the way that ideas could be sold using complex psychological techniques to stimulate motivation and change behaviour.

During the Second World War, Nazi propagandists were able to successfully adapt their strategy and output to the particular condition of the Middle East at the time, using the intended creation of a Jewish state in Palestine as the fulcrum of a campaign to attack international Jewry and the British occupiers of Arab lands that they could claim had been invaded and annexed and whose populations had been politically and economically marginalised. They were able to successfully sell this status quo as an existential threat to Arab nationalist political ambitions, to Islam and to the wider Arab nation. In the action they prescribed to counter these joint threats, they urged the Arab people to kill the Jews before they themselves could be killed, in effect inciting a war based on race hate, paranoia and psychological projection. If there was clear evidence needed of Harold Lasswell's categorisation of propaganda, after military and economic means, as the third implement of operation against a belligerent enemy, the Nazis provided it in the campaign they pursued in the Middle East. Whilst they succeeded in many of their propaganda aims in the region, they could not reproduce after their military defeat in May 1943 any comparable success on the battlefield or in the economic war.

For the British and their Allies, the victory in the Middle East over the Germans and the Italians in the Second World War replicated their eventual military success over Ottoman Turkey in the Great War. But where the successes of the First World War ended with Britain and France carving up of the region into zones of self-interest where their colonial and imperialist ambitions could be played out and strategic interests advanced, the military success of the Second World War in the region was to turn to ashes in little more than a decade of increasingly vexed and costly occupation.

The position and role of Palestine was to be central in this decline, and the British inability to construct a credible and convincing narrative around their eventual withdrawal from the country and abandonment of its people was to go on to define Britain's more fractious relationship with the post-war Middle East and the wider Arab world. Of the British experience of the Second World War in the region, it might be said that they had won the war but lost the peace; however, the notion in 1945 that affairs were going to deteriorate into a full-blown existential crisis during the decade to come would have seemed harder to predict.

CHAPTER VI

The Palestine Conundrum: Crisis Management and Reputational Deficit

'We plan to eliminate the state of Israel and establish a purely Palestinian state. We will make life unbearable for Jews by psychological warfare and population explosion. We Palestinians will take over everything, including all of Jerusalem.'
Yasser Arafat,
Chairman, Palestine Liberation Organisation

It is hard to overstate the levels of toxicity, anger and bitterness aroused by the subject of Palestine or to downplay its continuing role at the centre of the destructive and still widening fault line that divides the Arab world, the State of Israel and the international community. Even a century after the Balfour Declaration of 2nd November 1917 and the partition of the country following the establishment of the Jewish state in May 1948, young Palestinians you meet in Ramallah still look you in the eye and, unbidden, utter the disembodied word 'Balfour' with the significance of a loaded gun. The story of the British Mandate in Palestine, which ran from 1922 when it was finally granted by the League of Nations until 1948 when the British walked away from the Palestinian people and the two-state solution, has been told often and at length.

But alongside the facts of the occupation and its serpentine political, ethnic and religious complexities, the attendant packaging and presentation of the associated events have generally been both more opaque and less familiar. Why should this be? In broad terms, across the 26-year trajectory of the Mandate, the British were never able to construct a consistent or user-friendly rationale that made sense to

the outside world of what they were doing, or failing to do
their strategy was leading. For once, British propagandists
struggled to find ways of reconciling the competing narratives in play —
Palestine or window dressing a growing disaster without it continuing
to look and feel like one. It certainly played out as such, with all the
attritional consequences for Britain's reputation in the region, but not
before a slow descent through the agonising and humiliating steps of
crisis management and disaster recovery for which corporate players
now regularly scenario plan but for which British Empire thinking was
singularly ill-equipped.

It is rare for senior British politicians to make public statements about
past policy mistakes, especially ones with deep human consequences, yet
Britain's Labour Foreign Secretary David Miliband did just that during
a major speech in 2009 to the Oxford Centre for Islamic Studies, when
he suggested that the West must show greater respect for Muslims if it
wants to rebuild relations with the Islamic world. He went on to say,
'lines drawn on maps by colonial powers were succeeded, among other
things, by the failure – it has to be said not just ours – to establish two
states in Palestine.'[1]

Miliband, who built a reputation during his brief three-year tenure
in the job for both perceptiveness and willingness to listen, proposed in
his speech that British and Arab relations had been damaged by the use
of 'lazy stereotypes' by Western officials and conceded that his own use
of the labels 'moderate' and 'extremist' showed a lack of understanding
that risked 'undermining the force of our own argument.'[2] In his speech
he went even further, listing the Iraq war alongside the Crusades and
colonial-era division and subjugation of the Middle East as drivers of
bitterness, distrust and resentment in the region. 'When people hear
about Britain, too often they think of these things,' he said. The solution
he offered for the future of the West's relations with Muslim-dominated
countries 'lies in the building of broad coalitions based upon consent
among citizens, not just ruling elites.' His speech, in effect a plea for a
reset in public discourse and foreign policy, seemed prescient then and
remains so now.

The Terms of the Mandate

The compelling example of this failure in British policy, its flawed
implementation and colour-blind public projection, is nowhere better
displayed than in the unhappy and defining occupation of Palestine.
The rationale behind the British desire for the Palestine Mandate lay

In classic imperialist geopolitical strategy; by occupying Palestine up to the eastern border of the Red Sea, Britain could protect and control its maritime traffic through the Suez Canal. Added to that, the Mandate allowed Britain to create a land bridge from the Mediterranean to the Iraqi oilfields and a means of preventing any leakage of French ambitions from their power bases in Syria and Lebanon. Under the terms of the Mandate, Britain was to be 'responsible for placing the country under such political, administrative and economic conditions as will secure the establishment of the Jewish national home, as laid down in the preamble, and the development of self-governing institutions, and also for safeguarding the civil and religious rights of all the inhabitants of Palestine, irrespective of race and religion.'[3]

From the start, though, the British could not develop a credible narrative for the reconciliation of these competing agendas; their lives were quickly made impossible by the conflicting interests and demands of the different actors in this post-war regional drama, all of them anxious to adopt a leading role at centre stage. The cast comprised powerful voices, all pressing urgent cases for special treatment in the post-Ottoman Palestinian political settlement, among them Jews already living in their traditional homeland, Zionists and European Jews from the diaspora arriving in ever more frequent boatloads under an accelerated immigration programme, Palestinian Arabs whose houses and land were being put under growing pressure as the British sanctioned compulsory land grabs and Arab neighbours watching the build-up of the Jewish and Zionist powerbase and the occupation of the British with a combustible mix of anxiety and anger.

In all of this, the British justification for their presence in the increasingly fractious and volatile country spun the line that it was their role as honest broker rather than imperial self-interest which was the motivating force behind the military occupation. They were placed in the uniquely unenviable position of being accused of being simultaneously pro-Arab and pro-Jew; Britain spent time, effort, angst and increasing amounts of money not only trying to contain active insurgencies from Arab nationalists but increasingly Jewish ones as well. The Zionist agenda advanced relentlessly with the establishment of ever more communities and the import of weapons for self-defence, causing inter-communal fighting between Arab and Jew for the first time; the Arabs attacked the Jewish population in 1921 and again in 1926 during extensive mob violence; collusion of the British and the Jews in forming the notorious 'Special Night Squads,' a corrosive idea driven by British maverick army officer Orde Wingate, was seen by Palestinians as further evidence of the British 'holding back the democratic process they were supposed to foster under the Mandate.'[4]

Eventually, the pressure erupted resulting in a full-scale Palestinian uprising led by Arab nationalists Haj Amin Al Husseini and Fawzi Al Qawaqji in 1936. This in turn was forcefully repressed by occupying British troops over three ensuing years up to the start of the Second World War in 1939. Not only were the British struggling to contain events on the ground, but they were also battling world opinion which was moving increasingly in favour of accelerating the practical realisation of a Jewish state. The United States, still a relative newcomer in the power plays of the Middle East but destined to replace the British as the dominant force in the region after 1956, was becoming increasingly vocal and persuasive in its support for the Zionist cause and prepared to expend political capital in securing a successful outcome for post-Holocaust Jewish aspirations. In April 1946, the Anglo-American Commission on Palestine, chaired by Sir Norman Brook, recommended that '100,000 certificates be authorised immediately for the admission into Palestine of Jews who have been the victims of Nazi and Fascist persecution.' At the same time, it also recommended that 'Palestine shall be neither a Jewish State nor an Arab State; that Jew shall not dominate Arab and Arab shall not dominate Jew in Palestine.'[5]

This increasing conundrum was finally confronted by the British Cabinet in January 1947, when the Secretary of State for the Colonies reported to the Cabinet, 'the only reasonable solution of the Palestine problem is that recommended by the Royal Commission of 1936, namely the partition of the country between the Arabs and the Jews. This solution possesses an element of finality which is elsewhere absent.'[6] The British imperial will, its capacity to endure and ability to pay the price of occupation finally cracked under the pressure and they took the idea of partition of the country to the United Nations in 1947, anxious to hand off a problem which they had come to see as intractable, expensive and damaging to their long-term interests and the British reputation in the Arab world.

The ensuing years of wearying conflict and despair in Palestine have conspired to obscure this 'foster role' played by Britain according to historian James Renton, Senior Lecturer in History at Edge Hill University. Such an omission is tragic, as Mandate era misjudgements are being repeated, he argues, 'whilst Arabs and Jews played a fundamental role in the unfolding drama of Mandate Palestine, the driving force was imperial Britain. The old myth that Britain was merely 'holding the ring,' trying to keep the peace between two irrational, warring parties is a gross misunderstanding of history.'[7]

The Cost of Intervention

The information and communication demands faced by British public relations experts and propagandists in Palestine became impossible to meet, at least with conviction or authority. Insurgencies, both Jewish and Arab, the development of a political solution destined for the unsatisfactory compromise of partition and an international dimension spanning the domestic audience in Britain, the Arab world and a critical constituency in the United States made it impossible to set any objectives other than those of containment and immediate crisis management. Britain's intervention in Palestine was proving costly in political capital, resources, lives and increasingly its reputation for political judgement. It was these factors which fed into a communications plan aimed at selling the British sacrifices as worthwhile and necessary whilst at the same time doing everything it could to achieve a political solution and exit strategy which it could convince all audiences was just and workable.

In fact, from early on in its role as a Mandate holder, Britain had recognised that the Palestinian press was highly influential; there was a wide domestic audience that took an interest in what both Arabic and English language newspapers such as Filastin, Al Difa and the Palestine Post had to say, some of which concerning British policy and the British themselves was both uncomplimentary and provocative. As a solution to this problem, the government, under the guidance of a High Commissioner, first turned to censorship, both restricting public access to some information and putting the police in charge of enforcing the policy, a position which endured until 1927. However, this moved forward the following year when a press bureau was established in the administration Secretariat, and by 1938 it had become the Public Information Office (PIO). The advent of war witnessed a change in information culture, when the Palestine government belatedly recognised that information services could be made more central in the dynamics of influencing and seeking to control public opinion in the country; it was at this point that they started to try and build a more proactive and open relationship with the media. The PIO accordingly developed a twin track approach, as a PR machine to roll out community engagement programmes with the local population and as a producer of propaganda to boost internal security and keep people focused on the war effort.

The PIO delivered on this brief with what even now seems a relatively forward-thinking mix of PR tactics, including tri-lingual public information campaigns (English, Hebrew and Arabic) that distributed government information and publications, a fleet of mobile cinema vans offering villagers the outdoor night time movie experience (albeit the public information rather than Humphrey Bogart variety) and dedicated reading rooms providing direct access to a variety of official material set up in Tel Aviv and Jaffa.[8] Film was used as a public information tactic in Palestine but also at home, in one case specifically to pump up the attractions of a career in the Palestine Police amongst potential recruits in Britain. An effective and committed police force was recognised as pivotal to keeping a lid on the shaky tripartite stand-off between British, Jew and Arab. Produced in Palestine by the No.1 Army Film and Photographic Unit during 1945, the film 'Palestine Police' was handed over to the Colonial Office on 5th December 1945; it premiered to assorted dignitaries at the Ministry of Information on 7th January 1946 before being shown widely throughout the UK by Army mobile cinemas, as well as touring schools and boys clubs during that year.[9] For journalists, the PIO arranged weekly press conferences, served as a distribution agent for the British Ministry of Information (MOI) and provided press facilities, including the issuing of press cards, and a press service relying mainly on Reuters, the MOI and the BBC. The PIO also prepared news broadcasts and provided maps and photographs for local newspapers and it administered press legislation, newspaper rationing and, during the war, oversaw the censorship regime.

During the war years, British troops alongside wider audiences could watch films shot under the brand name 'War Pictorial News,' produced by the Ministry of Information Middle East, based in Egypt. These films were released with special commentary and titles, sometimes in Arabic or French, depicting different aspects of the war underway across the world; one example, 'Women Work For Victory' (no 104), focused on the war role that women from all over the region were playing by repairing damaged military electrical equipment such as binoculars and engine gaskets from a factory in Cairo. Claiming that: 'there are thousands of women working in the Middle East from 15 countries,' the commentary signs off in a particularly jingoistic vein: 'good luck to the women of the Middle East playing their part in the fight for freedom.'

Also looming large on the Palestinian communications spectrum was the powerful and authoritative medium of radio, one which was being exploited so effectively in the Arabic language by Italian and Nazi propagandists. In 1942, Axis radio was portraying life in Palestine as generally grim, 'swimming in a pool of blood,' its people ruled by a reign of terror dominated by the brutal British and the 'dirty Jews.'[10] Its accusations ranged from British violations of the holy places, the spread of famine and poverty and a hidden intention to annihilate the Arabs entirely. Recurring themes in these Arabic language broadcasts were consistent and predictable, including denunciation of Arab leaders who sided with the British, Arab and Muslim victimisation at the hands of the Jews and expansionist policies of the British and the Jews acting together in Palestine.

Whilst stations such as Berlin in Arabic focused on the association of Nazism and Islam in mutual opposition to British imperialism, the Arab Nation stressed in October that year that there could be 'no co-operation between Arabs and Jews in Palestine.'[11] It asserted that the Arabs had been the real owners of Palestine for thousands of years, putting forward the notion that if Jewish claims in Palestine were well-founded, then 'the Arabs can claim that they have a right to Spain and the Red Indians to America.'

Between 1934 and 1941, three British-governed radio stations were established in the Middle East: Egyptian State Broadcasting (ESB) in Cairo (1934), the Palestine Broadcasting Service (PBS) in Jerusalem (1936), and the Near East Broadcasting Service (NEBS) in Jaffa (1941). These three stations were modelled on the BBC and run as colonial or imperial stations, but they were also considered to be national stations. As a result, they operated as hybrid entities with overlapping and sometimes conflicting mandates.[12] The Palestine Broadcasting Service became an independent government department in 1945, when it had two transmitters in Ramallah and one each in Tel Aviv and Jerusalem. At that time, there were over 55,000 licensed radio receivers in Palestine, although the listening audience was much larger, especially in rural areas. Just as the significance of radio as the pre-eminent communications tool of the age was recognised by the British in Palestine and the Nazis in Berlin, so it was to be given comparable status by soon to be President Gamal Abd Al Nasser in Egypt after 1954.

Nasser, building on the experience and success of the Arabic language Nazi propaganda broadcasts so skilfully set up and managed by sympathetic Arab exiles during the war, was quick to harness the airwaves as soon as possible after his ascent to power on the realisation that he needed a weapon of maximum reach and penetration to deploy his propaganda war against the British, an aspiration as it happened that the Americans who were pursuing their own interests against the British in Egypt were only too happy to help subsidise.

Rationalising the MOI

In 1946, a major shift occurred in the internal organisation of the British propaganda factory, which has never been reversed, and which has had a long-term downstream effect on British government information culture and its ability to keep in step with foreign policy. In order to save money and resources after a debilitating war that had left Britain on its knees financially, the Ministry of Information was rationalised (in effect downgraded) to become the lesser Central Office of Information (COI), an institution which endured as such until its formal closure in 2011. Why did this seemingly bureaucratic change matter then and why does it still matter? And what was the significance for Palestine?

As part of the transformation, the new COI became non-ministerial. Its role would be to provide information, material and publicity advice and services for government departments at home and abroad. But, unlike its predecessor, the MOI, it did not continue to be responsible for government or departmental information policy and, most crucially was not represented as a standalone function in Cabinet; the case for information and propaganda could no longer be made by a dedicated minister with special responsibility and, importantly, direct knowledge. In effect, the administrative downgrade had not only relegated the status of information and communications at policy level, but it had made it much more difficult to integrate it with policy at all. This cathartic decision was first elucidated by British Prime Minister Clement Attlee who told Parliament in December 1945: 'in the view of the Government, the responsibility for the information policy of a Department must rest with its Minister. There must be effective machinery for co-ordination, especially as far as overseas publicity is concerned. Neither of these purposes requires a separate Minister exclusively concerned with information matters.'[13]

The ability to co-ordinate any effort to communicate British foreign policy overseas was effectively dropped and the responsibility for information that was not domestic was divided up between the Foreign, Colonial and Dominion Offices.[14] This disconnection was to hinder the propaganda efforts of Sir Anthony Eden a decade later, and has had a longer term negative impact on Britain's ability to establish a consistent narrative in the region, one from which it has arguably never quite recovered. Whilst Britain had to keep its own population onside during the Palestine Mandate years, this in practice never seemed to be the predominant challenge. The larger effort was spent in shaping the perspectives of three international audiences concurrently, selling each a variant of the facts on the ground with a spin that catered to their largely conflicting interests and objectives.

Public opinion in the United States needed to be shaped in such a way that the Anglo-American special relationship could survive the impact of the Jewish insurgencies and the British military response. Arab public opinion needed reassurance that the solutions to the stand-off between Arab and Jew would not result in the abandonment of the two state principle that would ensure the establishment of a Palestinian political entity, and the Jews both in Palestine and elsewhere had to be dealt with at insurgency level but also as political aspirants with a powerful international network (whose relationships Britain valued) and an unstoppable momentum towards inevitable statehood. The best Britain could do was lurch from containment to crisis management at every step of the process, perpetually looking for political compromise in a damage limitation exercise that spanned military engagement, diplomatic progress and, increasingly, finding an exit strategy that would deliver a measure of respectability to partition as a viable solution and at the same time preserve Britain's dignity and reputation, fast being undermined by the Americans amongst others.

Paying the Price for Past Mistakes

In a reversal of what it could now belatedly perceive as the reputational cul-de-sac of Palestine, Britain increasingly tried to pivot the narrative towards the United Nations as the competent international arbiter and problem solver, seeking to preserve its own interests by not committing further resources to administration, policing or infrastructure in the country.

In the process, Britain's perceived lack of progress caused frustration for the Americans who thought the British were simply backsliding. British propaganda was primarily reactive and defensive as it tried to preserve its reputation as a regional nation-builder, forced to refute the argument that its withdrawal from Palestine might be the thin end of the wedge and evidence of a wider policy of disengagement in the region. In addition, British propaganda emphasised the extent of its co-operation with the United Nations and promoted the mutuality of Arab-British friendship.[15]

With the ending of the British Mandate on 14th May 1948, and the declaration of the State of Israel immediately thereafter, the country was plunged into the first and most far-reaching of the Arab-Israeli wars, leaving the disadvantaged Palestinians dispossessed and defeated, in the midst of what became known as 'The Nakba' (the catastrophe or disaster), an event which caused the exodus of some 700,000 Palestinians from the fledgling State and is still marked by a day of national mourning in Ramallah, across the Occupied Palestinian Territory (OPT) and in Palestinian communities in the diaspora. By this time, the British were focusing their effort on nurturing King Abdullah of Jordan, Palestine's neighbour, even as storm clouds began to gather over their interests in Egypt.

Reflecting on the trajectory of the British Mandate years in Palestine, the combination of a failure of British vision, mishandling of events on the ground and dearth of a rigorous exit strategy all contributed to the lack of a just solution for the Palestinians, and it is this essential failure that has been at the heart of Britain's loss of reputation and decline as a power in the region, trumping the considerable contribution in capacity building that occupation made to the country's civil service, infrastructure, road network, schools and hospitals. At the same time, Britain's loss was America's gain; it enabled the US to take the opportunity to step in and fill the vacuum left by the reverses to British imperialist ambitions. This transfer of power and shift in regional ascendancy was to be further cemented by the events in Egypt, a mere eight years later when America again was to call the shots over a fatal failure in both British policy and communication. In hindsight, the high point of Britain's strategic solution to the Palestine question was most likely the Royal Palestine Commission's (the 'Peel' Commission) 1937 proposal of the two-state solution that it considered could be acceptable to both Palestinians and Zionists. But even here, there was 'blatant disregard' for its impact on the average Palestinian, according to historian James Renton.

With the passage of over 70 years since the Nakba, Britain is still forced onto the back foot in defence of its failure to secure a just settlement in Palestine, and the military campaign it fought is not a straightforward matter of national pride. The British action in Palestine was never recognised formally as a campaign; the 90,000 British servicemen who served in Palestine between 1945 and 1948 did not have the option of receiving a dedicated campaign medal, instead, they had to apply by post for a General Service medal, and even then were deprived of the opportunity of receiving it in person. For many years, the campaign was never mentioned at the Armistice parade in London with no opportunity to march past the Cenotaph, according to veteran Eric Lowe of Hayling Island in Hampshire. 'There's not even a definitive figure for the British troops who died; estimates suggest some 400 were killed or died of wounds. It took over 50 years for British veterans to get a memorial for the dead. In the end, the veterans had to pay for it from their own pockets,' he recalls.[16] Official figures, such as they are, now suggest that as many as 800 British servicemen lost their lives in the Palestine action between 1945 and May 1948 when the State of Israel was declared; many of their graves lie neglected or forgotten in cemeteries across Israel and the West Bank.

In a poignant ceremony in a windswept former Italian Prisoner of War Camp in Malton, North Yorkshire, the Palestine Veterans Association (PVA) dipped its standard for the last time on 20th October 2018 as a dwindling band of veterans realised that the ceremony would no longer be well enough attended to be viable. According to Nick Hill, PVA organiser, the veterans were treated 'as if they'd been involved in something dirty,' an embarrassing reminder of a disastrous British policy in Palestine. This largely forgotten part of Britain's Palestine narrative is telling for the insight it offers into British propaganda thinking at the time, the veterans always chiming an off-message and inconvenient note in a national self-justification otherwise focused on projecting a message of responsibility and orderly handover. In this failure, perhaps the more telling point is found in one of the enduring delusions of colonialist thinking, namely that lasting political solutions, peace and stability can be imposed by distant ruling elites engaging in nation building by drawing random lines on a map. But some, Israeli historians among them, believe that Britain was not the only coloniser in Palestine during the Mandate years. The Palestinian American academic Edward Said wrote, 'it is little short of miraculous that, despite its years of military occupation, Israel is never identified with colonialism or colonial practices.'[17]

Britain paid a high price for its failures in Palestine during the Mandate years and in the years immediately following the surrender of the Mandate to the United Nations. In 1955, as a direct consequence of its Palestine policy, the British government was still allocating a £10.7 million subsidy (about £200 million today) to the Jordanian Government to fund the Arab Legion and a further £2.5 million to the United Nations Relief and Works Agency (UNRWA) to help support Palestinian refugees living in camps. Over the ensuing decades, the reputational price tag for

Britain's Palestine policies is still being matched by a hefty and ongoing financial one.

To its credit, Britain is one of the very few donor nations that annually contributes 0.7% of its gross national income to foreign aid; in 2015 this was made a legal requirement by the UK government and that same year, the total spend was £12.1bn, the provisional figure for 2016 being £13.3bn.[18]

Across the five financial years starting in 2011/2, The UK Department for International Development (DFID) allocated over half a billion pounds (£507m) of its aid budget to assist the Palestinians.[19] This support, for the Occupied Palestinian Territory (OPT), which technically includes the West Bank, Gaza and East Jerusalem, is focused around three discrete areas: governance and security; rights and refugees (which includes providing assistance through the UN Relief and Works Agency, UNRWA); and economic development. Thus, the top priorities for DFID projects are promoting private sector growth to stimulate the Palestinian economy and spur job creation, support for development of Palestinian governance including public finances and the justice system, assisting the Palestinian Authority with building institutions that can deliver essential services to Palestinians living in the territories, including in the areas of security, health and education and humanitarian assistance to those most vulnerable.[20]

Contributions to support refugees cost about £33.5 million a year, whilst other DFID projects are intended to foster the development of Palestinian institutions and promote sufficient economic growth so that a future Palestinian state will be stable and prosperous, and an effective partner for peace alongside Israel. Around £25m a year is direct budget support to the Palestinian Authority (PA) to pay the salaries of selected PA civil servants. A current skirmish in the information war is being fought around this latter category; in 2016 accusations were levelled by former Conservative Cabinet Minister Lord Pickles that money earmarked for PA salaries was in fact going to remunerate Palestinians in the Israeli prison system convicted of crimes against the Israeli State.[21]

The former communities secretary also warned of reports that some NGOs supported by UK taxpayers' money were promoting violence on social media pages and called on Ministers to investigate urgently. 'DFID's stated goal is to help secure a lasting two-state solution. I regret the funding doesn't follow that laudable ideal,'[22] Pickles said. Following a review, as of October 2016, this money was redirected specifically at health and education workers; it is now used to pay the salaries of up to 30,000 Palestinian teachers, doctors, nurses and midwives and to ensure around 25,000 Palestinian children continue their education, are immunised, and have medical consultations. With a terrible inevitability, however, it is now the content of the school curriculum itself being questioned for its references to 'martyrs' in the nationalist cause.

Whether temporarily accommodating lighter shades of hope or darker dystopian visions, the information war in Palestine has rolled on across the decades since the Oslo Accords in 1993, often involving the same players and the same scenarios, but with worryingly diminishing returns. It is, to say the least, an unfortunate by-product of this history that the community engagement programmes on today's corporate governance landscape in the West Bank, covering issues such as water, health and tax bear some striking resemblances to those undertaken by the Palestine Public Information Office in 1938, as if the political agenda has been frozen.

Whilst these programmes are not being implemented through erstwhile British government sponsored authorities in Jerusalem, some of them are being funded by the UK alongside the US, European Union and others and are part of the new approach to institution building required for Palestine to become recognised by the international community and embraced as a full member of the United Nations (of which Palestine, along with the Vatican, currently only has Observer Status). There are, of course, many other distinctions at work in today's Palestine, some more nuanced than others and it is in the process of making some important technical advances towards statehood, for example in its membership of the International Criminal Court (ICC) and Interpol, which make direct comparisons between British and Israeli occupation a risky business.

But privately, some of those working on the ground in Palestine will admit to a weariness and sense of fatalism attached to the increasingly aid dependent culture in the West Bank (at one time there were as many as 2,800 NGOs and non-profits registered with the Palestinian Authority in Ramallah), the creation of a supplicant professional class, the cronyism and corruption of the flawed Palestinian Authority and, above all, of the lack of opportunity, jobs and hope for young people. The Palestinian human rights lawyer and former Palestinian Authority spokesperson, Diana Buttu, thinks the outlook is bleak. 'We are entering the worst phase in Palestinian history; we are in the worst place we have ever been historically since 1967. I firmly believe there is no Trump plan, no negotiation planned, he is simply implementing Netanyahu's wish list,'[23] she says. This view is reinforced at the highest level of Palestinian government. Speaking to British Parliamentarians in May 2019, Palestinian Foreign Minister Dr Riad Malki almost pleaded for tangible international leadership and support in the face of Donald Trump and Jared Kushner's 'Deal of the Century' which he described as a catastrophe with implications that spread far beyond Palestine and deep into the wider region. Donor countries have largely tried to manage the growing crisis rather than solve it, a weakness that Israeli President Netanyahu has increasingly begun to exploit, said Malki. 'Netanyahu enjoys impunity; he doesn't recognise accountability; the two-state solution is not on his radar. We will have no other course than to engage with actions that will protect our national interests,'[24] he said.

As you are readily told in the West Bank, smart young Palestinians all have a second passport and a Plan B; there is a passing resemblance in some of the cafés and shisha bars of contemporary Ramallah to the 'Interzone' of William Burroughs' Tangiers of the 1950s, a transient world in which everyone is waiting for something to happen, where 'economic laws, untouched by any human factor, evolve equations of ultimate stasis.'[25] Those such as investigative journalists who try and penetrate the carapace of the Palestinian political body armour are still the first to pay the price for daring to unlock the distinctions, in Walter Lippmann's words, between what is not in the public interest and what is none of the public's business.

CHAPTER VII

'The Anglo-French Aggression': Defeat in the Court of Public Opinion

'We will pray to God Almighty to help us in our fight against the tyrants. We will fight, fight, fight. We will never give in to the aggressors.'

Gamal Abd Al Nasser
President of Egypt, 1956-1970

EGYPT SEIZES SUEZ CANAL. The headline on the BBC News broadcast on 26ᵗʰ July 1956 was dramatic enough. But the details of the story were of the sufficiently hair raising variety to cause many British residents of the Home Counties to feel that their world had changed forever: 'Egypt's President, Colonel Gamal Abd Al Nasser, has announced the nationalisation of the Suez Canal Company to provide funding for the construction of the Aswan High Dam. The British Government and French stockholders who owned shares in the Suez Canal Company reacted with shock to the news. In a two-and-a-half hour speech delivered to a mass gathering in Alexandria, President Nasser said the Nationalisation Law had already been published in the official gazette. He said all company assets in Egypt had been frozen and stockholders would be paid the price of their shares according to today's closing price on the Paris Stock Exchange.'[1]

Who was this upstart? How could he have been allowed to cock a snook at Britain and France, the two imperial powers who between them had not only built the canal in 1869 but been responsible for managing the traffic through it, had secured the land on either side and appropriated a share of the deep revenue streams that flowed like honey down its

120 mile length with every cargo ship en route to and from India? The questions started to pile up quickly, as the true scale of this audacious and unilateral act of apparent banditry settled on a shocked Western consciousness. To the British public, it was as if the act were gratuitous, had come from nowhere, the whim of a little known Arab nationalist leader who had taken on himself the power to single-handedly disrupt the world order. Or so it seemed to the many for whom Egypt still typically remained an exotic, pink coloured shape on surviving imperial maps in British schools, merely the geographical convenience that accommodated the waterway connecting Britain to the brightest jewel in its crown.

But it was not long before the questions turned to a righteous kind of anger and triggered a further, more angst driven line of enquiry. What was the British government going to do about it, how would Nasser be made to pay and how was this stain on the national honour going to be erased? The answers to these questions and the responsibility for shaping the national response to the intricate and combustible consequences of the canal grab fell to a politician who many believed at the time might have been designed to personify the phrase 'cometh the hour, cometh the man' – the quintessential English Conservative Prime Minister, diplomat, soldier, Orientalist and gentleman, Sir Anthony Eden.

The course that Eden charted through the Suez crisis was both to define and destroy him, and at the same time to bring the sun down on the imperial chapter in British history that had reached its zenith by the start of the Great War and persisted until the British turned out the lights and closed the doors behind them on independence in Jordan in 1946, a partitioned India and Pakistan in 1947, a partitioned Palestine and Israel in 1948, an independent Sudan in 1956 and Cyprus in 1960.

In fact, the two principal protagonists in the Suez drama were already known to each other. Their only meeting was recounted in detail by the Egyptian journalist and Nasser confidante, Mohamed Heikal in his 1972 book, 'Nasser, the Cairo Documents.'[2] The two met for dinner at the British Embassy in Cairo on 26th February 1955, an inauspicious venue for Nasser who loathed the building for its colonial associations and what he perceived as its malevolent place in Egyptian history. Then British Deputy Prime Minister, Sir Anthony Eden astonished Nasser by greeting him in Arabic and proceeding to talk about the Qur'an and Arabic poetry and literature, saying that he had once thought about becoming an Arabist.[3]

After very distinguished military service on the Western Front, where he lost two brothers in action, Eden studied Oriental Languages at Christ Church College at Oxford University in October 1919, specifically Persian and Arabic. With Persian (Farsi) as his main and Arabic his secondary language, he graduated in June 1922 with a Double First. Of the meeting, Heikal recalled the immediate dislike the two men felt for each other. 'It must be rare for two men to sit down to break bread together who were so completely opposed in every way as these two. Every aspect of each man was completely the opposite of the other's. Heritage, upbringing, appearance, dress, experience, outlook, loyalties and ambition, everything conflicted. The dinner was not a social occasion, it was a confrontation between the ultimate representatives of two inimical ways of life, a confrontation which was both personal and national and which ended in tragedy.'[4] Nasser was already by that time an experienced orator and prime mover of shifting public opinion in Egypt and the wider Arab world, a masterful propagandist who had been engaged in longstanding and successful information warfare with the British; Eden, on the other hand, wrongly believed himself to be an accomplished PR strategist and media manager. In time, his approach to micro-management of Britain's media and PR war against Nasser and a fast modernising Egypt was to rebound on him and play a disproportionately significant role in public perceptions of the crisis and of himself as both bungling and dishonest.

Nasser, Revolution and Star Quality

Gamal Abd Al Nasser had a very clear and firm grasp on the relationship between public opinion and successful government and was well aware that part of his planned longevity in a precarious career would be linked to his ability to generate awareness and popular enthusiasm for himself and his policies amongst the Egyptian people and the wider Arab world.

To acknowledge the status and importance he attached to Egyptian and Arab public opinion, he was amongst the first to use the phrase 'the Arab street' as a way of articulating the constituency that he was principally addressing, a term that in its essence included a particular focus on the lower socio-economic orders and poor of Egyptian society.

As base material for PR sculpture, Nasser had a multitude of unique selling points, striking looks, charisma, a powerful speaking style, modernist views, a vision that could credibly project the rebirth of the Arab nation – and the aura and mystique of the revolutionary. Judged by the defining public relations principle of third-party endorsement, this image was to be powerfully reinforced through the photo-opportunities of the Nasser years: Nasser with Che Guevara, Nasser with Fidel Castro, Nasser with Ben Bella of Algeria, Nasser with President Tito, Nasser with Leonid Brezhnev – in fact, Nasser's progression through the starry corridors of the world's most era-defining and iconoclastic revolutionary leaders in itself tells part of his story and explains his status. He was also the Arab world's precursor to the glamour and superstar appeal of John F Kennedy. It had never produced a comparable figure and arguably never has since; he seemed to be a man made for the moment, a Titan who could tread the world stage with ease and project the new, modernistic and secular Arab voice with conviction and authority at the same time as retaining his Islamic credentials. To a traditionalist like Eden, Nasser's near iconic PR persona must have represented his worst nightmare.

Throughout the 1930s, Nasser had been a member of the Fascist sympathising Young Egypt Party and a major force behind the shift in Egyptian political thinking in favour of the potent mix of Arab nationalism and Islam as a counter to imperialism, Zionism, colonial subjugation and the economic exploitation of the Arab people by the West. He had come to world attention in 1952 as one of the officers who had led the American supported July revolution in Egypt that had toppled the British-backed King Farouk, becoming President in June 1956 (he finally appointed himself Prime Minister as well in the 1960s). In the course of his climb to the top of Egyptian politics, where he remained until 1970, he had removed his predecessor General Neguib from power, negotiated with the British over the withdrawal of their garrison from the Suez Canal, made Egypt into a one-party State and embarked on a large scale, highly effective lobbying operation against the British in their attempt to bolster the Baghdad Pact, Britain's last and ill-fated attempt to organise the countries of the Middle East into an interest group that could help maintain its position as the region's superpower and at the same time combat the spread of Communism. Specifically, failure to expand the Baghdad Pact membership in 1955 by the inclusion of Jordan and Syria lit the touch paper for the Suez conflagration, the British collusion with France and (unthinkably) Israel, and the US decision not to support the British military response or underwrite the pound on international markets, two decisions which proved both humiliating and decisive in the outcome to the crisis.

By 1954, Nasser was 'deeply conscious of the power of propaganda and was one of its most skillful exponents in the Middle East.'[5] Learning from the collaboration between the wartime Nazis and nationalists such as Haj Amin Al Husseini, Nasser saw radio as the pre-eminent vehicle for his propaganda campaigns, but was also determined to benefit from opportunities provided by the post-war explosion of the newspaper business; this was evidenced by his close and lifelong association with Mohamed Heikal, Egypt's most influential journalist whose powers Nasser drew on both as speech writer and mouthpiece for much of his life.

Nasser launched the 'Voice of the Arabs' (Sawt Al-Arab) radio station in 1953 as a way of starting a conversation with the Arab world about the potential of nationalism to break the international imperialist power monopoly. It proved a highly effective and pervasive propaganda tool, especially against the British, and Nasser referred to it as 'Egypt's general university.'[6] In his propaganda war with the British, Nasser's successful use of radio as a means of creating a strong personal connection, making an emotional appeal to Arabs across the region and setting the news agenda proved painful for Eden to take. His political antipathy became distinctly personal and a dedicated strand of his PR strategy was to demonise Nasser as a fanatic and dictator, a threat who he vindictively characterised as the new Mussolini, 'we all know how Fascist governments behave; with a dictator you always have to pay a higher price later on.'[7]

When Egypt recognised Communist China in April 1956, Britain and the US stepped up their propaganda war against Nasser according to Heikal, who counted nine British and American radio stations working against him. 'British newspapers were full of hostile articles against him. The Daily Telegraph published one article entitled 'The Master Plan of Nasser.' Heikal recalled that Nasser read this article, cut it out, wrote 'a good plan' on it and sent it to the Head of Egyptian Intelligence saying, 'if they are accusing us of doing all that then we had better do it.'[8] In the three-months in which Eden was forced to wait, from the nationalisation of the Suez Canal until an invasion plan and force could be assembled and co-ordinated with the French and Israelis, Nasser soaked up a storm of British negative PR and propaganda aimed at destroying his personal reputation through a combination of character assassination and stereotyping, painting him as both a tool of the Russians and an Arab tyrant.

On his accession to power, Nasser may have felt he needed help beyond his immediate circle with advice and tactical support to project his public persona more effectively and extend his publicity and media networks. In any event, he chose to reach out to one of Nazi Germany's most powerful and successful anti-Semitic propagandists to help in the development of a strategy to do this. In February 1956, Nasser hired Johann von Leers (1902-1965) as political and propaganda advisor at the Information Department of the Ministry of National Guidance.

As a leading Nazi propagandist in wartime Berlin, von Leers had written 'Judaism and Islam as Opposites,' an essay in which he argued that Islam and National Socialism had a common bond forged by shared hostility to the Jews.[9] Whilst in Egypt, he became known as the 'current Arab League representative for Germany in Cairo' and 'Arab League advisor on German affairs'[10] and, in time, converted to Islam taking the name Omar Amin. The fact that Nasser hired the former Nazi propagandist to work for Egyptian information agencies in the 1950s demonstrated his willingness to support ideas and ways of thinking about Israel and the Jews that had their roots in Nazi ideology and propaganda, according to historian Jeffrey Herf.[11] Von Leers, though, was not a lone standard bearer for Nazi propaganda expertise in Cairo at the time. In 1955, the Institute for the Study of Zionism was established there under the directorship of escaped Nazi Alfred Zingler, who had converted to Islam and taken the name Mahmoud Saleh. The Institute, which was heavily staffed by variously disguised former Nazis including Louis Heiden (the translator into Arabic of Mein Kampf), Dr Werner Witschale and former Goebbels employee Hans Appler (Saleh Shafar) was set up for the purpose of 'leading the struggle against Zionism and international Jewry.' Whether Eden and the British knew in detail about this connection and if it had any bearing on cementing his personal antipathies to Nasser and his demonisation of him as a Fascist is harder to know. In the aftermath of the Suez invasion, Nasser would go on to publicise the attack with 'a blitz of articles, films, photographs and specially commissioned magazines' that were distributed widely and aimed in particular at the United States, according to Shaw.

Eden as Media Manager

There is no doubt that in 1956, Anthony Eden's reputation reflected his time as the poster boy of British Conservative politics. Not only had the 57-year-old been the youngest Foreign Secretary in British political history, he had also held the post on three occasions. He had been Churchill's Deputy Prime Minister and was his natural successor. It would be no exaggeration to say that his political career had been glittering. Yet, although it was his chosen path, Eden's expectations did not start and finish with politics. He had done well academically at Oxford and had been a notably successful soldier on the Western Front, at one time the youngest adjutant in the British army. In addition, he was immensely hard working and accomplished, with a distinguished appearance, and had made a successful second marriage to Clarissa Spencer-Churchill, Winston Churchill's niece, who complemented him as part of a very socially prominent and glamorous couple. Clever and experienced though he was, Eden also had blind spots. One of them, oddly in the circumstances, concerned his relationship to the modernising Middle East. There is no doubt he suffered from quintessentially British patrician views when it came to the Arabs and the Arab world, equipped though he was with two of the region's languages and a great deal of Islamic history and cultural knowledge to back them up.

When Eden and Nasser met, Eden's attempts at Arabic and discourse on medieval poetry were perceived by the Egyptians to be part of a patronising tradition of British army officers more used to sitting around Bedouin camp fires in the manner of Lawrence of Arabia, an essentially romantic illusion they deemed out of touch with the revitalised Arab worldview of the 1950s. This placed Eden within an identifiably negative British stereotype, one associated with exploitation and subjugation. 'The British made two grave errors of judgement; they preferred to deal with the desert tribes rather than the city intellectuals and middle class and preferred to deal with royal families rather than the people. The British trusted the Bedouin, romantic as they were about people like Lawrence of Arabia, Gertrude Bell and Glubb Pasha...they were infected with the euphoria of Arabism and put their faith in the ruling families,' wrote Heikal.[12]

When Britain's Chief of the Imperial Staff, Sir Gerald Templer, returned from the Jordanian capital Amman, having failed to persuade King Hussein to bring Jordan into the Baghdad Pact fold, it created a loss of trust for Nasser and proved just the excuse he was looking for in order to ramp up his propaganda assault against the British and all their Middle East policies. The British response was to assume unusually high significance in the eventual outcome of the crisis, revealing some of the weaknesses in the Government information machinery created by the downsizing over the Palestine Mandate years but also, less predictably, in the decision by Eden to take a very personal role in defining the nation's press and PR strategy, perhaps provoked by his personal animosity to Nasser but also an inability to delegate, alongside the misguided belief in his powers as a media tactician.

It was unfortunate that, just when Eden needed a strong and experienced government information capability, he was faced with the equivalent of an engine that was now only firing on half its cylinders. The new Conservative government in 1951 had launched an enquiry into funding for propaganda purposes and subsequently started reducing the head count at the newly downgraded Central Office of Information (COI), successor to the MOI, from 1,413 to 974 personnel, a massive loss in capacity by organisational standards.[13] It also closed down the Crown Film Unit, stopped the distribution of films to cinemas and mobile screenings in factories and village halls, cancelled the government lecture service, cut the budget for exhibitions in half and cut back the Social Survey's spending and staff.[14]

But by October 1955, the shortcomings of this policy were already becoming apparent in two ways. Firstly, there was a growing recognition that Nasser's Egypt was exercising its influence against British interests using as its principal weapons press, radio and education. In a note on 'Middle East Oil' to the Cabinet on 14th October 1955, Foreign Secretary Harold Macmillan focused on both the means and resources required to ensure that public opinion in the region did not become so hostile to British oil companies that their commercial arrangements became impossible.[15]

'There is serious danger that the Middle East will slip away from us,' he wrote, citing both the Egyptian bid for cultural leadership of the Arab world and efforts by the Saudis to buy individuals abroad and neutralise British interests in Jordan. To counter these efforts, a propaganda front was opened up by the British Secret Service MI6 in 1955 to use the disaffected and out of favour British Saudi advisor, St John Philby, to write two articles in the Sunday Times exposing the corruption of the Saudi regime, then in the process of trying to lay claim to the strategic and oil rich Buraimi oasis. The effort was only revealed in 2018 by British historian James Barr, with the discovery of the diaries of a little known and secretive British spy John Slade-Baker, himself based in Beirut where Philby had fled from Riyadh. The antidote, Macmillan advised the Government, was to spend more money on spreading British influence through existing instruments of soft power, principally the British Council, alongside information-based initiatives that included increasing BBC medium wave transmissions in the region and providing technical expertise to help Iraq operate its new television station.[16] At the time Macmillan wrote his note and followed it up with detailed recommendations a month later, Britain was already spending a total of £15.3 million annually on the Middle East (about £300 million in today's money). In 1956, in response to recommendations, Government spending on the British Council was increased to £300,000 and an extra £75,000 was also allocated to information capacity.

Eden temporarily reinstated the MOI during the Suez crisis, but the damage was done and the attrition would turn out to herald a longer term slide in the COI's status and ability to project Britain's foreign policy narrative in the Middle East that would never be reversed, in due course leading one step closer to introducing the new concept and model of outsourcing as a potential secondary avenue for delivering government information campaigns. But in 1956, Eden must have felt shortchanged when, under severe pressure at a time of national crisis, he had to review his dwindling options in planning and implementing an effective response to Nasser's propaganda blitz.

Eden's first mistake was not to recognise that Nasser had in fact acted legally – the advice the British government took was that he was within his rights to nationalise the Suez Canal Company and offer shareholders fair compensation for their holdings as long as he allowed shipping to proceed through the canal unimpeded – after all he had not nationalised the canal itself. On receiving this advice in a written paper from Foreign Office official Richard Parsons, Eden's first reaction reportedly was to say, somewhat tellingly, 'this is no fucking good.'[17] His second mistake was to organise a tripartite military response with the French and the Israelis and plan to keep it secret, whilst at the time using newspapers and radio outlets, some of them like Voice of Britain based in Cyprus, to turn up the heat on Nasser himself by increasing the vilification and personal attacks.

The man who Eden signed up to run the disinformation campaign was Douglas Dodds-Parker (1909-2006), who had been in charge of the Foreign Office's disinformation service.[18] Heading a committee that included a clutch of secret service hands, Dodds-Parker worked on a twin-track communications strategy to counter Egypt's propaganda simultaneously in the Middle East and at home. He believed the two-pronged approach was working, but the stumbling block came when the British Cabinet, including Chancellor Harold Macmillan, advocated the re-introduction of censorship to mask the details of the preparations for the invasion.

Convinced by wiser heads such as former Ministry Of Information mandarin Walter Monckton that peacetime introduction of censorship would be madness, Eden then set about leaning on British media, including the BBC, to self-censor through the use of what were called D-Notices, in effect a complex system of embargoes that amounted to a kind of voluntary conspiracy to secrecy. D-Notices were not official and could therefore be passed off as voluntary, however, editors using

D-Notices were bound by an agreement not to tell their readers that the newspaper copy had, in effect, been censored. According to the official Ministry of Information account, 'In this way, Eden managed to get the press to censor itself during Suez while keeping the public in the dark about what was going on and giving the appearance that it was all done voluntarily in the interests of the country.' The account maintains that Eden went on to persuade editors to allow military censors to decide what information should and should not be published, in other words, he got them to agree to censorship in peacetime.[19]

Simultaneously, as he sought to mastermind the British government's information bigger picture, Eden was intimately involved often on a daily basis in setting up regular press briefings with chosen journalists to get his message out at the editorial and thought leadership level. He wanted the British electorate to understand and buy into his thinking about Nasser, the threat to trade posed by the canal grab and the wider strategic interests of Britain in the region so that he could prepare the psychological ground for public acceptance of the invasion. The audience in the United States was also on his mind at this time, and the Foreign Office was separately working on influencing public opinion in America to support Britain's position. These briefings were conducted under the rules of the parliamentary lobby system and were off the record, which is to say the information divulged could be used and referred to by journalists but not attributed to a named source. Briefing in this way can be risky as it depends on two key factors, trust in the integrity of the journalist relationship and taking a calculated bet on the fact that independent corroboration of the divulged facts won't be obtained from a third party who could inadvertently (or intentionally) blow the original source. Eden thought that he was a master of this type of media relations micro management, and it became his daily obsession.

Throughout his years as Foreign Secretary, Eden had courted many of Fleet Street's Diplomatic Editors and the man that Eden chose to use as the primary vehicle to get his views across to the British public over Suez was Times Foreign Editor Iverach McDonald (1908-2006), formerly the paper's Diplomatic Editor. The strategy was generally successful and Eden's private hard-line views on Nasser and his portrayal as a threat to national security fed through into subsequent Times editorials. A whole series of editorials, written either by McDonald himself or by the Times Editor William Haley, bore a noticeable similarity to what Eden had told McDonald during their first meeting, not only in their tone but right down to the phrases used.[20]

Eden can almost certainly be credited with some success in the presentational aspects of communicating Britain's case effectively to the public through the press. What cannot be sidestepped, however, is the outcome of Eden's overall Suez propaganda strategy, in which his media manipulation was just one part of a wider failure to prevent a general collapse of Britain's reputation for honesty and fair dealing in the region. The MOI archive account offers a damning verdict on Eden and his attempts to mastermind the crisis management and media handling of what rapidly became diagnosed as a national disaster. 'He had kept the press, Parliament and people in the dark about his real intentions, while secretly preparing for war yet insisting he was seeking a peaceful solution. His obsessive secrecy and his plan to keep the press from reporting his preparations for war meant that news of the biggest military action since the Second World War came as a bombshell to most people in Britain. He had neglected to explain to the British people why such a military invasion was necessary.'[21] It is hard to completely escape the parallel in this aspect of Eden's premiership with that of Tony Blair's flawed rationale and media manipulation prior to the invasion of Iraq over 40 years later, finally laid bare in the 2016 Chilcot Report. In his role as architect of Britain's information war over Suez, Eden can truly be said to have designed a house with no stairs.

A footnote to the media handling and ensuing public perception of the British and French invasion of Suez is offered in the account of Eden's broadcast announcing the event to the nation. It was something of an open secret that Eden's health had often been poor during his premiership and medical records released by the US National Library of Medicine confirm that he had a biliary tract injury which rendered him subject to recurrent fevers and post-operative disability at important times in his career and during international crises.[22]

Was this condition remotely relevant to his ability to handle every element of the crisis, compounded as it was through a sequence of events that would have tested any Prime Minister performing at their peak, starting with the Anglo-French landings on 6th November, the subsequent US withdrawal of support, the Soviet invasion of Hungary and UN intervention to police Suez before his enforced departure on holiday to Jamaica on 23rd November?

Eden's loyal wife Clarissa Lady Avon always maintained that his decision-making was unaffected by his health but the naturalist Sir David Attenborough, the person in charge of the BBC television news broadcast by Eden announcing the Suez invasion recalls arriving with a film unit at 10 Downing Street to find Eden prostrate and ill in his bedroom, unable to participate. He recalled that it was Lady Avon who personally caused him to do the broadcast, but only after she had used her own eyeliner pencil to add substance to his eyebrows and moustache which she considered gave him a very washed-out and exhausted appearance when she herself checked the outgoing pictures on the TV monitor.[23]

A Tale of Two Movies

A telling way in which to compare the respective British and Egyptian approaches to the propaganda dimension of Suez is to see it through the film maker's lens. This exercise, in particular, reveals much about the projection of the narrative constructed by each to justify their actions, and as propagandists well knew by 1956, film was among the most effective ways of packaging up a case and pitching it in the court of public opinion. But, as Walter Lippmann had so convincingly shown with his analysis of the news process in the 1920s, it is the selection of facts and their juxtaposition with opinion that present the real challenges to truth seekers. Thus, the British and the Egyptians both set out, in the immediate aftermath of the crisis, to influence opinion in favour of their respective accounts of the same set of events.

With astounding foresight and speed, the Egyptians captured the action of the Suez invasion in real-time, documentary style, releasing the result as a finished, English language film, entitled 'The Anglo-French Aggression against Egypt.' Although relatively little is known about the film's circumstances, it was compiled and distributed quickly, seemingly made in the period between the Anglo-French advance on Port Said, begun on 5th November and the British government's decision to make their own film in response, which was announced on 16th December. The film is considered by analysts to be a very cleverly made polemic, setting out to negatively influence international opinion about the British and French (and the Israeli 'war puppets'), casting them as imperialist invaders and treacherous war criminals, 'men who destroy what they claim to protect.'[24]

With some justification, though collusion was not to be formally admitted until 1967, the film makes direct claims about the machinations of Britain, France and Israel, referring to their 'secret arrangements' and the 'sinister imperialistic conspiracy' that led to the invasion. The commentary portrays the psychodrama of the invasion as a kind of national rape, bombing of civilian workshops, destruction of bridges, indiscriminate bombing of residential areas 'to destroy Egyptian morale,' and hospitals soon 'swarming with civilian victims.'

It does this in the context of opening sequences showing the improvement of living standards in Port Said post-nationalisation, juxtaposing civilian prosperity and purposeful activity with the subsequent ruthless barbarism of the Allied actions in cutting water supplies, creating a refugee crisis and starting an annihilation of 'the 23 million people in this part of Africa.' The defence of Port Said is depicted as a heroic people's resistance, the whole of Egypt classed as being with the defenders, 'joining in Nasser's prayer for strength and divine aid against the aggressors.' Though, a one-sided and in some respects inaccurate piece of reportage, the film in its design and construction was in essence a sophisticated expression of the atrocity propaganda medium, with enough elements of truth to make the overall projection of Britain and France's malign intentions and destructive capability hard to sidestep. From whichever starting point, the surprise invasion of a weaker, poorer nation state by two imperial world powers and their regional ally looked exactly what it was – bullying, unnecessary and indefensible. Neither the British nor French could ever have emerged well from this unbalanced but compelling account of events spun by Nasser's masterly grasp of the film documentary medium. Made by an opaque organisation, 'Egypt Today,' specially set up for the purpose, the 11 minute film arguably bears the hallmarks of Nasser's Nazi propagandist Johann Von Leers and his colleagues, whose intimate knowledge of how to mix a lethal cocktail of polemic with atrocity propaganda would by the 1950s have become ever more highly advanced.

The main British response, 'Suez in Perspective,' was released by the COI early in 1957 as a direct riposte to the charges levelled by the Egyptians in 'The Anglo-French Aggression against Egypt.' It was one of three films eventually made to both justify and promote the British position over Suez, the other two in the sequence being 'The Facts about Port Said,' a three minute aerial trip over the city to show how little of it had been destroyed, and 'Report from Port Said.'

'Suez in Perspective'[25] was commissioned from the British newsreel company British Movietone and its composition very closely reflects the style and tone of news coverage that cinema goers were used to seeing at that time alongside feature films. Using a lot of archive footage, it also included material commissioned by the COI, such as the aerial documentation of Port Said and the shots of the block ships that Nasser had placed in the canal to hamper the movement of international shipping. Tellingly, 'Suez in Perspective' was not for a domestic audience. Its distribution was designated as World Comprehensive, with major showings intended for specially invited audiences by overseas missions and the film was dubbed into a wide range of languages, including French, Italian, Finnish, Serbo-Croat, Latin-American Spanish, Arabic, Urdu, Hindi, Bengali, and Sinhalese, while a special German version was made in Germany. In the initial print-run, nearly 200 copies were despatched by air to over 70 territories.[26]

The pitch in 'Suez in Perspective' is, in many respects, the diametric opposite of 'The Anglo-French Aggression against Egypt.' The viewer soon learns that the invasion has been planned 'with care and skill,' the objective is to 'ensure minimum loss of life.' Rather than focus on collateral damage to infrastructure, the British film shows how much care was taken to ensure Port Said has remained intact. Civilian impact is contrasted through different treatment of civilian casualties, the Egyptian film showing Egyptian medical teams at work; the British version showing casualties from both sides and international medical staff. Children received the same divergence of documentary treatment, in the Egyptian version searching for water, whilst in the British one playing football with occupying British soldiers.

Both films go on to contrast the opposing takes on refugee movement, the supply of food aid and government support for civilians. Both also end with direct appeals from major players in the drama. Nasser himself is quoted, saying, 'the whole world is with us, and I wish to make it quite clear to the free peoples of the world that the ordeal through which the world is passing at present is the responsibility of the aggressors who invaded Egypt.' For the British, Churchill cites Britain's role as world policeman: 'in Britain we have the choice of taking decisive action or admitting once and for all our inability to put an end to strife.'

Considered analysis of both films shows quite quickly that the Egyptian version is vastly more effective than its British competitor, which is playing ideological catch-up from the first frame, back pedalling rapidly as its role as imperial power invading a free nation, supported by Israeli opportunists and French fellow travellers, is exposed with every frame as the fatal failure in policy it was. In effect 'Suez in Perspective' is an apologia for the failure of Eden's PR and propaganda strategy either to explain or justify the events which he had contrived to hide from most of the world. This failure is nowhere more evident than in the fact that the film was made for consumption by a large international market consisting of all of Britain's mystified friends and many equally baffled neutral observers.

Bitter and Painful Lessons

The facts surrounding the events of the Suez crisis are widely known to students of the episode's back story (there are at least 30 books and over 1,000 articles dedicated to aspects of the subject). The Anglo-French operation drew criticism from all quarters and, in December 1956, British and French troops were withdrawn from the city and replaced by Danish and Colombian units of the first United Nations Expeditionary Force (UNEF). The statistics do not make comfortable reading. Eden's invasion of Suez was costly for everyone; British casualties stood at 16 dead and 96 wounded, French casualties were 10 dead and 33 wounded, and the Israelis lost 231 dead and 899 wounded. The number of Egyptians killed has never been authoritatively determined, but Egyptian casualties of the Israeli invasion were estimated at 1,000–3,000 dead and 4,000 wounded, while losses in the Anglo-French operation were estimated at 650 dead and 900 wounded.

The financial cost was £275 million (£5.5 billion in today's values) but its knock-on financial effects were far greater; the pound came under sustained attack and Britain was forced to borrow heavily from the International Monetary Fund (IMF), the first time the IMF had been involved in such an international crisis. It was also indisputably the end of Britain's role as a world power; the process started by the exit from Palestine in 1948 was definitively concluded in the defeat at Suez in 1956; Britain's role as the Middle East's predominant superpower was over, and it gave way to the United States as the rising star in the region. The American veto over British intentions at Suez showed that the United States had a new ability and impetus to shape policy outcomes in the post-war Middle East, and it was to become an increasingly central player in the geopolitics of the region as it progressed through the 1960s and beyond, basing its more frequent interventions on a strong relationship with Israel and latterly Turkey as its anchor alliances. The symbolic importance of Suez was not lost on US Vice-President Richard Nixon, who openly celebrated the moment when he said 'for the first time in history we have shown independence of Anglo-French policies towards Asia and Africa which seemed to us to reflect the colonial tradition. This declaration of independence has had an electrifying effect throughout the world.'[27]

Suez had bitter and painful lessons for the British. Eden resigned in

January 1957 and did not produce his own account of the affair until 1960, when he recorded his thoughts about the Suez crisis in his book Full Circle.[28] The book, though, did not reveal much that was new, other than the personal antipathy felt between US Secretary of State John Foster Dulles and Eden and the major role America's positive hostility to Britain, as opposed to the anticipated hostile neutrality, had played in the outcome.[29]

One of the chief reasons for the notorious decision to collude with the French and Israelis in October 1956 was a need to fulfil the expectations his propaganda campaign demonising the Egyptian leader Gamal Abd Al Nasser had raised among Conservative Party ranks, elements of the press, and large swathes of the general public. It was this, as much as anything else, that led to Britain's disastrous police action in early November, the Cabinet's humiliation at the hands of the United States later that month, and Eden's resignation in January 1957.[30] This view is reinforced by the evidence of Foreign & Commonwealth Office (FCO) spokesman Richard Fyjis-Walker, whose role was to manage British radio broadcasts in Arabic from Cyprus into Egypt. 'Eden's obsession with Nasser was the equivalent of Bush's with Saddam, personal, irrational, unhelpful,' he recalled.[31] If Eden lost both the military and economic wars at Suez, he certainly lost the information war too. Two important factors played a role in this: in 1956, the British government information capacity and status were both at a low point following the downsizing after Palestine, and Eden's insistence on playing a hands-on role in personally micromanaging media briefings detracted from a unified and robust media initiative.

In the end, Sir Campbell Stuart's maxim that truth should be at the heart of a successful propaganda strategy would have served Eden much better, public opinion would have been both more understanding and therefore more accepting of subsequent events. It is unquestionably true that Eden's demonisation of Nasser badly backfired, making him look stilted and out of touch with the new generation of thinkers and leaders driving change in the post-war Arab world order.

The Suez crisis, according to one of Eden's official biographers, D R Thorpe, 'was a truly tragic end to his premiership, and one that came to assume a disproportionate importance in any assessment of his career.'[32] Nasser, on the other hand, was able to exploit his mastery of the propaganda medium to drive home his message with equal ease through radio, newspapers and film, successfully portraying the British and the French in the classic oratorical style and rhetoric of the time as colonial aggressors and imperialist war mongers. His media victory was to serve him well, making him the first superstar of the modern Arab era and delivering Egypt the political and moral authority to lead the Arab world well into the next turbulent decade up until the fateful 1967 war with Israel.

For the second time in only eight years, the British had been forced to place their intractable problems in the Middle East in the hands of the United Nations, compelled to reverse their way out of political and financial humiliation at the hands of the United States and close the door for the final time on the old certainties of empire. Not only had they contrived to lose assets, friends and credibility amidst the smoke-filled sky and twisted metal of Port Said but somehow despite their extensive efforts to control the news agenda they had lost the information war as well.

CHAPTER VIII

PsyOps, Information Operations and Saddam the PsyWarrior

'I do not mean by this that we should go on fighting according to the same formula of the October War of 1973. What I mean is that we should keep up the atmosphere of war to strengthen our political approach and enable ourselves to exploit any suitable opportunity which offers itself. To maintain an atmosphere of war and prepare for its requisites will enable us to enter any war successfully at the time of our choosing.'

Détente & The Arab-Zionist Conflict,
Interview given by Saddam Hussein to the Egyptian journalist
Sakina Al-Sadat on 19th January 1977

At just 26, Corporal Sarah Bryant seemed to have a bright future in the British army. In the pictures of her wedding day with husband and army colleague Carl in 2005, Sarah looks happy, confident and poised to take on the world. Yet, it was not to be. On 17th June 2008, Sarah became another fatality in the grim statistics that marked the progress of Britain's losing war against the Taliban in Afghanistan. A bomb hidden in a ditch near Lashkar Gah ripped apart her thinly armoured Snatch Land Rover in an instant, killing Sarah and SAS reservists Corporal Sean Reeve, 28, Lance Corporal Richard Larkin, 39, and Trooper Paul Stout, 31. Tragic as it was, Sarah's story wasn't just another statistic. She was officially the first British servicewoman to be killed on active duty in Afghanistan. What's more, she was a member of the UK armed forces psychological operations unit, known as PsyOps. Most of the general public didn't even know that PsyOps existed or what the term meant, so journalists wanted to find out what she had been doing and why she had been travelling in a war zone on a road that was so exposed. In the course of subsequent coverage, the army had to come clean about her job and what it entailed and, in the process, open the door to a world that had until then been almost entirely hidden.

It emerged that Sarah Bryant was a highly trained, Pashto-speaking member of a little known British Army unit called the 15 Psychological Operations Group; her outfit, 152 Delta Psychological Operations Effects Team, was part of the PsyOps Support Element attached to the Headquarters of 16 Air Assault Brigade, in turn part of Task Force Helmand. Bryant's job description, it transpired, was as a Target Audience Analyst. She had in fact already completed two tours of duty in Basra and Baghdad, where she had received a medal and commendation from a US Forces commander who had described her as a credit to the British Army.[1] This, in turn, prompted a whole series of further questions, amongst them, what part was the clandestine world of PsyOps playing in the war, and furthermore, what did being a Target Audience Analyst in Afghanistan involve?

Since the death of Sarah Bryant, the formal status and role of PsyOps in British military capability has become, broadly speaking, public knowledge albeit without operational detail. It turns out that 15 Psychological Operations Group was established immediately after the 1991 Gulf War when the success of US military psychological operations convinced the UK Ministry of Defence that the UK required a similar option. Since then, it has grown considerably and become subsumed into the British Army's 77th Brigade within Force Troops Command.

But it was not until October 2012 that the curtain was finally drawn back to provide a glimpse of the detailed activities of the Group, and only then because it was awarded an arcane honour by the British Army known as the Firmin Sword of Peace (surely something of a contradiction in terms). The occasion of the award even resulted in a photo-opportunity between Chief of Defence Staff Sir David Richards and Commander Steve Tatham, Royal Navy, on behalf of the Group. This award is given to units of the British Army that make a valuable contribution to humanitarian activities by establishing good and friendly relations with the inhabitants of any community at home or overseas. The citation noted that: 'a small team from 15 POG has been continuously deployed to Helmand for six years. Working predominantly with the Afghan civilian population, it has sought to inform, reassure, educate and through the promotion of free and unbiased discussion, persuade Afghans that their futures are best served not with the Taliban...but with themselves and their elected

1. The British capture of Jerusalem, 11th December 1917: General Allenby
(*centre*) making his proclamation on the steps of the Citadel. Sir Mark Sykes is
on the right and Major General MacAndrew, commanding 5th Cavalry Division
on the left. The official status of the proclamation was later withdrawn.

2. Max Von Oppenheim: member of the banking dynasty and social architect
behind the German Jihad in the Great War, a propaganda initiative designed
to spread the German sphere of influence and challenge British dominance in
the Muslim world.

3. Captured Muslim soldiers from Allied armies, sent as Prisoners of War to the German run Half Moon Camp (Halbmondlager) near Berlin where they were enlisted into the German Jihad. Here the first mosque on German soil was built.

4. Walter Lippmann, whose 1922 book 'Public Opinion' was the first to analyse the subjective bias of news, believed the process had to be actively managed by professionals. His highly influential views were listened to with equal respect by liberal democratic and Fascist leaders alike.

5. US film maker Lowell Thomas (right) pictured with T. E. Lawrence (Lawrence of Arabia), with whom he spent time in the desert making propaganda films which became instrumental in constructing the Lawrence legend. This picture was probably taken in London 1919 by his cameraman Harry Chase.

6. Haj Amin Al Husseini, Grand Mufti of Jerusalem, who based himself in Berlin after 1941. From here, he worked with colleagues to plan and manage the propaganda campaign against the British and the Jews who he saw as occupiers of Palestine and inimical to Palestinian nationalist ambitions.

تشهد بريطانيا تكتيكات حربية . ويفسح جنود المشاة الأقوياء المدربين طريقا للدبابات في شمال افريقيا.

الهزائم الدكتاتوريين محقق

7. 'The Downfall of the Dictators is Assured' (c. 1943), one of a series of Arabic language posters designed by Britain's Ministry of Information for use in the Arabic speaking world. Picture shows British soldiers advancing in front of tanks in the Western Desert.

8. 'Showboat,' a river steamer lent to the PR Section of the British Consulate-General, Basra, by the British Army Unit of the Inland Water Transport, draws away from her moorings at the waterfront of Ashar, circa 5th July 1944. The boat is fitted with a cinema-projector, loud-speaker and radiogram. Its voyage up the River Euphrates bringing propaganda films to the Marsh Arabs of Southern Iraq was judged a great success.

9. Film show of propaganda films provided by the British Public Information Office travelling cinema van in an Arab village in Palestine in 1943. The men are gathered in front of the screen, whilst a small group of women are relegated to the rear.

10. (*left*) This Ministry of Information publicity picture was designed to show that Muslims in Britain could expect to enjoy religious observance and their way of life without hindrance. Here Sheikh Hassan Ismail (in the centre of the photograph wearing a long patterned robe), the Imam of the Cardiff Mosque, is opening a new mosque in Butetown, Cardiff in 1943.

11. (*opposite*) Suez crisis, 1956: 'Salome,' British cartoon by Leslie Gilbert Illingworth, comparing President Gamal Abdel Nasser to the Biblical Salome, who demanded the head of John the Baptist. Nasser is shown receiving the head of British Prime Minister Anthony Eden, in retribution for Britain's decision to bomb Egyptian airfields.

12. (*above*) Defaced poster of Iraqi leader Saddam Hussein in prayer position but with blood covering his hands and face, taken some time in post-occupation Iraq. Saddam was a careful student of propaganda models.

13. (*right*) Iraqi Arabic language Psyop leaflet depicting Abu Musab Al Zarqawi, Leader of Al-Qaeda in Iraq, in a cage held by an Iraqi soldier whilst under assault from rats. The legend reads: 'This is your future, oh Zarqawi!'

14. Corporal Sarah Bryant: the first British servicewoman to be killed in Afghanistan was revealed to be a specialist, Pashto speaking Target Audience Analyst, part of the British Psychological Operations unit that was active in the country building links to the Afghan people.

15. 'Palestine-Falastin': Cuban pro-Palestine propaganda poster, 1984.

16. (below) Carefully posed for maximum projection of power and strength: the Shaikh Abu Ibrahim Brigade of Islamic State with its symbols: flags, camouflage uniforms, balaclavas and banners.

government.'[2] Furthermore, the citation revealed that the unit ran a network of radio stations employing local Afghans as DJs, broadcasting music, poetry, debate programmes and even a Helmandi soap opera, as well as producing graphical posters and leaflets to communicate in an area where literacy rates are only around 20%. Recent projects had included information campaigns to prevent children picking up spent ordnance, disseminating information from farming and veterinary workshops using their radio stations, and promoting debate on political issues of the day.

To the informed observer, this sounds like a very highly engineered community engagement programme built on the principle of persuasive public relations, albeit implemented in a fragile and post-conflict environment with soaring illiteracy rates, and thus technically challenging. It is reminiscent in its way of other public information campaigns in Afghanistan at the time, one of them a counter narcotics initiative started in 2004 by the British to persuade farmers to stop cultivating opium poppies and develop alternative crops, a brief which caused some serious head scratching over similar target audience selection problems that might have benefited from Bryant's skills. However, the bigger point about the PsyOps programme in Helmand, or for that matter in Basra and Baghdad is that it qualifies as being directly within the propaganda sphere and therefore part of the information war that is prosecuted in parallel with the country's military and economic wars.

To that extent it begs a few questions. Are we being asked to accept that this propaganda effort is neither transparent nor accountable and therefore not subject to any orthodox processes of scrutiny and evaluation? What 'unbiased' messages are being propagated, who approves them, and in what ways do they link into a wider and consensual national narrative? Like any service that consumes public resources, it needs to show activity, results and value, but under the umbrella of Information Operations (IO), the prevalent military management system for psychological warfare activities, this does not currently happen.

'Islam Is Our Way; Freedom Is Our Aim'
Yet, for those who cared to dig a little deeper, the activity in Afghanistan had its precedents. For the footprint of psychological operations can be found earlier in Britain's secret wars throughout the 1960s and 1970s when it was trying by every means to stem the tides of both nationalist and Communist insurgency that were threatening to engulf some of its remaining colonial interests. The failure of the Baghdad Pact and

the retreat from Suez, whilst a practical and reputational disaster for Britain, caused a necessary rethinking of the way in which British interventions in the Middle East were packaged up and sold. Henceforth, the propaganda dimension would no longer promote an overt imperial agenda based on a permanent regional footprint but would instead focus on a more subtle and persuasive information strategy centered on winning hearts and minds as a means to support British interests and foster alliances. Elements of the wars waged against the Mau Mau in Kenya from 1952 to 1964, and against Communist insurgents in Malaya from 1948 to 1960, both leaned on a psychological dimension to drive the propaganda initiative amongst the indigenous populations and at the same time provided a test bed for a type of information war that was prosecuted under the close control and direction of the military, a departure from the mainstream practice and narrative of propaganda.

From 1970 onwards, Britain was to refine this specialist branch of its propaganda business to further its agenda in the Middle East, by mounting a carefully calibrated information war on behalf of the new Sultan of Oman against Communist insurgents in the People's Democratic Republic of Yemen (PDRY), a country at the foot of the Arabian Peninsula and traditionally one of great strategic importance to Britain in helping protect the sea lanes from India. Subsequent accounts written by military historians and students of Britain's Special Air Service (SAS) have revealed that PsyOps was one of the four strategic pillars driving counter insurgency (COIN) operations against the Communist infiltrators from Yemen into neighbouring Oman. Tasked with the objective of securing the mountainous Dhofar region of southern Oman, a small number of SAS soldiers initiated a hearts and minds campaign alongside a civil development programme which offered the inhabitants both medical and veterinary assistance, and gathered intelligence to underpin a military response by the Omanis.

Branded 'Islam Is Our Way, Freedom Is Our Aim,' the campaign used information as a central building block to persuade the local population that they were being lied to and misinformed by the rebels.[3] To do this, the SAS established a government radio station, Radio Dhofar, and distributed many thousands of free Japanese transistor radios amongst the local people so that they could listen to broadcasts of official news. When the insurgents started to take these radios from local people, the SAS introduced a small charge for replacements, which made the insurgents unpopular and unwelcome as locals resented having to pay anything. To supplement the radio information campaign, the local teams also set up news and information bulletin boards in each village so that people could access more local news and keep abreast of wider developments in the programme, alongside the introduction of a regional newspaper. Despite a constant tussle of the airwaves between Radio Dhofar and Radio Aden, the Communist broadcast mouthpiece, the information war was eventually won by the Sultan of Oman and his British military supporters. The relationship between Oman and Britain, developed on the basis of this alliance formed to win over hearts and minds in the mountains of Dhofar has strengthened and prospered over the ensuing years to deliver an anchor for British interests and its presence in the Arabian Gulf; the relationship was further cemented in the Autumn of 2018 with the opening of expanded facilities at the south-eastern Omani port of Duqm, now able to accommodate Britain's largest aircraft carrier, HMS Queen Elizabeth.

Avoiding Information Fratricide

As it turns out, these days there is a whole industry dedicated to establishing the precise meaning of Information Operations. In what must qualify as a definitional hall of mirrors, even varying branches of the US Military think of it as meaning different things; the US Air Force and Navy, for example, tend to view IO as technical efforts to disrupt the flow of information over networks and the electromagnetic spectrum, whilst the Marine Corps and Army tend to focus more on human-to-human engagement. 'These differences make sense, given the different roles of each service, but they add to confusion in the broader debate,' according to the specialist information hub Real Clear Defense.[4] In fact, the US Army has changed its definition of IO several times over the past 25 years, even changing the term itself from information operations to information engagement, back to information operations, to a brief flirtation with inform and influence activities, and recently back to information operations, according to these experts. 'When you strip away all the buzzwords and politics, IO is nothing more than activities to encourage a desired audience to act (or not act) in a manner that is beneficial to the organisation conducting the activities,' Real Clear Defense concludes.[5]

This may be true, but it doesn't tell the whole story. The practice of Information Operations, of which PsyOps is just one component, is a management system designed to control the overall perception of a war space by outsiders, in that sense, reminiscent of Walter Lippmann's original description of propaganda contrived by the French High

Command at the Battle of Verdun. To that extent, it is a comparable system which manipulates the holistic information environment by controlling access to facts on the ground, sources, images and other information resources and assets that could be used to build an objective and truthful picture of the action underway and its context.

This causes real difficulties for those tasked with extracting the truth of events in such a way that the interests of public opinion are properly served, an issue that was compellingly written about by US investigative journalist Maud Beelman who identified the practice of IO as being amongst the official hurdles erected to make the truth harder to reach. 'IO, as it is known, groups together information functions ranging from public affairs (PA, the military spokespersons corps) to military deception and psychological operations, or PsyOp. What this means is that people whose job traditionally has been to talk to the media and divulge truthfully what they are able to tell now work hand-in-glove with those whose job it is to support battlefield operations with information, not all of which may be truthful.[6] While Beelman acknowledged the need for information war to balance deception of the enemy with authentic information for public opinion at home, she pointed out the associated dangers, 'sometimes the public can be willing to sacrifice detailed knowledge. But that can also lead to unaccountability and when information that is presented has been managed such, propaganda is often the result.'[7]

In the growing maze of definitions, there is something seductive about acquiescing to the notion that all of these mainstream and hybrid branches of propaganda, in the end, amount to the same thing. But this would be disingenuous as there are real distinctions that become clear when the engine of each is stripped down to its component parts; the process of technical comparison is always revealing as it confronts the detail often used as a smokescreen by insiders anxious to maintain their monopoly control over a field which, by its very nature, deters close scrutiny. Whilst the practice of PsyOps, if not the name, goes back millennia (military folklore claims the back story of psychological operations reaches to Alexander the Great and Genghis Khan), its modern formulation is a construct measurable in practical terms since the Second World War. The organisation and development of PsyOps are thus principally situated in a context in which it can be seen as the first real specialist branch of propaganda, and in that sense, contextually distinct from the broader idea of mainstream scientific propaganda. PsyOps, whilst under the direct ownership and control of the military as part of Information Operations, is in turn now part of the eve practice of perception management, an altogether more comprehensive definition of modern information warfare that embraces other aspects of propaganda, such as truth projection, operations security and public relations techniques, combining to construct wholesale alternative renditions of reality.

The ability and purpose of public relations in dealing with these credible renditions of reality, rather than simply projecting images, was part of its central rationale as envisaged by founder Edward Bernays, and it is this that makes PR part of the post-modernist interpretation of the universe in which relativism and individualism have replaced universal truths. Together, these forces have spawned the modern concept of the information warrior, the pursuer of war and foreign policy goals through the information medium. In modern conflict design, this new age manipulator of public opinion in the West has its Islamist opposite, the 'media mujahid.' Both are portrayed as consummate and committed strategists dedicated to the achievement of war and foreign policy aims and objectives through the medium of propaganda and media manipulation. This new archetype, a kind of communications and PR superhero (in the Marvel Comics mode), is schooled in multiple branches of propaganda and equipped with a range of information weapons and methodologies whose powers of projection can bring down a hostile regime with the precision of a missile. The information warrior is truly the post-modern propagandist of our time.

Drawing up the PsyOP Masterplan

In the US national planning grand scheme, PsyOp is a phenomenon that is not simply a tactical afterthought but a capability that exists and is propagated at the very highest level of national life. It has carte blanche to be used in any set of circumstances, peaceful or otherwise, in which it is deemed appropriate to be making a contribution to national security objectives or policy aims. Evidence of this lies with National Security Decision 77, 'Management of Public Diplomacy Relative to National Security,' which was signed by President Ronald Reagan as long ago as January 1983. It was a directive designed to comprise specific actions of the US Government to generate support for its national security objectives and to embrace a broad range of informational and cultural activities, also providing for the establishment of 'an interagency mechanism to plan and co-ordinate public affairs, information, political and broadcasting activities of the US Government.'[8] Following a further directive by President Reagan, his then Secretary of Defence Caspar Weinberger constructed a PsyOp Masterplan as the framework to deliver on this vision. Approved in 1985, the Masterplan offered up a new design for the US to perform worldwide psychological operations in support of national objectives in peace and crisis and at all levels of conflict.[9] One of the unique features of the 1985 Masterplan was that it called for the separation of psychological operations from special operations throughout the Defence Department, in effect so that PsyOp programmes could be given more room to be deployed wherever they might be required in support of national objectives, policy or strategy in peace or war.

Thus, over the intervening 35 years or so the theory and applied practice of PsyOp has gathered a large body of evidence that legitimises its status and provenance as a specialist military branch of the propaganda business, comprising academic papers, case studies, field manuals, training videos, personal accounts and comparative literature. PsyOP is an established part of the US army training curriculum; evidence of this turns up in the film 'PSYOP: The Invisible Sword,'[10] a public domain film made in 1996 and released from the US National Archives in 2015. Made for an audience of 'All Service Attendees at Non-Commissioned Officer Academies or Officer Career Courses,' the 15-minute film provides soldiers with an overview of PsyOp terminology and developments and some examples of how it can be used as both an offensive and defensive tool.

A glimpse inside the planning process confirms the scientific and psychological basis for the PsyOp model of propaganda. Central to this is the job of target audience analysis, the role in which Corporal Sarah Bryant developed her expertise. This is the starting point for all PsyOP and is broken into phases, starting with the identification of potential audiences. Once this is done, target characteristics including vulnerabilities, susceptibilities, conditions and effectiveness are analysed. 'Vulnerabilities are the four psychological factors that affect the target audience: perception; motivation; stress; and attitude.'[11] The term 'susceptibilities' is used to accommodate an analysis of the degree to which the target audience can be influenced by the messages it receives; 'conditions,' in turn, includes analysis of all environmental factors that affect the audience; and the key concept of audience effectiveness is the actual capability of the target group to carry out the desired response. The concept of audience effectiveness is fundamental to PsyOp success at strategic and tactical level...goals may require finding different effective audiences...who will have to be convinced by multiple messages.[12] This highly analytical and process-based approach to the operating model of PsyOp is designed to leave as little to chance as possible, at the same time taking the practice about as far away as one can imagine from the idea of opportunistic or creative campaigning.

The critical distinction between PsyOp and other forms of propaganda lies in its model of action-based response. PsyOP may ask target audiences to change their attitudes and perceptions about an issue but above everything it requires an audience to do something differently, to change its behaviour in some way. A classic example of this type of behaviour change would be persuading a group of enemy soldiers to give up, surrender and hand themselves in as the only logical step in their prevailing circumstances. The metrics of PsyOp are thus distinctive and compelling. In crude terms, the success of an operation to persuade enemy soldiers to give up and hand themselves in, as in Operation Desert Storm in Iraq in 1991, can be measured precisely by the numbers of enemy soldiers performing that task. This proof of effectiveness is one reason why PsyOp is perceived to be such a precision tool; its impact is evidence-based, not predicated on supposition or non-specific qualitative data.

The typical PsyOp operation uses a toolkit which is recognisable to most modern communicators, perhaps adapted for some face-to-face, close-quarters exchanges but classic tactics employ such devices as dual-language leaflets, native language radio broadcasts, news announcements and direct personal appeals. There are, though, some idiosyncrasies attached to PsyOp which may help to categorise its style but at the same time ramp up its status as a more mysterious branch of the business. In the PsyOp manual, the term 'white' is used to describe overt propaganda which the source takes responsibility for, 'gray' propaganda, on the other hand, is material that is distributed without an identifiable source. The third type, 'black propaganda,' is material produced by one source that purports to have emanated from another source.[13]

Saddam the PsyWarrior
The Iraqi invasion of Kuwait on 2nd August 1990 was a turning point in the development of the geopolitics of the Middle East, providing a trigger for a series of downstream events over later decades that have permanently changed its landscape, not least through the subsequent disastrous policy of regime change in Iraq and its associated ideological, political and social engineering. Less than a week after the invasion, on 7th August 1990, US President George Bush was authorised to initiate Operation Desert

Shield, the process by which the US and its fast gathering Coalition allies proposed to act to stop further Iraqi aggression.[14] On 17th January the following year, Operation Desert Storm, the second active phase to gain back control of Kuwait by military means got underway, with the aim of driving Saddam's forces out of Kuwait and re-establishing a legitimate government. In the five months or so between the two operations, Saddam turned his mind to ways in which he could win the phoney war by influencing public opinion inside Iraq, amongst Arab neighbours and more widely across the international community. How best to do this?

At that time, Iraq's information infrastructure replicated what might best be described as the traditional Soviet, one-party state model. Baghdad's Ministry of Information, headed by Latif Nussayif Jassim, tightly controlled access to and distribution of information within Iraq, including state television, radio and a carefully managed newspaper sector, as well as the broadcast of information outside the country. Foreign journalists wanting direct access to developments in Iraq were required to process their enquiries through the Ministry if they were to have any chance of securing a visa, a process which invited an unspoken quid pro quo agenda. This back-scratching set-up was typical of its time in many countries of the Middle East, few if any of which allowed an open information culture or freedom of the press. Thus, the conditions were in place for Saddam to establish and control the narrative which might explain his invasion and open up ways of attacking the US led coalition gathering to strike the Iraqis on their doorstep.

In addition to harnessing the traditional, creaking machinery of Baghdad's Ministry of Information, Saddam cast around for more innovative and subtle ways in which he might structure his information war. One option which he embraced was psychological operations, a type of propaganda, when set against the old systematic processes, he saw as offering distinct possibilities. As the bedrock of his propaganda strategy, Saddam looked to the model that the North Vietnamese had used against the Americans to shape international public opinion during the Vietnam War, in effect to portray America and its partners as embarking on another expensive and bloody mistake. The themes he took to populate this strategy were familiar, a war being fought by the poor against the rich and powerful, a conflict that would sow division at home and the prospect of another bloody and dirty war that would sap America's will and resources.[15] Saddam and his Revolutionary Command Council (RCC) sought to hinder any attacks on the country, at the same time discouraging participation in the UN embargo of Iraq, generating wider Arab support and rationalising the Kuwait invasion.

This strategy was also conspicuously successful in influencing public opinion in Palestine, where Yasser Arafat was hyper aware of the force which the 'Palestinian street' exerted on him and of the winds blowing through Palestinian public opinion. Saddam's struggle for survival against the US came to constitute a source of pride and identification in the Palestinian public consciousness, one which has yet to be entirely overwritten, and some analysts suggest that themes of his propaganda war against the Americans were in turn taken up by Arafat and his own information strategists to underpin their military struggle against Israel.

Some of the tactics Saddam deployed to achieve his propaganda aims were cleverly adapted from the PsyOp school of inducing maximum stress in the target audience. They included the systematic spreading of anxiety and panic (including in Israel) over the use of Scud missiles and their ever-present threat of chemical warheads; and Saddam's own personal appearances with Allied hostages, portrayed as 'guests' of the Iraqi establishment but increasingly positioned within strategic infrastructural sites that could become targets for Coalition bombing. The campaign used Iraqi TV as a relay to broadcast beyond its borders and, notably, also broadcast radio programmes to US forces gathering for the re-occupation of Kuwait – the most memorable of these being 'Baghdad Betty,' a character reminiscent of Tokyo Rose in the Second World War – who warned US servicemen that their wives back home were sleeping with a diverse range of bed partners, among them Bart Simpson and Tom Cruise.[16]

In time, as the war progressed, Saddam used other stress inducing tactics taken directly from the North Vietnamese PsyOp manual, the most notable being the illegal parading and interviewing of captured pilots, most of them in obvious physical distress. The first of these was Flt Lt John Nichol, a British Airforce Tornado navigator shot down on 17th January 1991 over southern Iraq with his partner, pilot John Peters. After three days of beatings, torture and psychological pressure he appeared on British television screens reading a script prepared for him by his Iraqi interrogators. 'I tried to put on a brave face, repeating the Iraqis' poor grammar to the letter, hoping the dreadful grammar would show that I was speaking under duress,'[17] he recalled. Nichol's performance had distinct echoes of the late US Senator John McCain who, as a US fighter pilot, bailed out over North Vietnam when his plane was shot down in October 1967. Badly injured on impact, he was subsequently paraded and interviewed on television, his treatment growing steadily worse as he refused both to confess or to accept an early release unless all other captured US pilots were released with him. After holding out for four days, McCain, at the point of suicide, agreed to write a confession. Looking back on his decision, he reflected, 'I felt just terrible about it... every man has his breaking point. I had reached mine.'[18]

Saddam's speeches at that time emphasised the attrition that would take its toll on any army choosing to invade Iraq, engendering images of plane loads of Vietnam style body bags on the way back to the States. To an extent, this PsyOp based campaign generated some results; there was an initial shift in international media coverage to reflect the potential downside on US public opinion of a long drawn out conflict. In time, Iraqi propaganda was undone by the failure of military performance to back up expectations.

PsyOP and Desert Storm

In the ensuing tussle for supremacy over the psychological and propaganda battlefields of Operation Desert Storm, US efforts to exert influence on the attitudes and behaviours of their Iraqi adversaries were highly effective; their campaign was estimated to reach 73,000 Iraqi soldiers and played a role in the surrender of 70% of all enemy prisoners of war (EPWs).[19]

Compared to their Iraqi counterparts, the US PsyOp campaign to support Operation Desert Storm was both systematic and well resourced. It used four methods to engage Iraqi soldiers: radio transmissions, loudspeaker broadcasts, leaflet drops and specially constituted EPW teams on the ground to open up conversations with specified units targeted for surrender. The operation used constant reinforcement to drive home the idea of the inevitability of death. It did this by dropping leaflets to announce specific bombing targets, then implemented the bombing and followed this up with further announcements of the bombing having taken place as and when indicated.

In these repeated communication and execution cycles, Iraqi soldiers began to see surrender as the only viable alternative to a death that would in effect be useless. Six broadcast platforms were established to support the PsyOp campaign, including three Volant Solo systems on converted C-130 aircraft and three ground stations, 'Voice of the Gulf,' 'Voice of America' and 'Free Kuwait People' according to the official case study of the PsyOp campaign to support Desert Storm.[20] In the main, programmes consisted of pre-taped messages broadcast each day for 17 hours, a standard taped message on an established surrender hotline being 'Your division will be bombed tomorrow. Abandon your equipment. Leave your location now and save yourselves!' US teams measured the effectiveness of these messages using complex parameters of audience exposure and resulting action relative to no transmissions being made. They calculated that impact on surrender reached about 34% and took the view that this relatively low percentage was as a result of cultural distinction. Due to the primacy of language channels that were visual rather than auditory, both leaflets and human engagement were ultimately more effective. In total, it was estimated that the campaign comprised 29 million 'in theatre' leaflets dropped, 17 hours daily of radio transmissions, and 19.5 days of aerial broadcasts.

It would be misleading, though, to characterise all US PsyOp activities as taking place at arm's length. During Desert Storm, frontline PsyOp squads from the US 4th PsyOp Group came within loud hailing distance of the Iraqi front lines in an organised attempt to induce mass surrender. Two to three-man squads equipped with loudspeakers loaded up with pre-taped messages would be dropped off by Blackhawk helicopter to do their work, sometimes only a few hundred metres from enemy positions.

One of the team members taking part in these operations, Staff Sergeant Edward Fivel, recalled how effective the approach could be, in one case, resulting in the eventual surrender of 400 Iraqi soldiers from a series of bunkers. 'We asked the pilot to land us on the ground not too far from the bunker. With what you might call serious reservations he eventually landed us, feeling a little protected, I guess, by the three Apaches and one Blackhawk whopping over our heads and to our right... the three of us were now on the ground...we picked up our loudspeaker equipment – the transmitter and the speaker – and ran about 200 metres closer to the bunker. We sat down and again started playing the surrender tapes....'[21]

Operation Iraqi Freedom

Some of the lessons learned in the deployment of PsyOp in Operation Desert Storm were immediately carried forward into the next US intervention in the region little more than a decade later. The US took the decision to conclude its unfinished business with Saddam Hussein and attacked Iraq itself on 20th March 2003. Operation Iraqi Freedom set out to effect regime change in Iraq, finishing the job that some US neo-cons saw the country as having ducked when their forces had stopped at the Kuwaiti border in the first Gulf War. However, the fact that the legal status of the invasion was, and remains, disputed removed the same sense of moral certainty, collective endeavour and righteous indignation attached to Desert Storm and underpinned the military action instead with an element of self-doubt and ambivalence. US and British propagandists had worked hard to present the Iraqi regime as unstable and a threat to regional security (the British 'dodgy dossier' was famously influential in swinging the British Parliamentary vote in favour of the war); at the same time, Saddam himself was personally demonised by Western media as a dangerous and unpredictable dictator sitting on an arsenal of chemical and other proscribed weapons (the so-called Weapons of Mass Destruction, or WMD) and with strong links to Al Qaeda and other jihadist organisations. The invasion and intended occupation of Iraq, to be followed by its political reconstitution and reinvention as a democratic state, required a heavy emphasis to be placed on a propaganda and information strategy that could rapidly be rolled out following the initial military phase of the intervention. In due course, this task of winning Iraqi hearts and minds was to attract a whole tribe of information warriors contracted by the US government to deploy a sophisticated programme of perception management and media manipulation that was breath-taking in its scale, ambition and resourcing. PsyOp was part of this elevated new approach to total information management of the post-war environment, and it went on to play a significant part in constructing the new reality designed to persuade Iraqis to turn their backs on the old certainties of Saddam's police state and embrace instead the sunlit uplands of the new post-war democratic vision of Iraq.

In an initial internal assessment of the role of PsyOp used in the military phase of Operation Iraqi Freedom, NATO analyst Lieutenant-Colonel Steven Collins expressed the view that it had been broadly successful, although difficulties remained in determining precisely what impacts had resulted from PsyOp activity and which had resulted from a combination of other initiatives. 'The use of mass media like radio, leaflets, and targeted media like e-mails against key decision-makers, and loudspeakers during ground operations, seems to have had an important impact,' he wrote in an internal NATO review of the operation.[22] Collins revealed that over 40 million leaflets were dropped on Iraq before the first attack on 20th March, with a further 40 million dropped during the campaign. Some of these threatened to destroy any military formation that stood and fought, while others encouraged the Iraqi populace and military to ignore the directives of the Baath Party leadership.

In addition to leafleting, radio formed a major part of the information assault, using both fixed transmission towers and aircraft to distribute messages. Local PsyOp radio stations were also set up outside major population centres; the British established Radio Nahrain (Two Rivers), an FM radio station, on the outskirts of Basra. In addition to setting up its own radio transmitters, the Coalition attempted to electronically jam Iraqi radio stations in order to gain a monopoly on the information available to the Iraqi people through this medium.[23]

Collins also revealed that Black PsyOp techniques were used during Iraqi Freedom, offering an insight into how this darker branch of the PsyOp business works on the ground. The Central Intelligence Agency (CIA) set up its Black PsyOp station, Radio Tikrit, in early 2003. It built its credibility by claiming to be managed by loyal Iraqis in the Tikrit area and by maintaining an editorial line slavishly supportive of Saddam Hussein. Within a few weeks, however, the tone changed, and the station became increasingly critical of Saddam. The Black PsyOp game plan is predicated on the target audience failing to see the ruse, with the attendant risk that, if it does, the credibility of the entire PsyOp operation is compromised. Other tactics successfully deployed in the initial PsyOp phase of the operation included text messages and emails sent directly to key decision makers in the Iraqi regime, some of which spelt out the personal and collective costs they would have to pay for their continued support of Saddam.

One result of the PsyOp activity that was not replicated in Iraqi Freedom was the level of surrenders experienced during Desert Storm and, whilst 250 Iraqis surrendered on the first day during the seizure of Umm Qasr, this initial trickle did not turn into a flood, according to Collins. Part of his assessment included the view that the 'shock and awe' element of the military campaign had largely failed, causing the US military and the PsyOp operation to re-examine its themes and messages.

In a hint of the anomalies and sometime absurdities that would emerge from the practices of perception management, military planners seemed to give little advance thought to any post-conflict PsyOp capability, with the result that Iranian agents, especially in southern Iraq, were in some instances able to fill the information vacuum. The US contracted companies to put virtually anything on the air rapidly to fill the void. This has led to some unintentionally amusing moments as the attention of the US media turned away from Iraq and contracted companies beamed parochial US news stories to bemused Iraqis, recalled Collins.[24]

As the occupation of Iraq deepened, the information war being fought inside the country by the US started to fall apart, its focus on US media at the expense of Iraqi audiences dooming it to chaos and failure, according to US Army Public Affairs Officer (PAO) Steven J. Alvarez, who was closely engaged with the effort on the ground. Alvarez' verdict on the professionalism of the US effort was damning and he believed that an informed Iraqi people could have slowed, if not stopped, the ensuing societal and cultural violence in their world.

'There is a direct link between Information Operations and influencing public opinion. The US Defense Department knows that Information Operations on the battlefield are critical to operational success in a fight against insurgents just as much as diplomacy is needed with military power. The Defense Department knows this and spent hundreds of millions of dollars trying to find the right public relations formula for Iraq, with very little success,'[25] he wrote.

Metallica and Barney the Dinosaur

Just where PsyOp could go as a branch of the propaganda business is the subject of constant speculation, if not obsession, amongst propaganda futurologists and war junkies. It is true that there are already some extreme examples of the genre to pick on which, when integrated with the possibilities of developing science, are a gift for blue sky thinkers. The British writer Jon Ronson, in his book 'The Men Who Stare at Goats,' looked into the doings of a secret US PsyOp special unit that was researching how to harness new ideas including even the powers of the paranormal and psychic projection in order to play with the minds of America's more recalcitrant enemies.[26] He exposed a number of proposals that were being worked up by this happy band of brother eccentrics, including creating a hologram of Allah which they planned to project over a target Arab city, with an accompanying electronic broadcast by Allah praising the virtues of the US. During the Iraq occupation, US PsyOp specialists acknowledged that they had pioneered experimental methods of interrogation, such as exposing uncooperative prisoners for extended periods of time to full-blast music from rock group Metallica or children's TV programmes like Barney the Dinosaur.[27]

Now, declassified analyses of US PsyOP campaigns in the Vietnam War support the accounts of some of these more speculative methodologies, tried out at the time on local Vietnamese villagers. Referred to as 'gimmickry' and deployed as part of a strategy to generate immediate results on the ground, the US 4ᵗʰ Infantry Division developed a device it called 'the magic box,' comprising two boxes with non-functional dials, gauges, antennae and remotely operated lights. US personnel told villagers that the device would detect Viet Cong, and that they would receive better treatment if they confessed before the device revealed them. When a known Viet Cong villager passed between the boxes, the hidden operator triggered the lights 'proving' the device's effectiveness and causing the Viet Cong in the community to confess. The Magic Box was from time to time supplemented by other gimmicks including the projection of images onto clouds and the use of ghostly loud speaker broadcasts as 'more or less desperate attempts to find a quick solution to show solid evidence of positive results.'[28]

Now it now looks as if the possibilities of the PsyOp revolution can go much further and sinisterly if some of the research already in the public domain is to be believed. The idea of creating weapons that can disrupt or alter the cognitive processes of enemy combatants is starting to become a reality, as the US military actively assesses the potential of neuro cognitive weapons which harness recent advances in neuroscience. The new fields of neuro-security and neuro-deterrence, situated somewhere in the biodefence domain, relate to weapons that will be developed to diminish or manipulate someone's thought processes. Neuroscientist and neuroethicist, Dr. James Giordano, a professor at Georgetown University Medical Center, Washington DC is leading a research group that is working on developing this new generation of weapons. He describes four broad categories: drugs; bugs; toxins; and bytes which between them can knock out every human sense, from perception to concentration, cognitive manifestations to motor skills, and neurological function to neuro-cognitive thought processes. To describe these areas formally, Giordano uses arcane and mystifying terms such as nano neuroscience, advanced neuro-pharmacologicals, neuro-imaging, neuro-manipulative devices, neuro-informatics and cyber-neuro-systems.

The US Army even holds an annual 'Mad Scientist Future Technology Seminar' which brings together scientists, sci-fi authors, futurists, government and private sector people, and academics to discuss the military implications of emerging science and technology, according to the writer George Dvorsky.[29] Among the items regularly discussed are electro-magnetic pulse (EMP) weapons, robotic swarming weapons on the nanoscale, and social networking attacks in which a soldier's friends, families, and colleagues could become vulnerable to virtual attacks, he says.

Most profound, however, is discussion on the potential for neuro-cognitive warfare. 'In the far term, beyond 2030, developments in neuro-cognitive warfare could have significant impacts. Neuro-cognitive warfare is the mashing of electromagnetic, infrasonic, and light technologies to target human neural and physiological systems. Weaponised capabilities at the tactical level will be focused on degrading the cognitive, physiological, and behavioural characteristics of soldiers,'[30] he wrote. It may be that the field of psychological operations is still in its infancy. Only time and a lot of applied science will surely tell what yet unknown fronts might be opened up for propagandists with the benefit of an entirely new set of tools in their kit.

CHAPTER IX

Alternative Realities: Perception Management, Outsourcing and Iraq

'If it bleeds, it leads' is an old adage associated with the press. The more lurid the content, the more fascinating it is to consumers.'

Steven J. Alvarez
Selling War – A Critical Look at the Military's PR Machine,
Potomac Books (2016), page ix

Information and the Role of the State

It is intrinsic to the process of government to try and manage the flow of information from its institutions in a way that best maintains a careful balance between its obligations and interests. In the totalitarian state, this is inevitably much more straightforward; information as a commodity is strictly rationed both as a way of controlling messages about what government is up to, but also as a means of shaping public opinion to endorse the prevailing political and ideological manifesto. Thus, at the time of Operation Desert Shield in 1990, and subsequently Desert Storm in 1991, Iraqi President Saddam Hussein could be described as sitting at the apex of a Soviet style command and control information and communications model whose purpose was to package up and propagate Iraq's official position on domestic and international issues. The Ministry of Information, with its chief official at ministerial level represented in the Revolutionary Command Council (RCC), was the gatekeeper to an information hierarchy which spread out from Baghdad to manage an ecosystem of people, offices and processes that embraced television, radio, newspapers and every aspect of the state's media persona. In this way, Saddam was able in the main to control the messages and images which the outside world could reasonably access about events in Iraq and the activities of the Iraqi government. This traditional model, with power concentrated at the centre, maintained a highly risk averse, cumbersome bureaucracy and closed information culture; its operational methodology carefully censored facts and opinions and built them around a series of official state lines which together made up the national narrative. Getting senior Iraqi officials or government ministers to express a personal or improvised opinion was an unwelcome and generally unrewarding journalistic move. This Ministry led, micro managed model, was the prevailing one across much of the Arab world at the time, reflecting an environment where the currency of information was highly valued and media liberties viewed as both dangerous and unwelcome. PR and press officers attached to the ministries to curate their respective official line lived with the fear that foreign journalists assigned to their charge might go rogue and release career-altering exclusives. The case of the freelance Observer journalist Farzad Bazoft, caught by the Iraqis and executed in 1990 for spying when he was found taking photographs near Al Iskandaria air force base south of Baghdad, is illustrative of the level of paranoia generated by classified regime sites and proscribed information at the time.

Whilst the nature and constitution of the one-party state makes the protection and management of its information a relatively straightforward process, for precisely the same reasons, it invites investigation by journalists who see it as a challenge to their professional ambitions and truth-seeking remit. In multi-party modern democracies, the task of governments to control the message they want to propagate and to protect the information they classify as confidential is necessarily much more complex. Lack of press censorship, freedom of information legislation and sometimes loosely applied codes of professional conduct make being seen to intervene in a state sanctioned process a much riskier business, as both British Prime Ministers Sir Anthony Eden and Tony Blair found to their cost during the Suez crisis in 1956 and Operation Iraqi Freedom in 2003. But the checks and balances of democracy do not deter Western governments from taking an equally active role in managing their information output and fighting the information war where concentration of effort can influence both policy and tactical outcomes to government advantage. Ironically perhaps, the practical challenges for both styles of closed and open information models are not dissimilar.

Declining UK Information Capacity

Since the Second World War, the scale and apparatus of the British information state has been subject to gradual attrition and downgrading of its status that has had a profound effect on its capacity and ability to wage information war. Statisticians would show this descent in an inverted curve from a high point reached in 1941 with the appointment of Brendan Bracken (1901–1958) as Information Minister, in charge for the duration of the war of a formidable information and propaganda machine organised as a fully realised government ministry. This was a complete turnaround from the situation at the start of the Great War in 1914, when it quickly became apparent that Britain had no propaganda machine in place; any activity was random and generally reactive with no systematic approach or plan, little human capacity and no sense of leadership or overt connection to the foreign policy agenda. That changed with the appointment of Liberal MP Charles Masterman as the first head of the newly constituted British War Propaganda Bureau (WPB). Masterman played a major part in bringing some order to the enterprise and was also the first person to import established talent and put it to work in the service of the country, engaging the writers John Buchan and Arthur Conan Doyle and the war artists Eric Kennington, William Orpen, Paul Nash, John Sargent and Stanley Spencer, amongst others. By November 1914, his Bureau at Wellington House had spent the princely sum of £1,444.00 on propaganda output, including 100,000 copies of the Prime Minister's speeches and 29,000 copies of Sir Edward Cook's pamphlet 'Why Britain Is at War.'[1] In 1917, the WPB in Wellington House was replaced by a new Department of Information nominally under government minister Sir Edward Carson but in practical terms run by John Buchan. This in turn became the Ministry of Information under press baron Lord Beaverbrook in 1918, with Lord Northcliffe placed in charge of propaganda to enemy countries.

The National War Aims Committee was set up in 1917 to focus on propaganda at home; this Committee worked closely with the Department of Information and with voluntary organisations like the Topical Committee for War Films. Though people were to find ways around it, censorship was instrumental in controlling the selection and flow of news from both the front line and the Cabinet Office. Censorship played a role in the monitoring, selection and rationing of information not least in the content of news. One of the most visible and dramatic cases of press censorship at work was in the closing down of Britain's oldest evening newspaper, the Globe and Traveller in November

1915 for having wrongly reported that Britain's most senior soldier Lord Kitchener had had an interview with the King and tendered his resignation. The police, in the shape of Chief Inspector Fowler, made a visit to the newspaper's offices in London's Strand with a warrant and seized all copies of the newspaper along with its printing plant.[2]

The MOI closed in 1918 and, after a fallow period, was fully revived by the Second World War to reach the height of its power in 1941 with Bracken's appointment as its sixth dedicated Information Minister (Bracken is also said to be the model for Big Brother in Orwell's 'Nineteen Eighty-Four' with the building his Ministry occupied, at London University's Senate House, dubbed the 'Ministry of Truth'). The MOI recruited many censor-minded ex-servicemen (including 300 former naval officers) and civil servants, but initially few journalists. Ultimately, by 1943, it employed 2,900 staff including around 200 journalists, according to the official MOI history.[3] Following the war, the curve started to invert rapidly, in 1946 the MOI being downgraded to the new Central Office of Information (COI) with no ministerial representation at Cabinet level, disconnected from the making of government policy and its business divided up between the Foreign, Colonial and Dominion offices. The final nail in the coffin of future ministerial status for the information function in British government was hammered in by Lord President of the Council, Herbert Morrison, at a Cabinet meeting on 4th December 1947. As part of a discussion on government publicity services, he told the Cabinet that, at an upcoming meeting of the Parliamentary Labour Party, he proposed to take the line that 'it was impracticable for a single Minister to assume responsibility for the handling of all government publicity, and to stress the difficulties which would arise if a separate Minister dealt with the publicity aspects of policies for which other Ministers were accountable to Parliament.'[4]

In 1951, COI headcount was reduced to a mere 974 personnel; the film unit, conference division and other important elements were closed completely. Thus, by the Suez crisis in 1956, British capacity to strategise and implement the information dimension of its foreign policy was significantly diminished, with no ministerial status, insufficient manpower and no co-ordinating function. The end game in this gradual process of attrition finally arrived in June 2011, when the COI was closed down completely and its functions merged into other parts of government, including the Cabinet Office, thus bringing to an end the formal commitment of the UK to an infrastructure designed to shape and manage its national brand and narrative. Why was this?

The finger can at least partly be pointed at lack of resources. 'This government has slashed unnecessary spending on communications,'[5] announced Conservative Cabinet Office Minister Francis Maude by way of explanation in an interview with the BBC. The BBC reported that the Cabinet Office had cut spending on advertising and marketing by 68% to £168m in the 2010 financial year. 'Scrapping the COI will remove an unnecessary layer of management, with individual departments able to deal directly with the advertising agencies working for them. There will still be a roster of approved advertising agencies, appointed by a new procurement board based in the Cabinet Office, to ensure the government can get the best deal for taxpayers when it buys marketing services,' it reported ministers as saying. The recommendation was to replace the COI with a new communications centre. Implementing this recommendation cost 400 jobs, closed the COI's network of regional offices around the country and loosened the grip of the government hand on direct information outputs. It also formalised one critical decision that had been in operation for some years, which was to give the green light to external suppliers to bid for government information contracts, opening up selective management of the national brand and accompanying narrative to private sector information warriors.

Currently, in order to help meet the national objective of establishing a secure and strong UK Union, the reconstituted Government Communication Service (GCS) is focused on undermining extremist propaganda, most especially of Daesh (Islamic State); it is doing this through its Foreign Office (FCO) Counter-Daesh Communications Cell, itself part of a 70 member Global Coalition, aiming to 'build resilience to extremist propaganda among vulnerable communities in the Middle East, and promote the positive action of the Global Coalition to support communities in Iraq and Syria liberated from Daesh,'[6] according to the 2017/18 Government Communications Plan.

The Plan also emphasises the partnership that the Home Office is forging between government departments, local authorities and civil society to counter extremist ideology in all its forms, linking with the Ministry of Defence to highlight the important role that UK armed forces are undertaking to defeat Daesh in Iraq and Syria.[7] A further focus is to combat the alarming increase in the disruptive communications of the Russian state. The Plan, though, does not reveal readily accessible details about these campaigns, or for that matter anything on overall staffing, although the GCS remains the major resource from which the Government draws its current stable of media professionals. However, it is transparent about its commitment to outsourcing. As many as 27 separate agencies are named on its Campaign Solutions Framework and a further 67 agencies appear as part of its Communication Services Framework. Thus, in theory, nearly 100 separate private sector suppliers could currently be engaged at any one time in promoting separate aspects of Britain's national information output, though still without ministerial representation, status or infrastructure.

However, analysis of Britain's future military needs is ongoing amidst the shifting sands of international power plays and ever diminishing resources, causing growing difficulty for planners. In that context, information warfare remains one of the main causes of insecurity for the UK, along with terrorism and cyber-attacks, with the first lines of defence being the intelligence agencies and the police with the military in a back-up role, according to Lawrence Freedman, Emeritus Professor of War Studies at King's College London. Whilst this is all reflected in the broad range of activities that come under the heading of national security, Freedman questions whether the balance is right. 'The Foreign Office has been run down over the years. What is the role of diplomacy, in addition to military measures, when addressing upheavals in the Middle East?'[8] he asks. This question is brought more closely into focus if it is really the case that the age of western interventions is over, an age which Freedman suggests began as the cold war came to a close with Operation Desert Shield in 1990, and has lasted up until the air strikes that have characterised the interventions in Libya and against Daesh in Syria and Iraq.

The Twin Gods of Outsourcing and Consulting
Outsourcing forms a critical part of the information puzzle and needs some contextualising, as it has not only been a standard bearer for globalisation but has come to pervade much of wider government thinking about the delivery of public services, including information and communications. The theory driving outsourcing appears simple, but is riven with complexities on closer examination. In essence a government seeking to maximise its budget bypasses an uncompetitive and inefficient public sector organisational model by using outsourcing to shrink permanent scale and cost in favour of targeted and temporary resourcing.

Outsourcing and consulting have between them created a cost base revolution for government, borne out by the related statistics, which have directly impacted the way in which the West has packaged up and sold its interventions in the Middle East. In 2016, the total global outsourcing industry was worth US$76.9 billion, with the largest share of revenue generated from Europe, the Middle East and Africa (EMEA), followed by the Americas.[9] Outsourcing by this definition involves the contracting out of business processes to third parties, usually in order for the business to avoid certain costs, including taxes. In 2016, business process outsourcing contributed a much smaller proportion of the industry's global revenue than information technology outsourcing, generating US$24 billion and US$52.9 billion respectively.[10] This level of commitment is amplified in the more mature markets around the globe. For example, the total annual value of outsourcing contracts agreed in the UK in the first three months of 2017 hit record levels of 1.4 billion euros, according to Information Services Group (ISG) in its quarterly outsourcing index. This is the highest total annual contract value recorded for the UK outsourcing market in any quarterly period ever recorded by ISG, which gave the value of outsourcing contracts across EMEA as 3.5 billion euros in the same quarter.[11]

The reach of outsourcing has extended beyond business into the frameworks and modus operandi that Western governments have adopted for their national information strategies. No longer able, or willing, to oversee and deliver the information dimension of war or foreign policy themselves, they have turned to a small and increasingly powerful cabal of private firms to do the work for them. In effect, they have delegated responsibility for this aspect of the national brand to independents, many of whom operate commercial contracts across national boundaries and are not especially subject to tight regulation or oversight. The delivery of these information contracts has consequently been undertaken largely outside the public view, beyond the range of national discourse and the subsequent lack of transparency in many cases has led investigative journalists to seek to lift the lid on the practice. It is, therefore, the general case that shrinkage of capacity in the state public information and media sector, coupled with the need to outsource in order to control costs and unlock creative thinking has evolved into a new age of specialist propaganda.

This new frontier of communications has been colonised by a sometimes-secretive breed of expert social architect who has pushed the boundaries of the ways in which information is used to support conflict. One combat zone where this connection has been most clearly defined is in the Middle East. With the launch of Operation Desert Shield in 1990, the wars against Saddam in Iraq and subsequently Al Qaeda in

Afghanistan became test beds for this new age marriage of convenience. Over the ensuing decades, the US increasingly engaged private contractors to manage those aspects of the military process beyond combat itself, drawing in sectors such as logistics and the personal security of civilian contractors involved in economic reconstruction and administration.

During the course of Iraqi Freedom in 2003, the number of US contractors in Iraq rose consistently to a high of 190,000 by early 2008, with a related bill of $15 billion.[12] Some of these contractors started to generate negative publicity, in one instance involving the massacre by a security convoy operated by the firm Blackwater of 14 Iraqi civilians in a Baghdad square in 2007.[13] In thrall to the new world of possibilities presented by outsourcing, US planners including the Pentagon sought to engage expert help to open up a propaganda front to sell the war narrative and win the domestic battle for hearts and minds.

The need for action was increasingly pressing as the Iraqis were also ramping up their efforts to exert some influence on world opinion through the media. In August 1990, as the Coalition troops sat inside Saudi Arabia just south of the Kuwaiti border, Saddam Hussein let some 100 foreign journalists into Iraq in order to try and set out his rationale for the invasion of Kuwait and lay out its historical context. Saddam's Information Minister Latif Jassim, gave the journalists an insight into Saddam's achievements, depicting him as an enlightened visionary in the service of the Iraqi people. 'Before the revolution that came in 1968, those who were barefoot were more than those with shoes, and illiteracy of the people was 70%. Everything you see nowadays in Iraq has been realised as a result of Saddam Hussein. You can ask anyone on the street, any shopkeeper, any taxi driver, any women or children - and they will say that President Saddam Hussein is the symbol of the whole country,'[14] Jassim enthused.

Citizens for a Free Kuwait

But much as Jassim would try and engage the media to focus the attention of the world on the persona of the Iraqi President, the success of the modernisation programme he had initiated and the justice of the historical narrative and policy of 'lebensraum' with which Iraq claimed Kuwait as its 19th Province, US attention was more focused on its own domestic audience and the job of convincing Americans that they should support the invasion of Kuwait and the war it would entail. In order to do this, the US and the Kuwaiti Government-In-Exile turned to the firm Hill & Knowlton (H&K), then the world's largest PR company. Nine days after Saddam's army walked into Kuwait, H&K set up an organisation called 'Citizens for a Free Kuwait' to co-ordinate the marketing campaign to reclaim the country, at the same time hiding sponsorship of it and any collusion by the Kuwaitis with the Bush government.[15]

Using Citizens for a Free Kuwait as a front, the campaign went on to engage over 100 H&K executives in 12 offices across the US, organising media briefings, distributing news releases and putting together a 154-page book called 'The Rape of Kuwait,' compiled by US author Jean Sasson and billed as 'The true story of Iraqi atrocities against a civilian population,' a pitch in some respects reminiscent of the French 'Red Book' of the First World War. At the time, even seasoned PR commentators were astounded by the scale and depth of penetration by H&K's campaign. The editor of US publication O'Dwyer's PR Services Report wrote, 'Hill & Knowlton has assumed a role in world affairs unprecedented for a PR firm. H&K has employed a stunning variety of opinion-forming devices and techniques to help keep US opinion on the side of the Kuwaitis....from full-scale press conferences showing torture and other abuses by the Iraqis to the distribution of tens of thousands of 'Free Kuwait' T-shirts and bumper stickers at college campuses across the US.'[16]

Alongside some of the more conventional strategies in the communications toolkit was an altogether more sophisticated and arcane style of propaganda which has come to be defined as perception management. This process involves the bringing together of a range of communications and PR skills in order to engineer a credible projection of reality that can be powerful enough to impose itself on the course of events, indeed, can set out to construct an altogether alternative version of the truth. In perhaps the most infamous example of this technique, H&K masterminded the seeding and dissemination of the 'incubator babies' story and the testimony of the Kuwaiti ambassador's daughter at the Congressional Human Rights Caucus held on Capitol Hill on 10th October 1990. In so doing, they were able to exert pressure and influence world public opinion against Iraq for what turned out to be entirely fictitious actions. As John Macarthur, author of Second Front wrote, 'of all the accusations made against the dictator, none had more impact on American public opinion than the one about Iraqi soldiers removing 312 babies from their incubators and leaving them to die on the cold hospital floors of Kuwait City.'[17]

H&K's manipulation and its practice of 'astroturfing,' the creation of fake communities of interest, was also condemned by the NGO Middle

East Watch, which investigated the affair after the recapture of Kuwait and chose to comment on the wider profanity of atrocity propaganda. 'The propagation of false accounts of atrocities does a deep disservice to the cause of human rights. It diverts attention from the real violations that were committed by Iraqi forces in Kuwait, including the killing of hundreds and the detention of thousands of Kuwaiti citizens and others, hundreds of whom are still missing,'[18] wrote Middle East Watch Associate Director, Aziz Abu-Hamad.

The Age of the Information Warrior

One of the great innovators and explorers of the practice of perception management is a little known US social architect, a mysterious though ubiquitous interpreter and shaper of public opinion whose reputation as a master manipulator has been honed in the service of US war planners in conflicts across the world, most notably in the Middle East. John Rendon, founder of the Washington PR firm The Rendon Group, plays to most of the 'eminence grise' stereotypes and prejudices associated with the world of top level communications thinkers in that he rarely steps into the light, does not generally do media interviews and is not dedicated to advancing his own public persona by sitting on panels or speaking at conferences. Yet his grip on the modern theory and tools of persuasion and their application to the shaping of public opinion led him to become the pre-eminent go-to propagandist of the modern US political age, a man with the ear of Presidents and the reach of an organisation supercharged by US Government dollars and carte blanche to get results no matter what. Rendon is still perhaps best known for his remarks made in 1996 when he first used the terms 'information warrior' and 'perception manager' in relation to his own role and modus operandi in the Gulf War. Before this revelation, these concepts were not even widely known or used within the PR business itself.

On the same occasion, when speaking at the US Air Force Academy in 1996, Rendon reminded the cadets that when victorious troops rolled into Kuwait City during Operation Desert Storm, they were greeted by hundreds of Kuwaitis waving small American flags. The scene, flashed around the world on television screens, sent the message that US Marines were being welcomed in Kuwait as liberating heroes. 'Did you ever stop to wonder,' Rendon asked, 'how the people of Kuwait City, after being held hostage for seven long and painful months, were able to get hand-held American flags, and for that matter, the flags of other Coalition countries?' He paused for effect. 'Well, you now know the answer. That was one of my jobs then.'[19]

Though his firm has a digital footprint and manifesto, Rendon himself has been assiduously careful never to become the story and in many respects this stance has simply deepened the interest of investigative journalists in his contracts, clients and personal backstory. Ironically, this includes his origins as an anti-war activist on the US political scene and a stint as Executive Director of the Democratic National Congress working for Senator and future Democratic Presidential candidate John McGovern. However, those convictions are firmly in Rendon's rear view mirror. These days a glance through the Rendon Group shop window reveals a range of products on the shelves encompassing the simple and the opaque, spread out under the collective banner of strategic communications and 'edge thinking.'

'Human Terrain Analysis' claims to provide clients with cultural and social intelligence in support of operations designed to fill an essential situational awareness gap. 'By leveraging our cultural and social experts, TRG has contributed to advancing the quality and fidelity of social and cultural modeling in support of next generation technology platforms for the United States Military.'[20] Bolted on to Human Terrain Analysis is the notion of Irregular Warfare Support. This provides research and analysis to help government and military clients in developing 'new approaches to countering and eroding an adversary's power, influence and will.' The psychobabble of high-level communications speak is a language designed to keep outsiders out and welcome those in the know, offering signposts to counter narcotic and military procurement framework agreements and inside track nods to experienced buyers of influence.

Over the years, the body of evidence linking John Rendon's activities in the Gulf, and especially Iraq, to the prosecution of the US Government's war aims and the ever-closer integration of the information dimension of war with the military and economic fronts has grown and become more compelling. In the process it becomes clear that the modern business of propaganda has morphed from its relatively humble and intellectually straightforward beginnings into an altogether more pernicious, complex brand of disinformation and psychological engineering. Though Rendon himself has seldom let his guard down, he gave one revealing interview to the American freelance journalist James Bamford in November 2005.

This appeared in the magazine Rolling Stone, under the headline: 'The Man Who Sold the War.'[21] Bamford was in turn interviewed about his meeting with Rendon by the independent news website Democracy Now[22] which shared his interest in the mysterious but influential figure whose thinking and methods had cast such a long shadow over the pursuit of US and Western interests in the Middle East. Bamford recalled Rendon's interpretation of the rationale for his involvement with regime change in Iraq as having been built on the success of his similar activities in Panama to replace the regime of General Manuel Noriega. 'The Rendon Group set up the Iraq National Congress because the Bush administration decided to do regime change in Iraq; we weren't attacked so we had to generate propaganda for it – the Information Operations Taskforce wanted to turn information into a major weapon to promote the war; we had to go on a propaganda war,' Bamford told interviewer Amy Goodman.[23] The Bush line was that after the first Gulf War the idea had been to oust Saddam Hussein and put the Iraqi exile Ahmad Chalabi in his place. It was John Rendon who came up with the idea of the Iraq National Congress as a vehicle to do this, and the organisation was subsequently paid $350,000 per month by the US as a retainer.

In his game plan to sell the US intervention in Iraq, one of the most contentious of Rendon's perception management strategies was to actively intervene in the outputs of news media in the region that the US saw as inimical to its interests. He became expert in real-time analysis of what Arab media and individual journalists were saying and writing so that he could target them with personalised communication that would cause them to alter their behaviour. At the height of his activities in Iraq, he was analysing in detail over 140 newspapers and a lot of broadcast media around the world, with a special focus on the Qatar owned Al-Jazeera broadcast news network, specifically targeted by the Pentagon for its anti-US line.

In time, Rendon came up with a proprietary tracking system called Livewire, which was an electronic media mapping methodology enabling him to analyse what governments around the world were going to be doing six hours before they did it, helping subscribers to get to policy makers in time for them to define a response. The Livewire system works by taking real-time news-wire services as they're filed, before they're on the internet, before CNN can read them on the air, and 24 hours before they appear in the morning papers and sorts them by key word. The system provides the most current real-time access to news and information available to private or public organisations. According to Bamford, the Rendon Group was directed to take a close look at the actual journalists who were reporting the news and analyse them. The plan then was to plant phony stories in news organisations around the world. 'The implications of such manipulation are considerable. You have a very dangerous situation when you have part of the government acting secretly to do something about foreign media that may end up deceiving US media. You formalise government deception and coercion of foreign journalists,'[24] he told Goodman.

In 2003, John Rendon was invited to give a talk on the subject of how best to use military information operations capability to a conference of military officials at King's College in London, according to the organisation Corpwatch. Leaked notes of the talk record him telling the audience: 'I believe that Operation Iraqi Freedom provided for all of us a ringside seat for a clash of cultures of communication. If you watched US or Western media, you saw the war portrayed one way. If you watched or listened to war news in the Arab media, you accepted delivery of a different set of news and information.'[25] Since Operation Iraqi Freedom, employees of The Rendon Group have gone on to provide communications support to the Pentagon and US embassies for counter-narcotics programmes, according to Lt Col James Gregory, a Pentagon spokesman.[26] That support includes tracking local print, radio, television and online reporting and helping countries such as Pakistan and Colombia conduct effective communications in support of US and partner nation counter-narcotics objectives. Those contracts were allegedly worth more than $11 million in 2011 and 2012. When Bamford was investigating the Rendon Group in 2005, he exposed 35 separate government contracts worth around $100 million.[27] Todd Gitlin, a professor at Columbia University in New York, has gone on record to accuse the Pentagon and Congress of failing to do their jobs by not informing the public or exercising due oversight on this issue. 'That the Pentagon outsources its public relations counselling is perhaps unsurprising, because their in-house efforts are so frequently ineffective,' Gitlin said. 'That they turn to a contractor who includes military deception as part of his expertise is also, I suppose, to be expected. Do members of Congress realise they are appropriating funds for these purposes?' he asked.

The Whistle-blower and the 'PR Industrial Complex'
The true extent and scale of the propaganda front in Iraq under US occupation was only finally revealed as recently as 2016, and only then because investigative journalists persuaded a British whistle blower to break cover and spill the beans on the largest single perception

management operation ever undertaken in support of national war aims. Martin Wells was a somewhat unassuming video editor from the English city of Bath; his services were for hire as a contractor in the UK and overseas markets where he plied his trade taking on short-term contracts generated through his agent. When Wells turned up for an interview in London at the British PR firm Bell Pottinger for an unspecified video editing role overseas, he had no idea where he would be posted and yet, having got the job on the spot, he found himself in the space of a weekend based in a highly secure building inside Camp Victory, near Baghdad, outside the all-important secure Green Zone where most international contractors lived and worked.[28] Wells soon discovered he was part of a huge operation based in Camp Victory in which executives of Bell Pottinger, working alongside US government employees, were engaged in a full-on secret propaganda war against Al Qaeda and other opposition groups inside Iraq, a war that carried a budget allocation for the British firm of $120 million a year.

The British company's conflict resolution division was employed by the Pentagon as part of its perception management operations between 2007 and 2011 in a contract that overall was said to have generated over $500 million, one of the largest PR contracts ever recorded. The Bell Pottinger team assisted the US Information Operations Task Force and Joint Psychological Operations Task Force in its strategy to dominate the information battlefield inside Iraq by producing and disseminating a range of faked information in a variety of formats. Wells' role in the operation was threefold, encompassing the generation of news stories, advertising and faked video CDs. 'We would do news stories for local news channels, making it look as if the footage was shot locally for Arab TV stations. We made what were called TVCs, which were television commercials saying Al Qaeda was a bad thing, and then we would make things called VCDs which used Al Qaeda video and propaganda and turned it into disks made to play on Real Player so it could be tracked,' he said. The 10-minute Video CDs were made exclusively from Al-Qaeda footage and had to negotiate an approval system which directly involved US Army General David Petraeus and the Pentagon, sometimes even the White House itself, according to Wells.

These fake propaganda CDs were encoded with tracking software, then left behind in Iraqi towns and villages by US marines whilst out on raids. Using Google Analytics to chart the individual connection of each CD to the internet, Wells was then able to monitor the location of individual CDs 'looking for a trail to someone who could possibly be a threat' and submit a daily consolidated report to his bosses.[29] The videos turned up in locations as far apart as Iran and the United States. 'If a video, 48 hours or a week later, shows up in another part of the world, then that's the more interesting one because that gives you a trail,' Mr Wells said. Lord Tim Bell, who resigned as chairman of Bell Pottinger in August 2016, was proud of the work his firm had carried out in Iraq. 'We did a lot to help resolve the situation. Not enough. We did not stop the mess which emerged, but it was part of the American propaganda machinery,'[30] he said. The conflict resolution division of Bell Pottinger subsequently closed in 2012 and the major players in that part of the company were soon off the scene.

However, whilst the Bell Pottinger contract for opening up the propaganda front in Iraq may have been the biggest and highest profile one on the block, it turned out to be just the tip of the iceberg. The joint Investigative Bureau of Journalism and Sunday Times exposé in October 2016 revealed that over 40 further media and PR companies were paid for their services in Iraq by the Pentagon between 2006 and 2008, revealing in turn just how pervasive the practice of outsourcing had become in the service of the US information war.[32]

The list of these firms included US companies like Lincoln Group and SOS International as well as Iraq-based firms such as Cradle of New Civilization Media, the Bureau reported. In 2005, it was widely circulated that the Lincoln Group, the Pentagon's go-to PR firm for Iraq wartime communications operations after the 2003 invasion, had embedded pro-US news stories in Iraqi press outlets. In November 2005, the LA Times reported that the Lincoln Group was helping the Pentagon covertly place 'dozens' of pro-United States stories in Iraqi news outlets. 'The operation is designed to mask any connection with the US military,' the Times recorded, adding that the Lincoln Group 'helps translate and place the stories. The Lincoln Group's Iraqi staff, or its subcontractors, sometimes pose as freelance reporters or advertising executives when they deliver the stories to Baghdad media outlets.'[33] The Times piece went on to make the accusation that the Information Operations Taskforce in Baghdad, as part of its psychological operations campaigning, had gone on to purchase an Iraqi newspaper and taken control of a radio station, using them to channel pro-American messages to the Iraqi public, though neither was identified as a US military mouthpiece. This work was allegedly worth $100 million according to estimates made by US TV station MSNBC.[34]

The Role of Public Affairs

Whilst the phenomenon of outsourcing has wrought massive and irreversible changes to the management and delivery of government services, the rise of this transcendent business model is not driven by economics alone. There are other powerful influences at work in shaping the landscape for outsourced services and one of them, at least in the case of the information capability within the US military, is directly to do with the knowledge and competencies of its internal public affairs (PA) staff that are tasked with managing the information dimension of the country's wars. We know this because a specialist directly employed in the field chose to speak out and expose the shortcomings of an aspect of the US war effort that he believes has wrought long term damage on the country's subsequent relationships with the Arab world. Steven J Alvarez served as a public affairs officer to US General David Petraeus in Iraq in 2004, where he was tasked with building bridges between the US military fighting the war and the US media reporting it. Alvarez, who from the start believed that the US was making a terrible strategic mistake by ignoring or downgrading Arab media and Iraqi public opinion at the expense of their US counterparts, had few illusions after only a month or so about the skills, knowledge and attitudes of most of his colleagues. Writing in his autobiography 'Selling War'[35] Alvarez blew the whistle on the blundering and ultimately self-destructive information war waged by the US during Operation Iraqi Freedom.

According to Alvarez, one of the principal disasters in Iraq was the failure of the public affairs cabal to link violence with communication; in fact, the inertia and inaction of the public affairs community caused further American bloodshed, he claimed. 'The public affairs community did too little, too late and the inaction of Public Affairs Officers (PAOs) at the highest levels and in critical roles in Iraq caused the climate on the streets that led to the deaths of US soldiers and Iraqis,'[36] he wrote. What caused this breakdown in both understanding and tactical handling of such a critical part of the war effort? Alvarez's reading of the capabilities of the public affairs corps was unflattering. 'We knew we were dealing with a not-so bright bunch that had at its core very close-minded and intellectually unsophisticated people who were incapable of thinking beyond press releases. Most felt that the only way to win in Iraq was through firepower...' he wrote. Alvarez found it ironic that in due course many of the concepts that he argued for in Iraq in 2004 were only two years later included in the 2006 counterinsurgency (COIN) field manual compiled by General Petraeus himself. 'The media directly influence the support of key audiences for COIN forces, the execution of their operations and the opposing insurgency. Recognition of this influence creates a war of perception between insurgents and COIN forces that is conducted continuously through the communications media,' the manual states.

The shortcomings of the public affairs capability were not made up for by the Defense Department's practice of outsourcing, according to Alvarez, who did not swallow the pill that throwing money at the problem would solve it. 'In 2005 and 2006, the Defense Department awarded hefty contracts to civilian companies and spent more than $120 million to improve the way it executed public affairs in Iraq. Nothing has shown that these contractors helped the military with interpersonal interactions with Iraqis or reaching out through Arab media engagement,'[37] he wrote. Alvarez goes on to make an impassioned plea for a public affairs capability that is built around total immersion of its teams in cultural and language training including regional expertise, a strategic knowledge of a country's media and its communications methodology, in other words a complete overhaul of the way that the US currently organises its public affairs and approach to information war as a whole.

Reforming the Smith-Mundt Act

Outsourcing has played a major role in the distancing of information war from the centre of public debate and at the same time enabled a disconnection between the role of the state and the private sector when allocating responsibility for the consequences of propaganda techniques such as perception management on the longer term relationships between the West and the Arab world.

The facts that are now known about the methodologies used by the West in its successive wars in the Gulf, Iraq and Afghanistan lead to the conclusion that nothing in the projection of warfare beyond its immediate context in combat zones can ever be as simple as it seems or taken at face value; evidence shows that perception and reality have in some respects become distorted through the prism of the professional propagandist in a way that now makes it hard to distinguish between the reality of events and a managed perception of them. Alvarez ends his treatise on the battle for public opinion in Iraq by suggesting that the propaganda machine overseen by Saddam's colourful Minister of Information, Muhammad Saeed Al Sahhaf (better known by the nicknames 'Comical Ali' and 'Baghdad Bob') at the time of the invasion in 2003 had distinct parallels with the one set up by the Coalition in due course to replace it. If the question of resources and competencies both feature high on the list of causative factors driving the modern phenomenon of outsourcing of specialist propaganda to contractors, there is a third reason which also deserves scrutiny. In the US, a low-profile piece of legislation called the Smith–Mundt Act has for many years made it illegal for US taxpayers' money to be used to propagandise American virtues and attributes to domestic audiences. This was viewed by legislators as necessary in order to prevent a similar information environment to the Soviet Union, where state-licensed propaganda could be broadcast in such a way as to distort public discourse and thus affect public opinion.

Over the years, the legislation has meant that huge amounts of American programming such as Voice of America (VOA), Radio Free Europe/Radio Liberty, and the Middle East Broadcasting Networks could only be viewed or listened to at broadcast quality in foreign countries. The programming varies in tone and quality, but its breadth is vast; it is viewed in more than 100 countries in 61 languages. The topics covered include human rights abuses in Iran, self-immolation in Tibet, human trafficking across Asia, and on-the-ground reporting in Egypt.[38] The Smith-Mundt Act effectively restricted these broadcasts. Senator William Fulbright, one of those who amended the Act in the 1970s, was responsible for moving to restrict the state sponsored broadcasts from domestic distribution, saying they 'should be given the opportunity to take their rightful place in the graveyard of Cold War relics.' Fulbright's amendment to Smith-Mundt was bolstered in 1985 by Nebraska Senator Edward Zorinsky, who argued that such propaganda should be kept out of America so as to distinguish the US from the Soviet Union where domestic propaganda is a principal government activity. Zorinsky and Fulbright sold their amendments on the basis that American taxpayers shouldn't be funding propaganda for American audiences.

It is not hard to see why, in the grey areas thrown up by aspects of this legislation, that the US government should not have thought a wiser course of action in its overseas wars was to use private firms to propagandise the attractions of US style democracy. In this way, any accidental or indeed intentional leakage of propaganda output in conflict zones such as Iraq or Afghanistan could not be so rapidly laid at the feet of the taxpayer.

The further reform of the Smith-Mundt Act in July 2013 has yet again changed the landscape for internal propaganda in the US, permitting the formerly banned broadcast of state produced programming that has until now been restricted to overseas markets. The Smith-Mundt

Modernization Act of 2012, which passed as part of the 2013 National Defense Authorization Act, means that thousands of hours per week of government-funded radio and TV programmes have been released for domestic consumption. Now the battleground for the application of specialist propaganda has shifted from the streets of Baghdad to those of places like St Paul Minnesota, where the large Somali population can now access VOA content produced for broadcast in Somalia, and previously only accessible there.

To some extent, the legislative framework and guidelines that have been developed to control the time and place of media broadcasts and transmissions of all qualities are caught in an endless loop trying to play catch-up with the technology via which they function. Rapid developments in satellite technology and their increasing accessibility to the private sector are bringing ever closer the nightmare for all governments of a digital free-for-all which simply cannot be effectively monitored or managed any longer. As far back as Operation Desert Storm in 1991, the first televised war, observers were noting that advances in satellite technology and suitcase-based earth terminals were making the issue of censorship moot. 'Civilian space-based reconnaissance systems will soon give the media unencumbered access to the battlefield. Any controls over what journalists report from future war zones must be self-imposed,'[39] wrote former director of Command and Control Policy of the Office of the US Undersecretary of Defense, Colonel Alan D. Campen in 'Information, Truth and War.' With time, this observation looks increasingly prescient; it has already been brought into sharp relief in 2019 by the real-time upload and broadcast via helmet cam of the massacre of Muslim worshippers in Christchurch, New Zealand.

CHAPTER X

'Companions of the Pen': Media Strategy in the Salafi Jihadist Utopia

'From the beginning of Western speculation about the Orient, the one thing the Orient could not do was to represent itself. Evidence of the Orient was credible only after it had passed through and been made firm by the refining fire of the Orientalist's work.'

Edward Said,
Orientalism, Routledge & Kegan Paul (1978), p283

Raqqa: Impossible to Live, Impossible to Leave

It is August 2014, and Islamic State (IS) is on the rise. Young, earnest and persuasive, IS Press Officer Abu Mosa is intent on delivering a compelling account of what daily life at the heart of the Caliphate is really like; he wants viewers to see at first-hand how the Islamist vision and ideology driving the Caliphate are working on the ground in Raqqa, a place where theology and society collide in a new style cosmopolitan community of polyglot jihadis who are living an Islamist dream of statehood unsubverted by the malign influences of modernism.[1] Like any PR executive tasked with giving VIPs a facilities trip to remember and an opportunity to sell the corporate line, he is careful to mix high level thinking and spiritual abstraction with on-the-ground local colour and human scale anecdotes, hoping the heady blend communicates a message that will attract more young Islamists from across the world to come and live the jihadi lifestyle free from the twin poisons of theological compromise and material decadence. Abu Mosa drives Vice News reporter Medyan Dairieh to a front-line sniper position opposite the last remaining Syrian army base in the area and, as we crouch down in trench lines and exchange fire with Syrian President Assad's forces only 400 metres away, we are reminded that personal sacrifice is part of the deal here and that, in Raqqa, even PR people are on the front line. However, this model of all-out commitment is too soon juxtaposed with a glimpse of medieval savagery and IS style justice that strips away any misplaced ideas of chivalry or sentimentality. As the car enters central Raqqa and passes a municipal park, we see countless heads of Syrian soldiers stuck on its spiked railings, their decapitated corpses strewn over the pavements which even now Raqqa's citizens are trying to negotiate in the course of their daily business. It presents a conundrum, grotesque yet compelling, incidental yet transformative, a small, horrifying glimpse of the price to be paid by enemies of the state and those labelled as apostates; Abu Mosa barely breaks conversational stride to acknowledge what we are seeing. Later, as part of this propaganda tour de force, the action moves out of town down to the Euphrates river gently winding its way under a blue sky for a chat with the Caliphate kids and a jolly bearded Belgian in charge of the 'media van.' Children, some as young as nine and branded in the way of lions as 'cubs,' are happy to talk up the Caliphate with suspiciously fluent slogans, many of them excited about going off to sharia training, the precursor to military training; all of them seem overly anxious to fight and die in the war against the 'kuffar,' or non-believers.

Abu Mosa expounds further on the seriousness of the business at hand, telling Medyan Dairieh self-righteously that his own kids won't be getting any sweets until the children of Deraa and Homs can as well. 'I don't return home for pleasure. I only go home when it is important or when I am sick. The family, honestly, is the least important thing. No-one would defend Muslims if we all sat at home with the family,'[2] he explains.

The film is notable for being one of the first to merge the reality of life in the Caliphate with the imagined life, reminiscent in its own way of the first revelatory glimpse behind the Iron Curtain into Soviet Communism at work in the 1950s, or indeed into the heart of a mysterious cult like Scientology, about which we had read and heard whispers but had no fully formed images or hard evidence. It is transfixing throughout, not only for its seemingly uncensored access to the places and the characters that represent this iconoclastic and game changing idea in progress, but for the glimpse it offers of ordinary daily life: commerce in local shops, social interplay, decisions about tax collection and religious instruction in mosques where worshippers are invited to acknowledge the omnipotence of the great spiritual architect himself, the black clad

Caliph Abu Bakr Al-Baghdadi. It is a deliberate and holistic portrait of the Caliphate and the society it advocates, a vivid colour postcard that looks improvised but is carefully written, an image that appears relaxed but is assiduously posed, the seamless blending of highly polished public relations and recruitment technique, a consummate, sophisticated and ultimately successful piece of propaganda that has already been watched by over 12.5 million people around the world, and is still notching up viewers in 2019.[3] The normalisation of the Caliphate in action, reflected in the smiling and benevolent faces of the IS religious police (the Hisbah) as they tour the town looking for infringements of the strict Sharia law, their over familiar and intrusive relationships with shopkeepers and citizens, all contribute to the acceptance of the reality of the new Islamist utopia. But the film shows above all that the pornography of atrocity propaganda is alive and well in Raqqa and has been carefully stage managed to evoke a kind of preternatural anxiety and barely latent terror which underpin every aspect of the regime's modus operandi. The viewer must appreciate or abhor the Caliphate through this lens. If you can ignore the decapitated corpses strewn about, the heads on spikes, the nervous hesitation of shopkeepers, the absence of women, the omnipresent guns and the occasional crucifixion in peripheral view, the overall portrait offers a seductive picture of life as it could be, rather than the way it is experienced for many radical Islamists frustrated at having to live marginalised and devalued lives in the West.

Yet little more than three years after this Vice News film was shot and the bucolic scenes of Islamic State's cubs at play in the gently rippling waters of the Euphrates seemed like a distant memory. Raqqa and its surroundings were steadily being degraded and obliterated by Coalition bombs and the advancing Kurdish military forces which between them were in the process of wiping evidence of the Caliphate's physical presence along with Raqqa itself from the map.

A drone flown over the city by the news organisation Associated Press on 17th October 2017 revealed a uniformly grey, dust shrouded and desiccated cityscape, a ghost town every bit as devastated as those cities in Germany like Dresden or Cologne, flattened by Allied bombs in the Second World War and ever since held up as examples of total destruction and the ultimate folly of war.[4] If visual proof were needed that the territorial ambitions and societal conceits of Islamic State had been crushed, it was provided by the devastated landmarks we had seen three years earlier, the main square where captured tanks had cavorted, the town hall where the black flags had flown, the sinister security buildings with their cell doors blown off their hinges, the empty and boarded up shops and the streets devoid of life. Where perhaps 100 IS fighters continued their resistance to the inevitability of military defeat from the depths of tunnel networks and isolated cellars, the total destruction of Raqqa and absence of life exposed by the dispassionate drone footage seemed more darkly symbolic of the legacy bequeathed to the world by the apocalyptic and medieval vision that Islamic State had been intent on realising there.

Prioritising the Information War

Closer consideration and examination of the ground-breaking Vice News film is rewarding because it offers a wealth of clues as to what made the Caliphate and its creator, Islamic State, masters of the business of propaganda and shows in the same breath what careful students they had become of modern public relations and communications practices and how they in turn had come to coalesce their knowledge, skills and effort into a media jihad. To realise such a film is no accident; it requires first of all the mandate and leverage of a media department embedded into the organisation at the highest level and authorised to generate coverage that both recognises and aligns with wider corporate objectives. It means putting in place a PR and media team trained and skilled enough to create a systematic communications programme of which film is simply one strand and it implies an overarching sophistication in how to combine the science of target audience analysis and selection with the practical ability to tap into their unconscious desires in such a way as to provoke an overwhelmingly emotional response. Above all, though, it reveals a maturity and deep knowledge of the way in which persuasive communications works at its influential best – when an independent, trusted third-party such as a professional news organisation provides the visual and verbal endorsement that Islamic State itself cannot deliver, affirmation when measured in global coverage that could be worth millions at the same time as being an effective recruiting sergeant for countless new converts to the cause. And it is certainly true to say that in the battle to establish its narrative both in the Middle East and across the wider world, Islamic State successfully delivered on its promise to wage information war with equal priority alongside its military and economic strategies, at the same time eclipsing efforts of the West or its Arab partners to compete equally in the battle for radical Islamist hearts and minds.

The question as to why and how this balance could have become so profoundly disturbed is the fulcrum of a wider debate about media, its access and distribution that is of equal concern to governments in the West and in the Arab world and exposes amongst other considerations the West's lack of organisation and method in pitching a counter-narrative that has been able to achieve comparable cut-through.

It took some time to crack the code that could unlock Islamic State's organisational and process model, and at the same time show that its media department and deployment of scientific propaganda to propagate its carefully constructed narratives were no accident but part of a wider methodology. On a January morning in 2014, in the northern Syrian town of Tal Rifaat, Syrian rebels entered into a fire-fight with a tall, gaunt man in his late 50s who they eventually shot and killed. They did not know who he was and certainly had no idea that they had taken out the strategic head of Islamic State, the man who had planned its structure and, in the process, created the most effective terrorist organisation of all time. The local rebels placed the body into a refrigerator, in which they intended to bury him and only later when they realised how important the man was, did they lift his body out again.[5] The man they had killed was an Iraqi, Samir Abd Muhammad al-Khlifawi, more commonly known by the pseudonym Haji Bakr. A former colonel in Saddam Hussein's intelligence service, he had been the primary planner who had mapped the organisational structure of Islamic State in a way that most resembled the Stasi centric model of East Germany, based on institutions and informers at every level of the organisational infrastructure in which no single person was beyond the reach or the gaze of the internal security apparatus and its informants. Haji Bakr left behind the blueprint for Islamic State in a folder full of handwritten organisational charts, lists and schedules which together show how to gradually subjugate a country. The German newspaper Der Spiegel gained access to the 31 pages, which together comprised a multi-layered set of directives for action, some already tested, and others newly devised for the anarchic situation in Syria's rebel-held territories. In the analysis of the documents that was to follow, the explanations and theories behind IS were tested against the evidence. Over and above its categorisation as a terrorist organisation or a mafia or criminal cartel, IS was judged to have little in common with predecessors such as Al Qaeda apart from its jihadist ideology, but rather to be an organisation whose only constant maxim is 'expansion of power at any price.' In amongst this detailed organogram, the establishment and operation of a dedicated media department and team was a principal part of its rationale, a capability tasked to deliver 'apocalyptic statements' and 'precisely implemented propaganda narratives.'[6]

Confirmation of the organisation and role of media activity at the heart of Islamic State's strategic purpose was subsequently confirmed by the organisation itself, despite a more general reticence about publicising its own internal priorities. In a film entitled 'Structure of the Caliphate' released in July 2016, it was revealed that the media operation did indeed have its own 'Diwan,' one of 14 such Diwans, or departments, which together made up the administrative structure of the organisation. In 2017, IS issued a Directive claiming that propaganda is a more potent weapon than atomic bombs and that it would continue to inspire terror attacks.[7] Titled 'Media operative, you are a mujahid too,' the IS Directive stated, 'it is no exaggeration to say that the media operative is a martyrdom-seeker without a belt.' The Directive was translated and analysed by King's College International Centre for the Study of Radicalisation & Political Violence (ICSR) in London, whose spokesman Charlie Winter said, 'the organisation has used propaganda to cultivate digital strategic depth. Due to this effort, the Caliphate idea will exist long beyond its proto-state.' Winter, who has done extensive work over a number of years in analysing Islamic State's propaganda strategy and output believes that the Caliphate brand is entirely unspontaneous, revolving around three axes: 'a coherent narrative that is at once positive and alternative; comprehensive, rejection based counter-speech operations; and the launching of occasional, carefully calibrated media projectiles.'[8]

The organisation has certainly absorbed the thinking and mechanisms required to set up and manage a modern media and communications department, with its attendant needs to build a team and programme capable of generating high impact results. In assessing the resultant structure, observers could be forgiven for thinking it most closely resembles a slick Western corporation invested heavily in a modern communications capability, comprising a network of local, regional and international offices and managing cross-border media initiatives bound together by signature branding, common graphics and clear messaging. Indeed, the IS media department has been systematically organised to enable the management of a range of media assets; its most recognisable include the A'maq and Nashir news agencies, the Al-Bayan radio station, monthly magazines Dabiq and Rumiyah, the Al Naba newsletter and its own video production house and picture distribution agency. In addition, it has been a major user of social media and messaging apps to build global networks and encourage individual two-way relationships, including popular channels such as Twitter and Facebook alongside lesser known ones. As one might expect, the monitoring of Islamic State's media outputs since it burst onto the world stage in 2014, has been obsessive, many observers and analysts closely watching both quality and volume as an instant barometer of the organisation's activity and health. Since the retaking first of Mosul in July 2017, and then Raqqa in November 2017, monitors have noticed that IS' media output has fallen off something of a cliff, reflecting both the loss of Caliphate territory and the fact that most of the production facilities were based in either one or both of these cities.

The BBC Monitoring Service, which produces detailed statistics on IS media outputs, reported that within hours of the group losing Raqqa, its output reached a numerical low point, dropping from an average of 29 items per day to just 10.[9] This low was apparent across all types of IS media content according to the BBC, which reported that the number of A'maq statements fell from 421 in September to 193 in October, while the tally of videos fell from 138 to 52, picture sets from 175 to 81, and video output from 15 to four.[10] The lack of video content is a particular setback for the group, which has relied heavily on slickly-packaged footage to get its message across. The media decline is also shown by the absence, or publication interruption, of two key IS media products – monthly magazine Rumiyah and Al-Bayan radio. Perhaps most tellingly of all, the IS media output that is still making it through is no longer depicting governance, public services and daily life in IS-controlled territory, an indication that promotion of the physical Caliphate as a destination has stopped at the expense of more instructional and motivational material directed at encouraging acts of random, outright terrorism. This coincides with analysis by other IS watchers, who believe that the media coverage is a reflection of changing policy in the now more mobile and back-footed Caliphate which is being forced to rethink its physical future in the Levant in favour of other destinations, like the North African Maghreb, which are further afield.

Atrocity Propaganda, Ritual and Power

When atrocity propaganda surfaced in the First World War as an especially high impact, grotesque branch line of the propaganda business, infamous examples like 'the crucified Canadian' became in time collectively known as 'bayonet baby effect' propaganda, capturing the idea of the ultimately unthinkable horror as a tool of the propagandist. Whilst the British pacifist and Parliamentarian Arthur Ponsonby managed to debunk many of these atrocity propaganda accounts as myth, others were shown to be authentic and these incidences together flagged up the arrival of a new and disturbing means by which the emotions driving public opinion in war could be dramatically manipulated. A hallmark of Islamic State, empowered by preceding jihadist organisations such as Al Qaeda, has been its strategy of elevating atrocity propaganda to new levels of prominence as the centre piece of its publicity assault on global media, both as a means of maximising coverage and as a way of putting across recurring key messages about its power, reach and core values.

Starting out with ritualised beheadings of individual hostages such as the US journalist James Foley and the British aid worker David Haines, the IS media planners gradually increased the scale and production values of these execution videos to aspire to cinematic quality outputs which were almost as if they had been made for commercial audiences around the world, which in a sense they had. Mainstream news media, online news programmes, video channels and app-based mobile platforms such as smartphones and tablets all hosted millions of plays of these videos before the authorities stepped in and laid down a partial censorship policy making them harder to access.

It appears that Islamic State has used trickery, in effect to overturn the accepted idea that atrocity propaganda exposes the brutality and moral depravity of an opponent and instead has subverted the concept to use as a tool to glorify its own medieval version of justice and thus parade it as a virtue. In this distorted mirror of the ultimate transgressive act, unthinkable barbarism becomes licensed retribution; torture and degradation of innocents become the natural and accepted corollary of perceived apostasy. As if by magic, atrocity propaganda communicates another set of messages entirely, rolling back the centuries to the Mongol invasion of Baghdad in 1258, when piles of severed heads lined the streets and the river Tigris ran with blood. The extreme nature of IS atrocity propaganda, typified in feature length films such as 2014's 'Clanging of the Swords,' becomes a way of desensitising its audience so that the acts of barbarity engage, subvert then corrupt the susceptible viewer who begins to see them as a legitimate show of power and justice, and thus acceptable at both a visceral and moral level. In this sense, Islamic State atrocity propaganda is the latest chapter in a long authoritarian tradition that in modern times stretches back to the Western Front and subsequently to Nazi hate speech, racial profiling, ethnic cleansing and ritualised killing of the Jews in Europe in the 1930s and 1940s before it reached Al Qaeda and then into the streets of Raqqa, the slopes of Mt Sinjar or the ancient amphitheatre of Palmyra. The question arises, is the rationale that enables this type of fascist propaganda distinctly psychological? Writing in 1951, shortly after the end of the Second World War, the Freudian psychologist Theodor Adorno claimed that the nature and content of fascist propaganda is psychological because of its irrational authoritarian aims which cannot be obtained by means of rational convictions but only through skilful awakening of a subject's archaic inheritance. 'The leader of the group is the primal father; the group still wishes to be governed by unrestricted force, it has a thirst for obedience,'[11] he wrote, claiming that the techniques of the demagogue and the hypnotist make the libidinal pattern of fascism and the entire technique of fascist demagogues authoritarian.

The evolution of this type of extreme fascist propaganda was not opportunistic or isolated. IS publicists had witnessed and even participated in a gradual reinvention of the propaganda porn genre; extremist Islamist trailblazers like the Jordanian Al Qaeda leader Abu Musab Al Zarqawi had successfully introduced the Internet as a vehicle for uploading and live webcasting the business of execution, making it for the first time globally accessible in the broadband-enabled home. At the time leading up to the killing of Ken Bigley on 7th October 2004, it was impossible not to feel a visceral and emotional response for the British engineer, confined in a chicken wire cage somewhere in the depths of Fallujah, before being beheaded live on the internet after publicly being made to beg British Prime Minister Tony Blair for mercy. If cases such as these had opened the door, it took an organisation with the media ambitions and savvy of Islamic State to elevate the genre to its next level, one which took the world entirely by surprise in its level of refinement.

Thus, global news audiences were treated to a succession of atrocity propaganda videos which, it transpired, were to initiate a race to the bottom of depravity, each successive production competing to outdo its predecessor in the psychological values of fetishised horror: the ritual immolation of Jordanian pilot Muath Al Kasasbeh (6th Feb 2015), the drowning of handcuffed prisoners in a metal cage with on board cameras (24th June 2015), the cinematically posed mass killing of captured Syrian soldiers by IS teenagers in the ancient amphitheatre of Palmyra (5th July 2015), and, perhaps the last word in the grotesque, a training video of brainwashed IS 'cubs' hunting down handcuffed prisoners running for their lives inside a warehouse killing ground, executing those they located at close range with handguns (28th March 2017).

At the end of 2015, the Washington Post was able to offer for the first time a glimpse inside the video making unit of Islamic State when it interviewed an imprisoned IS cameraman who had chosen to speak out about his life as part of the organisation's media machinery. Abu Hajer Al-Maghrebi, who spent nearly a year as a cameraman working for IS, recounted from a prison cell in Morocco how he would receive details of the day's shoot via a slip of paper bearing the black flag of IS, the seal of the media emir and the site of the shoot. He would often proceed, with other cameramen, to the scene of an unfolding bloodbath. Al-Maghrebi recalled the occasion he had driven two hours south-west of Raqqa and been part of a team recording the final hours of 160 Syrian soldiers who were stripped to their underwear, forced to their knees and massacred with automatic rifles.[12] His footage quickly found a global audience, released online in an Islamic State video that spread on social media and appeared in mainstream news coverage on Al Jazeera and other networks.

Al-Maghrebi was among a number of defectors to provide insider accounts of the mechanics of the IS media machine in action, describing what the Washington Post called 'a medieval reality show' in which camera crews fan out across the Caliphate every day, 'their ubiquitous presence distorting the events they purportedly are documenting.' Battle scenes and public beheadings are so scripted and staged that fighters and executioners often perform multiple takes and read their lines from cue cards, according to the Post. 'Cameras, computers and other video equipment arrive in regular shipments from Turkey. They are delivered to a media division dominated by foreigners — including at least one American, according to those interviewed — whose production skills often stem from previous jobs they held at news channels or technology companies, revealing that media and propaganda specialists led a charmed life in the Caliphate, highly paid, well respected and powerful, seen as the key to increasing recruitment and proselytizing the faith.[13]

Social Architects and Jihadi Salafist Doctrine
Of all the Islamist narratives in play in the first decades of the 21st century, Islamic State and its reimagining of the medieval Abbasid Caliphate has been by far the most compelling one and, in many respects, a natural extension of earlier versions which had more limited vision and more curtailed objectives, principally ones now associated with terrorism. First was the Taliban in Afghanistan, then Al-Qaeda, the construction of Islamist ideologues Osama Bin Laden and Egyptian doctor and former

Muslim Brotherhood member Ayman Al Zawahiri. Other offshoots and spin-offs followed, but Islamic State broke the mould, for the first-time occupying territory, appropriating borders, minting its own currency, raising taxes, appropriating oil revenue and paying a standing army. Islamic State can also make the claim to be the first Salafi jihadist state, in the sense that Salafi jihadism is a transnational religious-political ideology based on a belief in physical jihadism and the Salafi movement of returning to what adherents believe to be true Sunni Islam.

The terms 'Salafist jihadist' and 'jihadist-Salafism' were by general agreement coined by leading French Arabist and scholar Gilles Kepel in 2002 to describe a hybrid Islamist ideology developed by international Islamist volunteers in the Afghan Anti-Soviet jihad who had become isolated from their national and social class origins. Salafism, itself, is ascribed to a student of Jamal al Din Al Afghani (1838-1897), Islamic scholar Muhammad Abduh, who advocated a reversion to the teachings of the pious ancestors, *al salaf alsalih*, and doing away with the accretions that Islam had acquired across the centuries.[14] The proliferation of Salafi-jihadism, and its embracing of aggressive militaristic behaviours, ethnic cleansing and persecution of religious and other minorities, has meant that it has travelled hand in hand with the notion of radicalisation, one that has generally been inspired through a particular type of religious instruction available through mosque and *madrassa* networks across the Middle East, North Africa, Pakistan, Afghanistan and some more limited locations in the West.

Psychologists and behavioural scientists are trying to unlock the process of radicalisation itself, equating it to a form of brainwashing especially where young people are seduced into and then trained by the Caliphate. The Caliphate 'cubs' in particular bear the hallmarks of what psychologists categorise as menticide, most often carried out in purpose-built re-education camps; their mindless repetition of recurring slogans, range of inappropriate behaviours and espousal of ideological ideas beyond their rational comprehension all bear echoes of fascism, Nazism, and other cultist, extremist and eliminationist ideologies. But getting to the root cause of radicalisation is not easy, according to University of London researchers; they say attempts at general models for how individuals are drawn into or subsequently disengage from extremism may offer some dividends, perhaps, but they also risk downplaying human complexity and social and political contexts. 'Be that as it may, it is important, we argue, that policy-makers, politicians and researchers should be as transparent as possible about what model of the mind they are assuming and why. There may be a greater prospect of serious dialogue about the nature of radicalisation – its prevention and reversal – if we begin by reflecting harder on the casual use made of the terms themselves, the functions they may serve, and the built-in assumptions they may carry,' say the academics behind the 'Hidden Persuaders' project at the University of London.[15]

Packaging and selling such powerful and effective messages doesn't happen by chance. It requires messengers who are committed, knowledgeable and who understand the mechanisms and processes inherent in operating an effective media strategy. Islamic State's propaganda and media operations drew in a clutch of experts and ingénues alike, some of them experienced through working in Western media, others familiar with social media and digital communications, and more simply there to learn and get up to speed. IS even successfully coerced one of its own Western hostages, amongst whom there were a number of working journalists including the American James Foley. With echoes of the British broadcaster Lord Haw-Haw in Berlin in the 1940s, IS managed to 'persuade' the captive British photo-journalist John Cantlie to present a series of programmes under the banner 'Lend Me Your Ears' to talk viewers through the inevitability of the West's military defeat to the forces of IS in successive battle scarred towns from Kobane in north-west Syria to Mosul in northern Iraq. In 2019, the final whereabouts of Cantlie along with any proof of life are still not known, although the content of his programme making for the IS media machine was later extended to reporting on other social and political aspects of the Caliphate in action, such as its system of Sharia Courts.

The use of a foreign journalist like Cantlie for propaganda purposes was almost certainly amongst the innovative ideas of IS' Head of Propaganda and alleged Minister of Information, Abu Muhammad Al Furqan and its Head of Media Operations, US born Ahmad Abousamra, a shadowy but central figure in its media jihad and perhaps the most significant of the social architects behind the selling of the Caliphate's vision to audiences around the world. Killed in a Coalition airstrike in Syria as late as January 2017, Abousamra was a Boston-raised computer scientist, a dual US and Syrian citizen who had left the US for Pakistan in 2006 to emerge, within a decade, as the mastermind of the IS media effort. Amongst his responsibilities was the editorship of the magazine Rumiyah, and it was in these columns, under the heading 'Among the believers are men,' that his own obituary was published.[16] The extended article in the eighth issue of Rumiyah was able to fill in some of the gaps about Abousamra's movements that had puzzled Western intelligence agencies and analysts. 'Fearing that he would be one who speaks hypocritically, he pursued the course to which he called others, so his end was as he wished: to be killed for the cause of Allah on the frontlines,' the article stated of the man it called Abu Sulaiman ash-Shami.

Abousamra's death was one of a number in the media team that degraded its overall capability over the course of 2017, when it was increasingly on the back foot and under growing pressure. The organisation's propaganda head and founder of its first media organisation, Abu Muhammad Al Furqan, was reportedly killed in September 2016, and its spokesman and most public face, Abu Muhammad Al-Adnani, killed in August of the same year. The US Brookings Institute identified Al-Adnani as Taha Sobhi Falaha, a Syrian national from Idlib, who pledged allegiance to Abu Musab al-Zarqawi in 2002-2003.[17]

Abousamra was on the FBI's 'most wanted' list, with a $50,000 reward outstanding for his capture. His journey had allegedly taken him to both Pakistan and Yemen, where he had undertaken military training in camps in 2002, but he succeeded in gaining a computer science degree in the US before finally leaving in 2006. The Rumiyah obituary confirmed Abousamra's travels and also revealed that he had in fact come close to succeeding with a plan to launch an attack inside America. 'However, Allah decreed otherwise, and He does what He wills,' the magazine said. 'Their plot was discovered just days before the operation's appointed time.' Instead Abousamra went to Syria and joined the Nusra Front. He supposedly asked them to send him on a martyrdom operation when they wouldn't transfer him to Iraq, but this was not his fate. Instead, the magazine recalled that Abousamra went on to 'discover the treachery of the Nusra front' and reaffirmed his oath of allegiance to ISIS leader Abu Bakr al-Baghdadi. He fought with the rank and file and was finally selected for a martyrdom operation—before being whisked from it at the last minute to join the media propaganda efforts.[18]

#mediajihadgoesdigital
It is mid-October 2017 in London and the sky is darkening with the approach of a storm which is carrying sand all the way from the Sahara. The sun has been completely obscured and a strong wind has begun to blow in gusting squalls up the Thames. Small clusters of people are standing watching this extreme weather event from the windows of King's College, part of London University situated just north of Blackfriars Bridge. Inside the College's International Centre for the Study of Radicalisation and

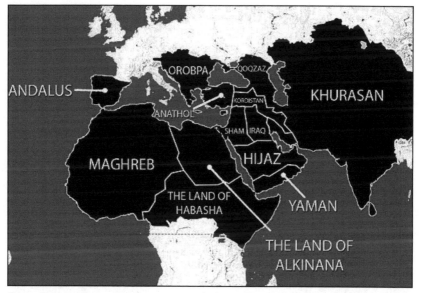

Part of an online campaign to spread the realisation of Islamic State's grand scheme, this map draws on history and legend to show the constitution of its new world order.

Political Violence (ICSR), a conference is underway, bringing together a powerful and expert group of academics and researchers into the causes and consequences of violent online political extremism. Gathered under the banner of VOX-Pol, the European Union funded academic network set up to research 'the prevalence, contours, functions and impacts' of this phenomenon and the responses to it, they are sharing their latest intelligence and findings that together spell out the current state of play with the Caliphate's digital jihad.

The use of social media and online platforms to build networks and disseminate online propaganda has been one of the most active and successful channels of Islamic State's strategy for its media war. Global online brands such as Twitter and Facebook, alongside lesser known names such as Telegram, have been part of the Caliphate's total media approach, seeking to open up targeted and personalised dialogue with its worldwide audience of disciples, fans, wannabes and potential recruits. This type of two-way communications is reflective of modern thinking about methodologies of persuasion and influence, a technology enabled pathway via which brands and consumers enter into an ongoing dialogue that shapes and customises their relationship. The psychology and dynamics driving this communication make it more complex, elaborate and individualised, and consequently much more difficult in which to intervene. Not only is the content less orthodox and uniform than standard propaganda, but the technological dimensions of the digital format make it infinitely harder for the concerned authorities to firstly monitor and then control the output itself. The evidence shows that it has taken Western agencies too long to come up with ways in which to deal with the issue effectively and, at the same time, it has flagged up their own shortcomings in mounting an effective counter-narrative with which to engage the younger, more mobile audience that inhabits the chatrooms of the Web and holds real-time digital conversations around the globe.

Notably, online jihadist propaganda attracts more clicks in the UK than any other country in Europe, a report by the UK based think tank Policy Exchange found in 2017.[19] This has caused the British government, in conversation with its partners in the fight against global terrorism, to begin to work more closely with the big social media companies such as Google and Facebook to try and close off some of these loopholes. Co-ordination and integration of these efforts is increasing, and the evidence is beginning to suggest that the tide against online jihadist content may be turning, in some places even quite quickly. Organisations like Vox-Pol and others track very closely, and in some cases respond to, the online jihadist traffic and output of Islamic State and other jihadist extremists, so that an increasingly accurate picture is now available of the operational intricacies of the effort along with details of the output.

An example of this is the detail gathered by Vox-Pol researchers of just one day's output from the IS media team in April 2017, a moment when the organisation was beginning to feel the increasing weight of external military pressure. They reported that on Monday 3rd April, 2017, IS uploaded its daily propaganda content to a variety of social media and online content-hosting platforms. This content generally included videos (in daily news format and other propaganda videos), 'picture stories' (a photo montage that tells a story), brief pronouncements similar to short press releases, radio podcasts and other documents (such as magazines). Over the course of Monday afternoon and evening, 153 unique Twitter accounts were identified that sent a total of 842 tweets with links to external (non-Twitter) web pages, each loaded with an item or items of IS propaganda. 'We identified only 10 of those Twitter accounts (7%) as being independent, third-party mainstream accounts. The balance of accounts was identified as being pro-IS. Fifty of these accounts appeared to be throwaway accounts created on Monday morning,' researchers revealed.[20] Their findings challenge the notion that Twitter remains a conducive space for IS accounts and communities to flourish, although IS continues to distribute propaganda through this channel. However not all jihadists on Twitter are subject to the same levels of disruption: 'Our analysis rests on datasets containing 722 pro IS accounts and a convenience sample of 451 other jihadist accounts, including those supportive of Hay'at Tahrir al-Sham, Ahrar al Sham, the Taliban and Al Shabab, active on Twitter at any point between 1st February and 7th April 2017.' The findings of their research revealed that Twitter is just one node in a wider jihadist social media ecology. Pro-IS accounts were linked to as many as 39 different third-party platforms or content-hosting sites. Of these six remained prominent across the three time periods: justpaste.it, IS's own server, archive.org, sendvid.com, YouTube and Google Drive.[21]

As the restrictions imposed by social media platforms have increased over the last two years, IS and its supporters started to use Telegram, a messaging app which offers encryption, ensuring the privacy of users. Telegram has 100 million active monthly users, and many of its groups are private; because of the network's security features, extremist material can be hard to identify.

Where they get through, violent photos and videos on bigger platforms such as Facebook and Twitter are generally removed within days. Evidence also suggests that IS is trying to distribute a softer style of material, such as cartoons, with which to penetrate digital security cordons. Early in 2017, a channel on Telegram and a since de-activated channel on YouTube began releasing narrative animated stories which veered away from the brutal and shocking images that the Caliphate had previously been pushing. One, specifically aimed at children, was titled 'The Ruler and the Brave' and told the story of a country that had become disillusioned with its tyrant leader. The leader, the video explained, would lie to his subjects about 'brave men' who dared to stand up to him. These 'brave men' turn out to be IS militants.

The Counter Strategic Communications Effort

Shared intelligence begins to enable the pulling together of the pieces of a complex jigsaw that builds into a collective picture that in turn reveals some of the reasons behind IS' success in its online recruitment and propaganda strategy. One of these emerges from research in Kuwait, which shows that proper information campaigns are badly needed in the country to replace existing counter-narratives that are too weak and ineffectual. The core task is to reach out to a second generation of children who have borne witness to the destruction of their family units and who, in profiling exercises, are found to be most at risk and in need of having their cognitive, mental gaps filled; they are often also children who live on the margins of Kuwait's urban centres, poor and with little access to the fruits of the conspicuous capitalism readily on display in the Gulf. The finger is also pointed at the need for a more closely regulated strain of religious teaching across the mosque and *madrassa* network to replace the distorted version of Islam that is sometimes propagated by Imams and other more extremist Salafist hate preachers, giving children religious information that is fundamentally flawed, leading to subsequent decisions which can promote engagement with jihadist recruiters and be counter-productive to their life chances.

Evidence is growing of the role of radical Salafist preachers as new spiritual authorities in the jihadist recruitment and retention chain, with recent research showing that two charismatic preachers especially have created strong audience networks via social media and TV outlets amongst jihadist fighters active in Syria.[22] Ahmad Musa Jibril, a Palestinian-American cleric born in Dearborn, Michigan, does not explicitly call for violent jihad but supports individual foreign fighters and justifies the Syrian conflict in highly emotive terms. 'He is eloquent, charismatic and, most importantly, fluent in English,'[23] say researchers. Musa Cerantonio, a 29-year-old Australian convert to Islam frequently appears on satellite television and has become an outspoken cheerleader for IS. Both men are very different and consequently have different appeals. 'Ahmed Musa Jibril is a subtle, careful and nuanced preacher, whilst Musa Cerantonio is much more explicit in his support for the jihadist opposition in Syria,' the report says.

In Saudi Arabia, where there is a full-time ongoing effort to counter online extremism, Saudi researchers discovered over 200 Facebook pages leading to terrorism and violence with over 150,000 active participants, 10% of them who disseminate information and pictures. 80% of participants are on average between 18 and 24, of whom 75% are male. Realising they needed a counter awareness programme, the Saudis came up with 'Al Sakinah' (Spirit of Tranquility); they also started closing accounts they found and, through the 'Sawab' programme, actually began engaging in online dialogue with 150 jihadis, 58 of whom abandoned their extremist stance after these interventions. Whilst these efforts are effective to some degree, the consensus of the experts seems to be that more evidence generally is needed with which to underpin Western policy development, as definitive online research itself is very difficult to assemble.

In its report, ICSR stated that propaganda is central to the Islamic State's survival, both as a group and as an idea.[24] Its author, Charlie Winter, believes that there are no easy answers when it comes to counter strategic communications. 'People think you can undermine ideology by making videos but it is important to understand there are so many audiences you have to reach. You are not just managing a battle against Islamic State,'[25] he says. Winter contends that the West needs to start developing stronger stories of its own, even engaging role models to help people identify more closely with general concepts. 'We need to start offering people an alternative narrative rather than counter-narrative; we need to think carefully about how we deal with that. Defining one that works is tricky; one that doesn't counter but prevents, which puts activism over just producing literature. Activism is working with people, giving them purpose.' He refers to a London based NGO called the London Tigers which is a project working with children that reaches out to them before they can engage with radical activity.[26]

Beyond the introduction of schemes and programmes that reach more directly into communities, the UK and US have, along with partner countries, also ramped up efforts to restrict access to extremist online content spread by IS and other jihadist organisations. The Global Coalition against Daesh, of which there are 74 member countries around the world, reports that Daesh activity on Twitter has fallen 45% since 2014 and points to greater steps being taken by global online brand names such as Facebook, who will now act fairly swiftly on user reports of extremist content on its pages. The Coalition, formed in 2014, is committed to degrading and ultimately defeating Daesh, with one of its strategies to 'tackle its propaganda and its destructive and hateful messages by exposing the organisation's falsehoods that lie at the heart of its ideology, and to present a positive, alternative future for the region.'[27] As part of its activity, the organisation hosts a counter-messaging facility on its website that communicators can use as a resource to help establish narratives that counter some of the specific myths propagated by IS in its media campaigns.

One example is confronting the myth that Daesh generated a strong economy in Raqqa, the counter-message being, 'False. Women were taxed for giving birth and residents were forced to swap valuable US dollars for worthless Daesh dinars. Many Raqqawis saw their entire life savings wiped out by Daesh's self-serving policies.' Counter messages are also constructed to emphasise that local and foreign IS fighters were deeply divided; IS rules of behaviour actually baffled most Raqqawis, the brutal punishment regime created a climate of fear and the system of rule was rife with hypocrisy. The Coalition's Counter-Messaging Working Group is jointly led by the United Arab Emirates, the UK and US, supported by the Coalition Communications Cell. This draws on the expertise of the Coalition members, the US State Department's Global Engagement Center (GEC), and the UAE-based Sawab Center, bringing together all the strands of the ongoing work to undermine Daesh's claims to statehood, its military success and false religious narrative. One of the objectives of this strategy is to act as a centre of communications gravity and co-ordinator for other players in the information war, including civil society, religious communities and their leaders as well as commercial partners, in order to build resilient communities better able to respond to the challenge of extremism. Launched in July 2015, and physically located in the UAE, the Sawab Center focuses on interrupting IS communication and recruitment by turning up both the volume and intensity of online debate representing 'moderate, tolerant, and positive approaches in the region,' at the same time seeking to expand its own networks of message carriers and influencers.[28]

It is hard to question the commitment of partners in this project to make progress in the ongoing information war with IS and other jihadist centred organisations. But there must remain some doubt as to the effectiveness of the initiative, based on its relatively low profile and soft statistics. Not many are aware of the Counter-Messaging Workgroup and, of those who are, large numbers cannot in a practical context know what it really means. The idea, in itself, of narratives and counter-narratives is one which professional communicators may understand but which does not necessarily resonate at a populist level. In any case, and this must be the wider point, the counter-narrative strategy itself looks quite narrow and content light. It is all very well to construct individual messages that take down specific IS false claims, it is quite another thing to construct a counter-narrative that sets out the case for a rethinking of the wider relationship between the West and Islam, one which is based less on strategic and financial self-interest and more on positive alternatives. These need to be founded on the principle of equality in relationships, and situated in a political and social context where civil and human rights are at the centre rather than periphery and in which institutional, commercial and cultural power is deployed for the benefit of populations as a whole rather than for the longstanding elites who have engineered the systems and processes that sustain their domination of the economic and political landscape.

But in the ongoing struggle waged in the digital combat zone, the flux of information war throws up episodic claims by both sides for victory or defeat. Towards the end of April 2018, the law enforcement authorities of the European Union member states, Canada and the United States claimed they had disabled much of Islamic State's online propaganda machine in a joint takedown operation led by the Belgian Prosecutor's Office.[29] Claiming to have disabled IS's news, radio and features operation, Europol's Executive Director, Rob Wainwright, said, 'with this ground breaking operation we have punched a big hole in the capability of IS to spread propaganda online and radicalise young people in Europe.' The claim was echoed by EU Commissioner Dimitris Avramopoulos, who stated, 'Daesh is no longer just losing territory on the ground, but also online. We will not stop until their propaganda is entirely eradicated from the Internet.' However, some observers of IS online information outlets observed that, shortly after the Europol announcement, the A'maq News Agency appeared to be right back in business, sending out its news releases once more.

In what seems an even more sinister sign for Western agencies, the IS film 'Harvest of the Soldiers #25' was posted on 17th January 2019, listing all foreign soldiers recently killed by IS units across a number of apparently co-ordinated military operations in West Africa, Khorasan (Afghanistan), the Caucasus, China and Iraq, among them suicide bombings, martyrdom attacks, and explosive ambushes. Alongside the film, a 16 page newsletter, Al Anba, posted on 16th January listed, often alongside pictures and graphics, the details of these various episodes.[30] The seeming co-ordination of these events and their relation to each other, let alone their proactive promotion, must be a further cause for deep concern about the currently accepted Western definition and narrative of progress. The veracity of this alternative version of events has been borne out to some degree by the bombings of Christian churches in the Sri Lankan capital of Colombo in April 2019. Shortly after the deadly attacks, a further video was released by the IS media department of its leader, Abu Bakr Al Baghdadi, carefully and deliberately posed in the style of an armed mujahid, claiming the Colombo bombings as retaliation for the final assault on the Caliphate in Syria and Iraq.

CHAPTER XI

Public Diplomacy, Soft Power and the Resetting of Relationships

'Pan-Islamism is dormant – yet we have to reckon with the possibility that the sleeper may awake if ever the cosmopolitan proletariat of a 'Westernized' world revolts against Western domination and cries out for anti-Western leadership. That call might have incalculable psychological effects in evoking the militant spirit of Islam – even if it had slumbered as long as the Seven Sleepers – because it might awaken echoes of a heroic age.'

Arnold J Toynbee
Islam, The West and The Future, Civilisation on Trial,
Oxford University Press (1948)

It is November 30th, 2017 and I am entering a grand period building on the corner of London's iconic Parliament Square. The occasion is a highly significant one for me and a group of colleagues, present and former, who have between us spent many years supporting a small NGO dedicated to giving Arab politicians, activists and thinkers a platform in British Parliament. The Council for Arab British Understanding (Caabu) was formed in 1967 by a cross-party group of British Parliamentarians in response to the military defeat of Arab forces by Israel in the six-day war of June that year, the subsequent annexation by Israel of the West Bank and West Jerusalem and the creation of a further generation of permanent Palestinian refugees. The founders believed that it was of critical importance for the Palestinian and wider Arab point of view to be represented amongst British lawmakers, and furthermore that the values of conflict resolution, civil rights and human rights should form the paramount basis for the development of future British foreign policy in the region. Tonight is the 50th anniversary of the founding of Caabu which, across its lifetime, has served as one of the principal mechanisms through which British Parliamentarians of both Houses have been able to experience the issues faced in Palestine and neighbouring Arab countries by visiting and witnessing conditions there at first hand. The perceived value of this more direct engagement is reflected in the fact that there are many serving and former Parliamentarians in attendance tonight alongside a plethora of Arab ambassadors, journalists, commentators and Middle East watchers. The turnout is a tribute to the organisation's reach and influence, and it is no surprise that the Conservative Government's Foreign Office Minister, Alastair Burt MP, is the first of a clutch of speakers who also include the Shadow Foreign Secretary, Labour MP Emily Thornberry and the UK's first British-Palestinian MP, Layla Moran.

After he opens up with some words of congratulation, Burt makes clear that this evening his intention is not to focus on the intractable issues that define the political deadlock in which Palestine and the wider region are gripped, or even the recent centenary of the Balfour Declaration with which Britain was intimately concerned, but the subject of the wider relationship between the United Kingdom and the Arab world.

Sidestepping the thornier territory of Balfour, he focuses instead on the UK's strong bonds with the region, emphasising that security and stability matter to Britain and are the propellers driving the deployment of humanitarian, diplomatic and military assets towards peace efforts in the region. It soon becomes clear that this evening Burt is intent on focusing on Britain's strategy of building relationships in the Middle East through the use of public diplomacy and soft power. 'It's not all about speaking softly and carrying a big stick,' he suggests, 'but more about engaging jaw-jaw instead of war-war.' It is the business of building mutual understanding which is where soft power comes into play, he says right on cue. This is the trigger for Burt to list the ways in which Britain is able to exert the levers of soft power and in the process widen and deepen its relationship with the Arab world starting with the English language, that of science, IT and international business. 'We are the preferred destination for Arab investors. Our education system continues to be a magnet, with over 20,000 students from the Gulf alone choosing to study in the UK. BBC Arabic and Persian services also play a vital role in promoting the British brand, providing trusted and impartial news in the region,' Burt continues, warming to his theme. He touches on annual film festivals, the importance of culture, the Tunisian version of Macbeth in Arabic, and the poetry of Mauritania in his quest to trawl the sunlit uplands of public diplomacy and the benefits it can deliver across the region. In some respects, it is both apposite and refreshing for these generally underplayed aspects of Britain's relationship with the Arab world to be a focus of the occasion and it is left to the UK's first British-Palestinian MP, Layla Moran, to berate the government for its ability to mark the centenary of the Balfour Declaration without having explicitly accommodated any Palestinian dimension. But the bigger and more awkward question that nags away after this summary analysis of British power and influence in the region is more fundamental: who can really articulate the rationale or quantify the effort driving public diplomacy and soft power and where would we turn for a definitive account of the big picture? Should we still think of public diplomacy and soft power between them as propaganda at best or even cultural imperialism at worst?

Two Intersecting Circles

Like much of the language of communication and persuasion, that of public diplomacy and soft power seems exclusive to insiders. It is tough to know whether the obscurity of language is associated more with embarrassment about an abrogation by stealth of hard power or the inherent complexity of the idea itself, which is anything but straightforward. The term was only coined in 1965 by former US diplomat Edmund Gullion and his definition aggregated different strands of thinking which in themselves were not particularly innovative but when packaged conceptually as a big idea delivered a sum much greater than its parts. His concept of public diplomacy, which in time has been generally adopted by governments and civil society, deals with the influence of public attitudes on the formation and execution of foreign policies. It encompasses dimensions of international relations beyond traditional diplomacy.

For example, the cultivation by governments of public opinion in other countries, the interaction of private groups and interests in one country with another, the reporting of foreign affairs and its impact on policy, communication between those whose job is communication, as diplomats and foreign correspondents; and the process of inter-cultural communications.[1]

The sub-text of public diplomacy, however, is that of power and influence by means other than a big stick. In particular, the travelling companion and outcome of public diplomacy is generally soft power, a notion devised by Harvard Professor Joseph Nye to express the indirect behavioural influences that governments can exert on others through the means expounded by Alastair Burt in his speech, namely culture, values and ideology that direct nations toward interdependence over confrontation. In the modern age, the argument for public diplomacy advanced by academics and the political and diplomatic class is that it puts the human dimension of communication and interaction at the centre of relationships in a far less manipulative way than propaganda ever did. It can be argued that the concept of public diplomacy echoes the theme of modern symmetrical communications in its intention to establish and develop a true dialogue between sender and receiver, with the objective of establishing a relationship of equals as opposed to ruler and ruled. In theory at least, anyone can engage in public diplomacy; it is not exclusive but an open access instrument of persuasion by mutual attraction. As the American academic Nancy Snow, Professor Emeritus at the College of Communications at California State University, writes, 'today a citizen blogger is as much a public diplomat as any Undersecretary of State for Public Affairs and Public Diplomacy. Likewise, an exchange student or scholar can transform his thinking and behaviour through direct, face-to-face engagement with host nationals and then build on the relationship through social media.'[2]

Beyond the organ of the Government set up to handle information about the United States and to explain our policies, 'what is important today is the interaction of groups, peoples, and cultures beyond national borders, influencing the way groups and peoples in other countries think about foreign affairs, react to our policies, and affect the policies of their respective governments,'[3] Snow argues. Even a hard-core believer in the virtues and impact of public diplomacy such as Snow has to reconcile the similarities that characterise public diplomacy and propaganda, conceding at some point that 'these two circles do intersect, but neither circle is within the other.'

The argument goes that the best of public diplomacy far outweighs the worst of propaganda by providing a truthful, factual exposition and explanation of a nation's foreign policy and way of life to overseas audiences, encouraging international understanding, promoting dialogue and displaying national achievements overseas. But even if one accepts the distinctions between the two, it is still hard not to conclude that public diplomacy and soft power may simply be palliative terms which side step the less convenient truth that the unpalatable face of propaganda is alive and well and living in a kind of semantic witness protection programme. Neither does the fact of public diplomacy, whether actively nudged and funded by governments or not, take on the argument that we should be constructing a much more visible and accountable mechanism for setting out and communicating our national brand and narrative, part of which should be our public diplomacy effort.

To some extent, these weaknesses have already marked out public diplomacy as a flawed and vulnerable concept; in 2018 Russia expelled the British Council from its offices in St Petersburg and other Russian cities on the basis that its staff had been using the Council as a cover for spying. 'If someone allows you in their home, act decently,' Russian Prime Minister Dmitry Medvedev was quoted as saying in the weekly Itogi newspaper. 'After all, it is known that state-financed structures like the British Council conduct a mass of other activities that are not so widely publicised...they are involved in gathering information and conducting espionage activities.'[4] The agenda driving this latest action was almost certainly linked to Britain's sanctioning of Russian diplomats in London after the attempted assassination of Sergei and Yulia Skripal, but the British Council with its language teaching programmes and cultural exchanges is not the first standard bearer of public diplomacy to attract accusations of cultural imperialism or worse. Longstanding instruments of US soft power in the Middle East, such as Voice of America and USAID, have been attracting negative headlines amongst conspiracy theorists for decades. So, where best to take a critical look at the latest generation of soft power instruments promoting US and Western interests in the Middle East whereby one might assess their impact on public opinion?

'The World is a Geospatial Pinball Machine'

Beyond the usual generalities about cultural exchange, one of the best public disquisitions on US public diplomacy '2.0' was offered in a speech by the Obama administration's Undersecretary of State for public diplomacy and public affairs, Tara D. Sonenshine, in an address she made to the Washington Institute.[5] Sonenshine, a former National Security Council official, referenced the Arab Spring as having marked a shift in US strategy in the region towards young people as the region's future agents of change. 'They are the emerging leaders and innovators who can lead their countries and economies to greater productivity and global understanding,' she said. The emphasis on leadership is especially interesting as it reflects a wider recognition of the need for change in the next generation of leaders in the Arab world, away from the old command and control style, along with its authoritarian psychology and suppression of civil and human rights. In his 2012 manifesto 'My

Vision, Challenges in the Race for Excellence,' Muhammad bin Rashid Al Maktoum, the Ruler of Dubai, wrote, 'today's Arab crisis is not one of money, men, morale, land or resources...the real crisis is rather one of leadership, management and perennial egotism.'

Reflecting the findings of much contemporary research in the region, Sonenshine focused on the vulnerability of young people to violent extremist ideologues who use false messages to recruit them into terrorism, revealing that the US Center for Strategic Counterterrorism Communication developed an approach to sow doubt about the extremist world-view among those being targeted by terrorist recruiters. 'From digital engagement in Arabic, Somali, and Urdu, which includes aggressive use of online videos, to creative strategies that reach audiences on the ground in their home countries, we are contesting the communications space used by Al-Qa'eda and its supporters,' she told the audience. If the first strand of the strategy is to refute the false narrative of distorted theological interpretation, the second is to construct a positive, alternative narrative which offers a combination of hope and the more solid possibilities of educational and economic opportunity. As with the British world-view, the teaching of English tops the list. 'It is the language of finance, science, diplomacy, banking, and international law. It also enables young people to study in the US and access the training that will maximize their potential for more prosperous futures,'[6] Sonenshine said. One operational example of this strategy is the English Access Micro-scholarship Program, first initiated in Morocco in 2003 with 17 students, which targeted non elite students from 13 to 20-year olds in the Middle East and North Africa (MENA). Since then, its growth has been rapid; now the programme reaches 18,000 students, with more than 80,000 alumni in 85 countries, in the process expanding this type of English language outreach to journalists, educators, entrepreneurs, religious leaders and other key influencers across the region. In doing so, it seems apparent that Sonenshine, Burt and others across Western government might simply be extending the philosophy first exercised in the region in the 1950s that asserts the moral authority of the English speaking world, a cultural extension in its way of the stereotyping with which the West is still regularly accused in its dealings with the Arab world.

The US strategic approach to public diplomacy now has both commercial and digital dimensions, flagging up the potential for a more mixed public-private sector involvement which may increasingly point the way for the future. A working example of this new model of commercial partnership is offered by the US government, Coca-Cola and Indiana University which has launched a one-month entrepreneurship education program that kicked off by bringing 100 MENA young leaders to the US in its first year. The self-interest in this scheme is clear, but there is mutual benefit too and one can see the potential for empowerment and change through this more inclusive alliance of complementary interests. Building and connecting networks is also central to this expanded vision of public diplomacy; the US embassy in Syria has increasingly used digital outreach and social media tools in order to bypass the Al Assad government and connect directly with the Syrian people, an example of how digital networks offer a further channel for relationship building, both widening and deepening the reach of soft power.

Rebranding the 'Arab Street'

Identifying and analysing shifts in public opinion in the Arab world presupposes agreeing a working definition of the concept itself, something which has been notoriously difficult to do and a rock against which many analyses have foundered in the past. This is because generalising about Arab people is traditionally a dangerous game; use of the Arab world as a collective term to imply a simplified approach can be misleading. Arab leaders themselves have in the past made political judgements based on assessing both national and regional sentiment, attempting to quantify the process by expressing the notion of the 'Arab street' as a barometer of public opinion. Gamal Abd Al Nasser, who was the first to articulate this idea, was not alone; Yasser Arafat too paid close attention to the mood of the 'Palestinian street.' This term has largely become discredited as an overly simplistic caricature of the evolution of public opinion which now increasingly characterises modernising Arab societies. The 'Arab street' was generally taken to describe a litmus test of thinking amongst the lower socio-economic layers across Arab populations, but it masked the complexities inherent in such an exercise. The contemporary Arab world currently has a combined population of 422 million spread across the Middle East and North Africa (MENA) who can be called Arabs because Arabic is their mother tongue,[7] and over half of whom are under 25 years old. A further definition of an Arab country is that it is a member of the Arab League, which is a regional organisation representing all Arab countries.

However, Arab people also tend to be defined by sub-sets of data including population density, disposable wealth, lifestyle, educational opportunity and consumer habits, indicators which collectively show the widest spread between the Arabian Gulf and North Africa. Yet the notion of collectivity is sometimes also expressed by shared financial, economic and political institutions and interests, amongst which are the Gulf Co-Operation Council, the Arab League, OAPEC and the United Nations. These in turn offer a further source of generalisation about a macro Arab point of view, accommodating attitudes, perceptions or behaviours within a range of shared preoccupations that also include the injustice of the occupation of Palestine and animosity to the State of Israel. Although a recent alliance has emerged between Israel and some Gulf states, 87% of respondents in the 2017 Arab Opinion Index said they would oppose their country diplomatically recognising Israel. Whilst it is ever clearer that the Palestinian cause no longer resonates with all Arab leaders, it is still compelling to the rebranded 'Arab street'; 77% of respondents say that the Palestinian cause concerns all Arabs and not the Palestinian people alone.'[8]

A further challenge in accommodating the notion of Arab public opinion is the traditional difficulty of testing and measuring it regularly, if at all. Until recently, there has been little work done by the research industry or government with which to offer comparative analysis of public opinion over time in a way that allows general conclusions to be drawn.

At one time, principally because of government restrictions, commercial sections of embassies, chambers of commerce and specialist journals were the only sources of first-hand data which formed the basis of statistical analysis and commercial decision making. However, this is changing as the countries of the Middle East liberalise their markets and grow new generations of consumers whose cultural choices, spending patterns and social views need to be taken into account by the private sector, including advertisers and the media. Young people aged 15 to 24 constitute approximately 20% of the populations in Egypt, Iraq, Lebanon, Libya, Morocco, Oman, Sudan, Syria, Tunisia, Yemen, Jordan, Algeria, and Saudi Arabia, according to Youth Policy Organisation. In the Arab countries' populations, young people are the fastest growing segment; some 60% of the population is under 25 years old, making this one of the most youthful regions in the world, with a median age of 22 years compared to a global average of 28.[9]

Organisations like Gallup, the Arab Barometer and the Arab Opinion Index are now able to carry out regular polling in some countries, a process which has started to reveal consistency in the low opinion held amongst Arab populations of the West, its policies and interventions in the region.

Arab public criticism of the United States in the region hit new troughs in the post 9/11 years (11th September 2001), mainly due to widespread disillusionment and disengagement with US foreign policy. The extent of this was shown in an opinion poll, 'Impressions of America' taken in six countries on behalf of the Arab American Institute by Zogby International one year after the invasion of Iraq in May 2004; this showed overall public attitudes toward the United States were extremely unfavourable, 'even though the governments in those countries— Saudi Arabia, Jordan, Morocco, Lebanon, Egypt, and the United Arab Emirates (UAE)—have excellent relations with the United States and the first four are among America's oldest Arab friends.' Unfavourable ratings in Egypt and Saudi Arabia even reached 98% and 94% respectively, while in Morocco, the UAE, Jordan, and Lebanon they reached 88%, 73%, 78%, and 69%.[10]

Successive consumer polls, perhaps unsurprisingly, show that a generation later public opinion is still largely negative. The 2016 Arab Opinion Index, for example, found that among foreign powers only Israel was perceived to be a bigger threat to the Arab world than the US; some 82% of survey participants in 12 Arab countries said they believed the US posed a threat to stability in the region, according to the poll unveiled in Washington, DC in April 2017.[11] The Index, an annual survey first conducted in 2011, came on the heels of the US bombing of Syria in response to the alleged use of chemical weapons by President Bashar al-Assad's regime.

Of the 18,310 survey respondents contacted in 2016, 77% said they had negative views of US foreign policy toward Syria. Imad Harb, director of research and analysis at the Arab Center in Washington DC, an affiliate of the Doha-based group, said he couldn't predict how the recent US military action would change regional opinion. However, US foreign policy in the Middle East remained unpopular across the board, with 80% of respondents reporting negative views of US actions in Palestine, and more than 70% reporting negative perceptions of US involvement in Iraq, Yemen and Libya in 2017.[12] The latest destructive ingredients to throw into the stew of Arab public opinion on US foreign policy have been provided by the unilateralism and big stick diplomacy of Donald Trump, both in the withdrawing in 2018 of $65 million of funding from the United Nations Relief and Works Agency (UNRWA), responsible for education, health and the welfare services of five million Palestinian refugees[13] and the wholly controversial and provocative decision to move the US embassy in Israel from Tel Aviv to the shared city of Jerusalem, a decision perceived by some Palestinians as driven by a global evangelical Christian conspiracy seeded in the US.

Overall, there is now an accumulation of statistical evidence to show that America and its foreign policy in the Arab world remains highly unpopular. How can that change unless both policy and action on the ground actively work to shift the attitudes of revitalised and reconstituted Arab public opinion which is fast leaving old notions of the 'Arab street' behind? If the US has some uniquely difficult challenges to overcome in shifting Arab public opinion, it has company in the West amongst those who have also pursued the more coercive options of hard diplomacy and military intervention as their default foreign policy positions. Britain too is at the forefront of those fighting to repair the state of public opinion brought about by their policy stance, not only in the region but at home as well where government decision-making has been widely questioned. British Parliamentarians have famously had trouble supporting some of the unconvincing national narratives constructed to support past interventions, the 'Weapons of Mass Disappearance' that British MP Robin Cook so effectively ridiculed in the House of Commons after the invasion of Iraq offering one example, the failure to approve the bombing of Syria another.[14]

The UK opinion poll conducted by Arab News, the Middle East's largest English language daily and the research organisation YouGov in September 2017, revealed that negative Arab sentiment about flawed Western foreign policy in the region is echoed in similar views amongst the British themselves. The 'UK Attitudes Towards the Arab World Poll' found that only around one in 10 Brits believe that British foreign policy in the Arab world has been a stabilising force in the region; with as many as 83% of those polled saying Britain was wrong to go to war in Iraq.[15] The findings further reflect public opinion in the region, showing that over half (53%) of British people feel that the UK government should formally recognise Palestine as a state and under a third (31%) believe that the Balfour Declaration is something to feel proud about.

The poll is also a wake-up call for what will almost certainly become further deterioration of our relationship with the Arab world unless the twin instruments of public diplomacy and soft power are brought to bear on improving cultural, educational and commercial links. One in four Brits, across all ages and stages of life, claim to know little or nothing about the Arab world and less than a fifth have ever travelled to Arab countries. Perhaps most disturbingly of all, nearly two-thirds of respondents (63%) believe that Arabs who have migrated to the UK have failed to integrate in Western societies and live in isolated communities, in turn creating growing potential for anti-Muslim hate crimes. Taken together, these numbers begin to tell a story about the reasons for the failure of the West to win over modernising Arab public opinion which has become a more quantifiable and thus coherent expression and manifestation of a collective Arab sensibility and consciousness. This notional community could now be said to share issues and interests that transcend nationalist or political difference to promote a world view that accommodates commitment to moderate Islam alongside acknowledgement of the need to modernise government institutions, civil society and their associated models of leadership.

Following the cathartic events of the Arab Spring of 2011, the countries of the G8 came together in 2013 to form the Deauville Partnership as a way of developing and nurturing the West's relationship with these reforming countries, dealing with the major players for the first time as a collective force, including Egypt, Tunisia, Morocco, Libya, Jordan and Yemen. The Deauville Partnership, itself supplemented by the Arab Partnership Initiative to support these countries in the security sector, focused on widening and deepening the reforms sought by the nascent Arab revolution, most especially in the areas of investment, trade, women's rights, access to capital markets and development of small business capacity. The 'Forsa' (Opportunity) small business initiative to support entrepreneurs was one example of this programme. This has been the single most concerted and coherent response of the West to nurture the reform agenda; could it be the start of a different pattern of thinking that might challenge past interventionist models that have stalked Western policy in the Arab world?

The Arab Spring, whilst it has stalled in some countries and run into a range of obstacles in others is still on the march, still redrawing the map of the Arab world. The latest of these cathartic revolutionary movements occurred in Algeria and Sudan in the Spring of 2019, comprising a second wave of popular nationalist and political uprising that has toppled the authoritarian regimes of Abdulaziz Bouteflika in Algeria and General Omar Al-Bashir in Sudan. In the process, this Algerian 'Smile Revolution' and Sudanese 'Nile Spring' are opening up the prospect of fresh approaches to the organisation of both government and civil society, driven by an increasingly activist middle and professional class and fueled especially by young people with ambitions to build more prosperous and democratic countries with stronger, more representative and outward looking institutions.

These movements in themselves are beginning to show the scale, potency and impetus of public opinion that has been either suppressed or latent throughout the decades of authoritarian rule aided and abetted by the military and reinforced by lack of media and individual freedoms.

Aid, Development and Peace Inequality

Over and above educational, cultural or commercial initiatives, the most mature and largest scale instrument of Western soft power has been the provision of aid, spread across a wide project spectrum. Whilst there are long standing disagreements in the international community about the ethics, politics and culture of aid, there can be little doubt that it has been widely and effectively used to achieve a variety of both immediate and longer term ends, from feeding starving and displaced populations in regional disaster zones such as Iraq and Syria to supporting more arcane corporate governance projects like security sector reform in Tunisia and Palestine in order to lessen the destructive potential of fragile and post-conflict states. As with other parts of the developing world, there is an ongoing intellectual tussle about the provenance of the aid agenda in the Middle East, Palestine being perhaps just one prominent example, where it can be seen as either directly or indirectly linked to the exercise of soft power by the West, but where its harder edges are associated directly with humanitarian needs in conflict zones which have often been paralysed as functioning political states. Recent evidence suggests that the official British attitude to aid is shifting to link budgeted aid programmes with the opportunities for procurement of related British goods and services, an idea that has grown in attraction since the UK's aid budget was fixed by law at 0.7% of GDP and increased external scrutiny for measurable payback from aid spend has come about as a direct consequence.

The UK provided over £13 billion in overseas development aid (ODA) in 2016, which made it the third largest global donor country in ODA spending terms. The largest spending donor remained the United States (£24.9 billion), from a global total of £86 billion.[16] British aid is either classed as bilateral or multilateral, with the greater share (£8.5 billion) categorised as bilateral. In 2016, UK bilateral aid to Asia rose to £2.3 billion, driven largely by increases in aid to Jordan and Syria, areas affected by the Syrian humanitarian and refugee crisis.[17] Tellingly, though, the British government also spent over £1 billion on government and civil society which covers public policy, human rights, conflict prevention and resolution, and peace and security; this was the third largest area of British aid spending. Not all aid goes through the Department for International Development (DFID) though; the Foreign and Commonwealth Office (FCO) also provided £504m of ODA in

2016 through core departmental policy programmes, international subscriptions and aid-related frontline diplomacy.

These policy programmes supported a wide range of UK foreign policy and UK aid priorities in the majority of Development Assistance Committee (DAC) listed countries. As well as scholarships, FCO programmes include small-scale interventions in support of diplomatic activity and longer-term capacity building. This work contributes to strengthening global peace, security, governance or prosperity in support of the UK Aid Strategy and its most significant allocations are to the Chevening Scholarships Programme and the Magna Carta Fund for Human Rights and Democracy. It is an anomalous by-product of Britain's legal commitment to spend 0.7% of its GDP on aid that the overall annual aid allocation is going up so fast in step with the country's GDP that planners are not consistently able to find enough legitimate projects which they can endow with funding.

Not all development aid is judiciously spent, and it may be that those projects that are unhappily revealed to be either suspect or incompetent have the reverse effect on public opinion and are reflected in more sceptical public attitudes. This was the case in the exposure by the investigative BBC programme Panorama of weaknesses within the £9 million Free Syria Police programme being administered by the widely respected UK advisor Adam Smith International (ASI), a management consultancy that has been instrumental in delivering the UK's aid vision overseas and has won aid contracts worth £537 million from the British government over a five year period.[18]

ASI faced accusations that the project was wasting British taxpayers' money and worse that employees were being forced to work alongside Islamist extremist organisations such as Jabhat Al Nusra enforcing Sharia law in order to make headway in setting up and managing the police stations included in the programme specification. The accusations drew comment from Crispin Blunt MP, then Chair of the powerful Parliamentary Foreign Affairs Select Committee, who criticised prevailing standards of governance in the aid business: 'there must be more accountability for what you support. There needs to be oversight,'[19] he told reporter Jane Corbin. This lesson may well be in the process of being learned, as ASI was temporarily banned from applying for further Government contracts. But despite occasional aberrations, much of the aid business still remains invisible to the public, who are not generally privy either to project or budget details.

It is hard to quantify the precise link between aid programmes on the ground and any related shift in public opinion towards donor states. But spending on public diplomacy programmes is far outstripped by the disproportionate resources that the world continues to spend on creating and containing violence, as opposed to peace. In 2015 alone, UN peacekeeping expenditure of $8.27 billion totaled only 1.1% of the estimated $742 billion of economic losses from armed conflict. Those activities that aim to create peace in the long term (peace building) totaled $6.8 billion, or only 0.9% of the economic losses from conflict according to the World Economic Forum (WEF).[20]

But future improvements in peace are fundamental to greater investment in peace-building and peace-keeping, according to the WEF. Peace-keeping operations are measures aimed at responding to a conflict, whereas peace-building expenditure is aimed at developing and maintaining the capacities for resilience to conflict. Peace-building expenditure aims to reduce the risk of lapsing or relapsing into violent conflict by strengthening national capacities and institutions for conflict management and laying the foundations of sustainable peace and development. These numbers suggest a serious under-investment in the activities that build peace and demonstrate that the international community is spending too much on conflict and too little on peace.

Given the fact that the cost of violence is so significant, the economic argument for more spending on peace is indeed powerful. 'Furthermore, a new phenomenon is emerging as some countries grow more peaceful while overall levels of violence increase: peace inequality. This drives a broader dynamic of greater economic inequalities between nations, as the least peaceful countries spiral into greater violence and conflict, they are also further set back economically,' says the WEF in its annual report.

Constructing an Alternative Narrative
Since he was elected US President on 8th November 2016, Donald Trump has consistently flagged up fake news as a commodity which is knowingly used by mainstream news organisations to lay traps for him and tell damaging lies about his intentions and policies. The term itself has now passed into the language as if it is a new phenomenon which has been a direct by product of the internet age, driven by mysterious 'bots' in remote eastern European villages churning out thousands of false stories in order to generate a clickbait cash return. In fact, as the pacifist Arthur Ponsonby pointed out in 1927 in his book 'Falsehood In Wartime,' fake news stories like 'the crucified Canadian' and 'the corpse utilisation factory' were first used a century ago by propagandists anxious to leave a trail of

disinformation with which to confuse and disadvantage an enemy, and became a regular feature of wartime atrocity propaganda. Over the course of 2018, the hunt for fake news and its perpetrators intensified as ever more contaminated news matter was discovered through systematic searches by interested parties as disparate as Facebook and the US government. So ubiquitous has fake news become, and the fear that it will obscure the legitimate news agenda, that the British government announced as early as January 2018 that it was launching a dedicated fake news unit to counter disinformation by 'state actors' and others, generally taken these days to mean the Russian state.[21] This new national security communications unit will be able to more systematically deter our adversaries and help us deliver on national security priorities, according to a Downing Street spokesman, who emphasised, 'we are living in an era of fake news and competing narratives.'

The development was announced in the shadow of a British Parliamentary Committee carrying out an inquiry into this growing phenomenon, in the process of requesting information from social media companies such as Facebook and Twitter, including on Russian state activity during the EU referendum of 2016. Political reporters were told that the Government will respond with more and better use of national security communications to tackle these interconnected and complex challenges.

This announcement about the bolstering of Britain's dedicated information capability followed hard on the heels of a prior Downing Street announcement in which it had confirmed that a special unit had been set up in the Prime Minister's Office to offer communications consultancy services to countries in the Middle East and North Africa (MENA) to help them improve the images of their own governments.

Specialist areas of operation within this initiative include crisis communication, and 'establishing political clarity.'[22] Contracts are already in place between this unit and government clients in Tunisia and Jordan and others are in the pipeline yet no-one has sought to point out the tensions between these two latest stand-alone communications units, the first of which appears to be countering attempts to bring down the state through the manipulation of information, the second a simple public relations move to help allies polish their image. The inherent contradictions in this government position seem to have escaped any criticism.

The British Government Communication Service (GCS) is currently responsible for planning and managing British national information output, but since the existential cuts of 2011, it has been operating in an oxygen starved environment with fewer resources than ever. Now it is having to live in uneasy tandem with at least two dedicated single-purpose units that appear to be accountable directly to Downing Street via the Cabinet Office. This seems to be moving Britain further away from control of the national brand and narrative which might realistically pull together its separate strands into a coherent and credible information strategy. It surely has reached the moment when, as former national information advisors such as David Kilcullen have proposed, we need to develop a capacity specifically for strategic information warfare and an integrating function that 'draws together all the components of what we say and what we do.' In this way, we can develop the connected approach we need to shape our national narrative in a way which makes holistic sense of both our policy stance and interventions in the region.

Whilst there may be no appetite for a return to the old bureaucratic, top-heavy Ministry style, there may be more mileage in examining the merits of creating a senior role for an information tsar tasked with pulling such an information capability together, combining the direct engagement of public diplomacy, the systematic use of modern persuasive public relations and the narrower, selective skills of psychological operations and information operations where the context is specifically military, an idea ironically not so far from the system proposed by Harold Lasswell in 1927 to ensure that an information specialist got a seat at the top government table.

A New Paradigm for Relationships
In the midst of rethinking our communications capability and purpose, we may never find a better moment to assess the way in which our attitude to public information and the construction of our national brand and narrative has developed over the last century. This becomes a meaningful exercise not only in order to make judgements about the historical course of events but also to evaluate what has been truly effective in moving public opinion, both domestically and internationally. The trail of propaganda and false narrative that the West has dispersed across the region over the last century encompasses an uneasy mix of self-interest and deception, bequeathing a legacy that has served to perpetuate misunderstanding and obscure policy objectives.

The introduction of systematic propaganda by Sir Campbell Stuart was a significant factor for Britain in the First World War and the parallel development of atrocity propaganda brought into play a genre of information war which in some respects became a motif for the century of conflict that has characterised the progress of certain Middle East countries from Mandated imperial territories in 1922 to modern, independent states in 2019. Along the way, propaganda and information war have progressed through a series of technically complex and serpentine models which include systematic and scientific propaganda, psychological operations, perception management, public diplomacy and soft power.

These initiatives and campaigns between them have carried a cost for the West, not simply in quantifiable financial and human terms but also in the more qualitative realm of credibility and weakened relationships as measured through the prism of public opinion. It is possible to argue, for example, that the national narrative that accompanied Britain's invasion of Suez in 1956 was so destructive and with such long term implications that even the substantial reverse engineering subsequently carried out by the Central Office of Information was never able to fully repair the country's reputation for honest dealing in the region or, in the same breath, that the contribution British expertise made to the US led campaign of perception management to wilfully distort the information environment in Iraq after Operation Iraqi Freedom in 2003 created an enduring lack of trust and confidence in Western information practices and their destructively opaque motives.

The point at issue is that the information war waged in parallel with the military and economic war, Harold Lasswell's so-called third implement of operation, may be seen in the end to have had just as major an effect on outcomes, perhaps not on the immediate battlefield but on confidence, trust and thus public opinion, all more fragile commodities but equally instrumental in achieving a longer term geopolitical endgame.

At the same time as the West has been pursuing its information wars across the region, the Arab response has resulted in a propaganda narrative and style more actively managed and better integrated with its own need to project a more confident sense of sovereignty, national identity and political purpose. This was true of Arab political leaders such as Gamal Abd Al Nasser and PLO head Yasser Arafat, both of whom showed themselves to be highly capable of creating and projecting popular profiles for both their political projects and personal agendas, each with an instinctive mastery as persuaders; they were able to cleverly package simple yet potent messages which cleverly harnessed the national mood and at the same time shaped public opinion more widely in the region. Other leaders such as Saddam Hussein were perhaps less immediately intuitive but became technically skilled in their reinterpretation of external propaganda models and their adaptation of aspects of them to the domestic and regional circumstances of Iraq and its regional military confrontations with the United States and Israel.

Above all though, it is Islamic State which has learned the most conspicuous lessons from Western propagandists, reflected in the highest priority which they attribute to information war and the status they confer on the information warrior as a jihadi and martyr of equal worth to those Islamist foot soldiers who wear the explosive belt. These two major positions are further reinforced in the evidence of the lessons Islamic State has learned from modern Western communication theory and practice, including the construction of sophisticated media departments, the calibrating of professional teams with complementary expertise and a range of tactics reflective of mainstream thinking about how branding and dialogue are used to engage a modern, diffuse and geographically dispersed audience. Especially significant is its focus on the high impact, visual recall of atrocity propaganda to make a strong emotional connection, the use of the paraphernalia and psychology of fascist propaganda to encourage dependency amongst its followers, and the innovative steps the organisation has taken to use social and digital media and dedicated apps as tools for increasingly customised and personal two-way communication.

Ending the Age of Intervention

There are significant trends in play, which between them, are likely to have a major impact on the future development of information and propaganda alongside economic and military conflict in any ensuing interventions in the trajectory of the Middle East. First of these is the growing reality that the age of direct and large-scale Western military intervention is over, the latest evidence of this provided by the projected withdrawal in early 2019 of the last US forces engaged on the ground in Syria. The events of the first decades of the 21st century in the region have now shown conclusively that the West is no longer prepared to pay the financial or popular price of failure that this modus operandi has entailed. It can be argued that, as a direct consequence, the role of diplomacy should now increasingly extend to include public diplomacy alongside state diplomacy as both Britain and the United States consider how they might maintain their dwindling influence in the ongoing post Arab Spring realignment of the region.

Secondly, there is no doubt that some key regional players are increasingly seeing international diplomacy as the primary exit route from the cul-de-sac of military confrontation and existential crisis that has held the region in its grip for decades. The debilitated Palestinian Authority which, since the Oslo Accords of 1993, has been responsible for governing prescribed areas of the West Bank and Gaza is focusing its main effort away from propaganda war with the occupying Israeli administration in a conscious effort to extricate itself from the old confrontational patterns.

The Palestinians, who are still formally intent on establishing an autonomous political state within recognisable and internationally agreed borders ('the two-state solution'), are instead refocusing on a broader front that includes a package of alternative approaches, including tacit approval of the activist Boycott, Divestment and Sanctions movement alongside a diplomatic push to gain admission to a clutch of international organisations which collectively can reinforce their status as an independent nation. Included in this initiative are the International Criminal Court (ICC), which allows them to pursue justice for crimes committed within Palestine, the cross-border police organisation Interpol and the United Nations, of which Palestine has only achieved Observer Status. The Palestinian government is also actively pursuing other measures of definitive political progress, already successfully lobbying Britain's Labour Party and the Irish and Swedish governments to commit to the full recognition of the State of Palestine and seeking to recruit NGOs and civil society organisations to advocate for their national aspirations.

The recognition that diplomacy and the pursuit of statehood by other means may never replace Israeli accountability as a goal, but which may in the end still have better outcomes than confrontation, is another reason that the Palestinians continue the process of building stronger government institutions, directing their information capacity at crafting more direct relationships with citizens and delivering more tangible diplomatic outcomes that move the conversation beyond mere rhetoric. In their strategy of building modern and more effective government institutions and processes, the Palestinians share similar goals and objectives to many other modernising Arab states, all of whom are placing information and communications capacity at the heart of their modernising exercises.

A third trend is the containment and partial halting of Islamist extremism as a force, both on the ground and within its own existential narrative. With the falls of Mosul in July 2017 and Raqqa in November

2017, the physical expression of the Caliphate as a recreation of a single entity spanning a borderless Iraq and Syria soon ceased to be a practical reality. The degrading of the Caliphate became more marked over the course of 2018, stripping it back from occupation at its height of the northern half of Iraq, the north-east of Syria and elements of Kurdistan up to the borders with southern Turkey as far west as Kobane. The vision projected by the propaganda of Islamic State, of a modern-day Salafi jihadist project populated by a multinational coalition of hard core ideologues is temporarily on hold, its nucleus in Raqqa blown apart by Coalition bombs and Kurdish Peshmerga ground attacks. Observers have noted that, since the fall of Raqqa, the content and output of IS propaganda has changed in tone and message to focus on persuading IS sleepers and isolated 'soldiers' to commit random acts of war and terror around the world rather than spinning the former vision of the Caliphate as a jihadi lifestyle choice. Whilst Islamic State has been under siege physically, the evidence is also beginning to suggest that its online activities are finally being challenged too, by a more effective and penetrating counter strategic communications effort co-ordinated in the Gulf.

However, the IS propaganda machine is still able to function albeit at a somewhat curtailed level, producing material including films and newsletters which detail its co-ordinated operations across many interconnected fronts, from China to West Africa, and which are directed at audiences of jihadists spread across sympathetic Islamist organisations including the Taliban, Boko Haram, Al Shabab and Al Qaeda in the Islamic Maghreb. This output, much of it in Arabic, includes films such as 'Harvesting of the Soldiers #25,' Arabic language newsletters and sophisticated infographics. Nonetheless, a lower level war is ongoing and specialist work continues across the academic and professional communities in the West to better define the identifying characteristics of Western recruits to the jihadist cause in an effort to stop the migration of the idea, its ideology and physical manifestation.

New research has identified three different character types that particularly lend themselves to radicalisation as foreign jihadist fighters, according to Dr Petter Nesser of Norways's *Forsvarets forskningsinstitutt* (FFI); these are entrepreneurs, misfits and drifters.[23] It is the entrepreneurs who are able to mobilise the most meaningful threats, which are in turn likely to rise in direct proportion to the interventions in the Middle East by Western governments, [24] he says.

Qatari Twist in the Saudi Tale

A corollary of this third trend, and one whose impact took many observers by surprise, has been the appearance of a liberalising spirit in the region, one which caused Saudi Arabia, the political standard bearer of Sunni Islam, to seemingly effect a pivot into the modern age during the course of 2018. Like a series of dominoes, the country's reforming leader Prince

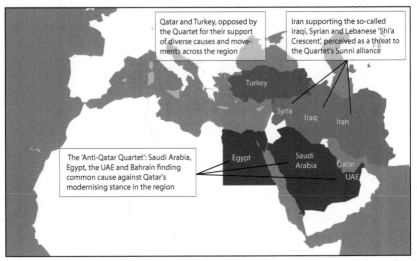

Qatar and Turkey, opposed by the Quartet for their support of diverse causes and movements across the region

Iran supporting the so-called Iraqi, Syrian and Lebanese 'Shi'a Crescent', perceived as a threat to the Quartet's Sunni alliance

The 'Anti-Qatar Quartet': Saudi Arabia, Egypt, the UAE and Bahrain finding common cause against Qatar's modernising stance in the region

Middle East Alliances Today: The above is a simplification of a complex web of relationships, but it tries to capture some of the bare bones of the various political axes motivating some of the headlines today.

Muhammad Bin Salman (MBS), toppled many of the most longstanding populist obstacles to social progress in the Kingdom, delivering highly visible freedoms for women including the purchasing and driving of cars, access to movies, piloting aircraft, and jogging in public. Women candidates were also permitted for the first time to stand in some local political elections. As part of the same reforming package, the ubiquitous religious police (the Mu'tawwah), the guardians of propriety and protectors of virtue, were also required to accept curbed powers, no longer able to stop people at will or beat transgressors for infringing the country's draconian dress code. Some greeted this apparent social revolution as part of the ongoing Arab Spring movement, detecting an opening of the door to change that might signify a deepening maturity in the Arab world, one potentially capable of accelerating the resetting of relationships with the West.

In time, this liberalising trend was revealed as a smokescreen for a parallel agenda, one which in its process of realisation revealed a remarkable step change in the Kingdom's capacity to wage information war and, at the same time, move the centre of political gravity further into the heart of the region. Alongside its more emollient, reforming persona, the Saudi regime doubled down on its suppression of civil and human rights including the coup it staged involving some of the Kingdom's wealthiest citizens who, accused of institutional corruption, were incarcerated in the Riyadh Ritz-Carlton hotel without trial until, rumour has it, they bought their freedom with large sums of cash. Beyond its own borders, the Saudi government actively pursued its enemies and prosecuted a deeply damaging and globally unpopular war in Yemen as a response to what it saw as a regional power grab by neighbouring Iran.

Most unexpected of all, in its newest role as information warrior, Saudi Arabia planned and managed a sophisticated information and propaganda campaign to degrade and destroy the reputation of its immediate neighbour Qatar, which it alleged was a state sponsor of terrorism across the Middle East. To do this, it garnered support from Arab allies including the United Arab Emirates, Bahrain and Egypt (forming 'the anti-Qatar quartet') and mounted an economic blockade of the tiny Gulf state that even required Qatari aircraft to change their routes in order to avoid Saudi air space. During the intensive Saudi lobbying that accompanied this set of events, the international community remained equivocal in its support, scrambling to marshal a response to the action and decipher its opaque logic. Whilst moving to complete its historic land, maritime and air blockade of Qatar, Saudi Arabia embarked on the mother of PR wars, one which in its scale and ambition showed it had absorbed many of the lessons of the West's interventions in the region and at the same time deployed newly enhanced communication skills that have been methodically incorporated into government practice across the region since the Arab Spring. In the battle to engage hearts and minds and dominate public opinion in the Gulf and internationally, some estimates suggest that by the middle of 2018 the country had spent up to $1.5 billion on a mix of PR and lobbying initiatives, a sum that has been matched and even exceeded by Qatar itself, which has embarked on its own PR and information counter blitz.[25]

Stitched into this PR war, there is much at stake. What seems like an unequal struggle between Saudi Arabia, the Titan of the Gulf and an anchor Western ally in the region, and tiny Qatar, a more enigmatic and free-thinking player in regional politics, will have a major impact on the leadership and future direction of the strategically important Arabian Gulf. Qatar, which has been gaining the upper hand in the war of public opinion, epitomises an ascendant view amongst countries of the broader Middle East that the Saudi quartet represent between them an autocratic conspiracy against the aspirations for political change that they have opposed since the uprisings of 2011. Qatar increasingly promotes an image as a champion of change, more comfortable to be in dialogue with Islamist and revolutionary movements, including Hamas, if the region is to move beyond the old typecast image. This bid for ideological and moral authority, as an architect of the Arab world's future direction, is at the heart of Qatar's positioning in its PR war, one in which it has engaged some unlikely and controversial allies.

As part of its strategy to win hearts and minds in Washington, Qatar reached out to the US-based Jewish community in order to press its case, hiring the specialist Jewish lobbying firm Stonington Strategies, according to the Times of Israel.[26] This was, in itself, a response to the Saudis reaching out to the Jewish lobby through its own proxies, in one case using the specialist Jewish lobbying firm Bluelight Strategies to persuade Washington to up its pressure on Qatar to fall in line with Saudi thinking, according to the newspaper.

Two major factors are helping to drive Qatar's perceived success in the PR war. Firstly, the depth of its pockets means it can spend to attract requisite expertise and fund both people and advertising. Secondly, through the technical expertise and network of the Al Jazeera media empire, it has developed a world-beating brand which has enabled it to dominate the Arab media landscape. Over time, Qatar's strategy to build bridges with the US, whose Al Udeid Air Base it hosts, has paid off; estimates suggest that in order to win hearts and minds in Washington, it retained up to eight firms in the US in 2017 and then assembled a bank of advisers that included many former US government officials. PR slogans ('America's strongest ally in fighting ISIS'), leaflets, advertising and digital campaigning all featured heavily in Qatar's campaign.

The complexity of this PR war and the scale of its penetration of the dialogue of Western and Arab governments has been both unexpected and powerful. Amongst other lessons, it shows how the role of information and propaganda in pursuing policy aims has crossed the divide in the Middle East from being a primarily Western tool to one which is now in the mainstream of Arab government thinking and capacity. A significant transfer of knowledge and expertise has taken place since Operation Iraqi Freedom in 2003 and the uprisings of the Arab Spring of 2011 which shows that the battle to control public opinion both within and beyond the region has assumed new and dramatic proportions where more than ever is at stake in influencing the public mind, dominating the news agenda and crafting a vision of the future. At the same time, events have shown the practical difficulties of managing the downside of a more open, proactive information culture and policy, notwithstanding the input of professionals; the Saudi state is learning the bitter lesson that the technical skills of media strategy and PR campaigning must travel hand in hand with those of crisis management and disaster recovery, two sides of the same perception management coin.

These events are collectively beginning to show that information war, alongside soft power, is becoming the principal battleground in a new phase of conflict both intra regionally and in the relationship between the West and the Arab world; engaging in and winning this war will be the big prize as the 21st century moves out of its first decades. Public opinion, for so long at the periphery of power play politics and strategic and military interests, is going to occupy a much more central role in the future of the region than it has in the past, and those who can best influence and control it will find themselves the new masters.

The predominantly youthful and increasingly connected Arab world is no longer prepared to play simply by the rules of the old elites and vested interests in the way of past generations; already young people are changing traditional social and educational patterns, becoming entrepreneurs and informed consumers, assuming high profile leadership roles, moving more comfortably around the world and looking both east and west for inspiration and alliances.

It is up to the West to respond with policy initiatives that reflect some of the opportunities presented by this more three-dimensional vision of the world, ones that can offer something new and more imaginative, that should challenge the next generations of leaders to think beyond the stale and the failed. In 'What Went Wrong?: Western Impact and Middle Eastern Response,' his 2002 analysis of the crisis in the Muslim world that anticipated the catastrophe of 9/11, the historian Bernard Lewis floated the idea that civil society would seem to offer the best hope for decent coexistence between Islam and the West, based on the value of mutual respect. This view has many supporters, among them former British Foreign Secretary David Miliband who proposed in his prescient speech in Oxford in 2009 that the time has come to assemble broad coalitions and alliances that are inclusive of all citizens, not simply the old elites. Leadership skills, stronger and more modern institutions and participative government help build more inclusive societies; sectarian tolerance and resolution of the refugee crisis in a region still in chaos are priorities for Western and Arab governments to tackle together. This message is gaining traction amongst those thinking about building institutions and governments designed to deliver a subtly different shaped and powered future. If British and Arab relations really have been damaged by the use of 'lazy stereotypes,' we need to think as Miliband suggested about how we use language and terms such as 'extreme' and 'moderate.' If we continue to invade countries as we did Iraq in 2003, we also need to understand the link with the 'bitterness, distrust and resentment' in the region that will follow.

Now a century on from the Paris Peace Conference of 1919 and the downstream treaties of 1920 at Sèvres and San Remo that led to the redrawing of the modern Middle East, and it is apposite to reflect on the outcomes for a region that has gone on to suffer ensuing decades of recurring military, economic and political strife. The major events and milestones that have marked the passage of Western intervention over the 20th century and into the 21st include names and events whose associations are now indelibly marked as steps in the progressive decline of the West as a major interventionist power and influence in the region. The Palestine Mandate, the Suez crisis, the Iraq wars and the campaign for Libyan regime change have all reserved a place in a Western consciousness that has increasingly struggled to come to terms with uncomfortable themes of self-regard and self-interest at the expense of national self-determination as envisaged by US President Woodrow Wilson and the nascent League of Nations in 1919.

Instead Western interventionism has been challenged by a new order of regional empire building and ideological ambition driven by Russia, Turkey, Iran and the Kurdish drive for a political state. The events of the Arab Spring in 2011 and of the 'Nile Spring' in 2019, whilst still truncated in their political outcomes have begun a process that has exposed the green shoots of a new and dynamic generation of Arab public opinion unhooked from the old stereotype of the 'Arab street,' which is fast carving out new spaces for young and more insistent voices.

This trend looks irresistible and unlikely to be denied, destined to grow whatever the short term obstacles placed in its path. It is time for Britain and the West to respond to this major opportunity of a fast galvanising and activist Arab world by closing the gap between what we say and what we do and in the process to set the old aside and embrace the new.

Chapter Notes

Chapter One

1. Lasswell, Harold D, *Propaganda Technique In The World War, The Matter In Hand,* (New York: Peter Smith, 1927) p9. ISBN 978-1-61427-506-0.

2. Lasswell, Harold D, p27.

3. https://www.alaraby.co.uk/english/comment (accessed18th July 2018).

4. *Attitudes Towards the Arab World* – a poll among UK residents, Arab News, You Gov, Council for Arab-British Understanding, 16-17 Aug 2017; total sample size 2,142 adults.

5. https://www.youthpolicy.org/mappings/regionalyouthscenes/mena/facts (accessed 4th July 2018).

6. Lasswell, Harold D, p27.

7. *Guardian,* Julian Borger, Diplomatic Editor, Thursday 21 May, 2009.

8. *2015 Global Peace Index Report,* World Economic Forum, https://www. weforum.org .

9. *2015 Global Peace Index Report,* World Economic Forum, https://www. weforum.org .

10. Watson Institute of International Public Affairs, Brown University, Providence, RI, 9th September 2016.

11. *Guardian,* 23 April 2014.

12. Knightley, P, *The First Casualty,* (Andre Deutsch, 2003), p486, ISBN 0-801880-300.

13. Rampton S, Stauber J, *Weapons of Mass Deception, Liberation Day,* (USA Jeremy P Tarcher, Penguin 2003), p5, ISBN 1-84119-837-4.

14. *'Airforce Intelligence & Security Doctrine, Psychological Operations,'* Air Force Instruction 10-702, Secretary of the Air Force, July 19, 1994.

15. Winter, Charlie, *'Media Operative, You Are a Mujahid Too':* The International Centre for The Study of Radicalisation and Political Violence, King's College, 2017.

16. Utting, Dr Kate, *'The Information Campaign and Countering Insurgency: Lesson From Palestine 1945-1948,'* Defence Studies Department, King's College, London.

17. Freedman, Lawrence, The Transformation of Strategic Affairs, Adelphi Book, 2006.

18. Freedman, Lawrence, The Transformation of Strategic Affairs, Adelphi Book, 2006.

19. FBI, Most Wanted Terrorists, Brookings Institute, (accessed January 2017).

20. *BBC News*, 10th May 2017.

21. *BBC News* (https://bbcnews.co.uk ,19th September 2017.

22. *Global Issues*, https://www.globalissues.org/article/157/war-propaganda-and-the-media.

23. The UK Chartered Institute of Public Relations (http://www.cipr.co.uk).

24. Bernays, Edward L, *Crystallizing Public Opinion, Introduction*, Stewart Ewen, (New York: Ig Publishing) , ISBN 978-1-935439-26-4.

25. PR Census 2016 PR Week/PRCA/Yougov.

26. Nato Review, Summer 2003.

27. Global Research, Dissident Voice, 5th July 2016.

28. *Ibid.*

29. Rampton S and Stauber J, *Weapons of Mass Deception, Liberation Day*, (USA Jeremy P Tarcher, Penguin 2003), p71.

30. USC Center on Public Diplomacy.

31. Rugh, W, '*American Soft Power and Public Diplomacy in the Arab World.*' Palgrave Communications, 2017, 3:160104 doi: 10.1057/palcomms.2016.104.

32. Keohane, Robert O and Nye, Joseph S, *Power and Interdependence in the Information Age*, Foreign Affairs, Vol. 77, No. 5, September/October 1998, p. 86.

33. Brown, John, '*Public Diplomacy & Propaganda, Their Differences,*' American Diplomacy, Foreign Service Despatches and Periodic Reports on US Foreign Policy, 2008.

34. TNA CAB/129/78 Middle East Oil.

35. British Council https://www.britishcouncil.org (accessed July 2017).

Chapter Two

1. *Arab News*, 25th September 2017.

2. *Ibid.*

3. *Country Studies*; https://www.countrystudies.us/Egypt/20.htm.

4. Said, Edward, *Orientalism*, (London, Routledge & Keegan Paul 1978), p3, ISBN 978-0-141-18742-6

5. Said, Edward, p4.

6. IWM Digital Archive, collections/item/object/1060023688.

7. Le Bon, Gustave, *The Crowd*, Study of The Popular Mind, The Era of Crowds, (Aristeus Books 2014).

8. Lippmann, Walter, *Public Opinion*, Leaders and The Rank And File, (Jefferson Publication 5th December 2015). ISBN-13 978-1512179316.

9. Le Bon, Gustave, *The Crowd*, Study of the Popular Mind, the Era of Crowds, (Aristeus Books 2014) ISBN 9781502303264.

10. Le Bon, Gustave, *The Crowd*, Study of The Popular Mind, The Era of Crowds, (Aristeus Books, 2014).

11. Freud, Sigmund, *Group Psychology and The Analysis of the Ego*, (printed by Amazon) ISBN: 9781500715427.

12. Freud, Sigmund, *Group Psychology and the Analysis of the Ego*, the Group and the Primal Horde, (Printed by Amazon).

13. Adorno, Theodor, *Freudian Theory and the Pattern of Fascist Propaganda*, (The Essential Frankfurt School Reader, 1982), p126.

14. Jerrold Post, Prof, *Yasser Arafat, Psychological Profile and Strategic Analysis*, International Policy Institute for Counter-Terrorism, 2002.

15. Freud, Sigmund, *Group Psychology and the Analysis of The Ego,* The Herd Instinct, (printed by Amazon).

16. Trotter, Wilfred, *Instincts of the Herd in Peace and War,* England Gegen Deutschland, (Trs Marco Pedulla, Independently Published). ISBN: 9781520332611.

17. Trotter, W, *Instincts of the Herd in Peace and War,* England Gegen Deutschland, (Trs Marco Pedulla, Independently Published).

18. Toonpool: https://www.toonpool.com (accessed 10th July 2018).

19. Harold Lasswell, 1927, attrib.

20. Curtis, Adam, 'Century of The Self, Part 2': 'The Engineering of Consent,' interview with Edward L Bernays, (BBC2, March 2002).

21. Bernays, Edward L, *Autobiography of an Idea,* (New York, Simon and Schuster, 1965).

22. Ewen, Stuart, *Crystallising Public Opinion,* Introduction, (New York, Ig Publishing).

23. Davies, Nick, *Flat Earth News,* (Chatto & Windus, 2008), p69. ISBN: 9780701181451.

24. Lipmann, Walter, *Public Opinion,* The Nature of News, 1922, Chapter 23.

25. *Ibid.*

26. TNA, Education, Britain 1906 to 1918, gallery-6-propaganda-case-studies.

27. TNA, Britain, Propaganda 1914-1918.

28. TNA, 'Battle of The Ancre,' public screening, (London: Kew, 23rd February, 2017).

29. Reuters, World News 24th May 2017.

30. The New Arab, 1st December 2016.

31. Fourth Annual Gulf Studies Forum in February, Youtube.com, (accessed 4th February, 2018).

32. *The Times,* Oliver Wright and Francis Elliott.

33. Medialine: http://www.medialine.org (accessed 10th July 2017).

34. *Ibid.*

35. Interview with author, Caabu, (Council for Arab British Understanding, London 25th September 2017).

Chapter Three

1. History.com: http://www.history.com/topics/saladin (accessed 15th August 2017).

2. Bernays, Edward L, *Propaganda,* Introduction, Mark Crispin Miller, 2005.

3. Ferguson, Niall, *The Independent,* 27th October, 1998.

4. Badsey, Dr Stephen, *Britain World War One,* BBC History.

5. www.firstworldwar.com.

6. Lewis Geoffrey, Islamic Quarterly 19, 1975,The Ottoman Proclamation of Jihad in 1914.

7. Rogan, Professor Eugene, *The Fall of The Ottomans,* A Global Call To Arms, (Penguin Books 2016), p72.

8. *Daily Telegraph,* 10 Aug 2014.

9. Rawi, Ahmed K, *John Buchan's British Designed Jihad in the Novel Greenmantle,* Jihad and Islam in World War One, edited Erik-Jan Zurcher 2016, ISBN 978 90 8728 2394.

10. IWM, Propaganda, Film, 'With Lawrence In Arabia': A Lowell Thomas Adventure Film 1927, IWM1131a.

11. Stewart, Rory, 'The Legacy of Lawrence of Arabia,' (BBC, October 2016).

12. Gardner, Brian, *Allenby*, Allenby and Lawrence, (London, Cassell & Co, 1965), p207.

13. Penguin: https://www.penguin.co.uk (accessed 15th May 2017).

14. IWM, *'Film of Lawrence of Arabia'* / film collection/propaganda/, Lowell Thomas, HA Chase, IWM42.

15. IWM, Digital Archive, IWM Ref1131a.

16. Lean, David, *'Lawrence of Arabia,'* Columbia Pictures, Dir David Lean, produced 10th December 1962.

17. www.history.net/lowellthomas.

18. Thomas, Lowell, *With Lawrence In Arabia*, (Hutchinson & Co, 1924).

19. Thomas, Lowell, *With Lawrence In Arabia*, (Hutchinson & Co, 1924), Foreword, vii.

20. IWM, Film Content, *'General Allenby's Entry Into Jerusalem,'* Topical Film Company, Collections IWM 13.

21. Jawahirriyah, W, *The Storyteller of Jerusalem*, 2015, (Interlink Books, January 2014), p353, ISBN: 978-1566569255.

22. *IWM*: Digital Archive, *'The New Crusaders,'* Film Collections IWM17.

23. *IWM*: Digital Archive, *'Advance of the Crusaders Into Mesopotamia'* Film Collections IWM79.

24. Urban, Mark, *Generals: Ten British Commanders Who Shaped The World*, (Faber & Faber, June 2006) ISBN: 978-0571224876.

25. Gardner, Brian, *Allenby*, Allenby and Lawrence, (Cassell & Co, 1965), p160.

26. *IWM*, *'General Allenby's Entry Into Jerusalem,'* Digital Archive Topical Film Company, Film Collections, IWM 13.

Chapter Four
1. *TNA*, cabinet papers/themes/wilsons-fourteen-points.htm.

2. *TNA* CAB 24/72: The Memorandum respecting Settlement of Turkey and the Arabian Peninsula.

3. *TNA* CAB 24/72.

4. *Ibid.*

5. *Ibid.*

6. *Ibid.*

7. Ponsonby, Arthur, *Falsehood In Wartime, Propaganda Lies of the First World War*, (Chatto & Windus, 1928). ISBN: 978 0939484393.

8. Ponsonby, Arthur, Chapter X111.

9. Ponsonby, Arthur, *Falsehood In Wartime, Propaganda Lies of the First World War*, (Chatto & Windus, 1928). ISBN: 978 0939484393.

10. *Ibid.*

11. *The National Archive* (TNA), Education, Propaganda, 1906-1918, Gallery 6, case studies.

12. BBC/Arts &Entertainment/17 February 2017.

13. The British Library (TBL), 10R/L/MIL/7/1873, *'Report on the Treatment of British POWs in Turkey, 1918,'* Lord Justice Younger.

14. Von Ludendorff, Erich, *My War Memories 1914-1918*, (London, Hutchinson & Co).

15. Stuart, Sir Campbell, *Secrets of Crewe House, the story of a famous campaign*, Foreword, (Hodder & Stoughton, September 1920).

16. The Open University, http://www www.open.ac.uk (accessed4th June 2017).

17. Stuart, Sir Campbell, *Secrets of Crewe House, the story of a famous campaign*, Foreword, (Hodder & Stoughton, September 1920).

18. *Ibid.*
19. Office of the Historian, Foreign Relations of the United States, 1917-1972, Public Diplomacy, World War One,history.state.gov/historicaldocumentsfrus1917-72PubDip/d1
20. www.revisionist.net/Introduction to the Propaganda Factory.
21. Creel, George, *How We Advertised America,* (New York: Harper & Brothers, 1920), Second Lines.
22. www.history.net.
23. Lasswell, H, *Propaganda Techniques in the World War,* p34.
24. Von Ludendorff, Erich, *My War Memories 1914-1918,* (London, Hutchinson & Co).

Chapter Five
1.   *TBL*   bl.uk/world-war-one/articles/the-legacy-of-world-war-one-propaganda.
2. Reynolds, David, *'The Long Shadow,'* BBC, 16th January 2015.
3. www.britannica.com/biography.
4. D'Amato, David, *Libertarianism,* Mussolini and the Press, pub 28th January 2016.
5. *Ibid.*
6. Herf, Jeffrey, *Nazi Propaganda for the Arab World,* (London, Yale University Press, 2009), p74, ISBN 978 0 300 16805 1.
7. Herf, Jeffrey, p64.
8. Rubin, Barry; Schwanitz, Wolfgang, *Nazis, Islamists and the Making of the Modern Middle East,* (Yale University Press, March 2014) ISBN: 978-03001-40903.
9. Nazi Collaborators: The Grand Mufti of Jerusalem, 10. www.zionism-israel.com/hdoc/Mufti_Fatwa_1941.htm.
11. Welch, David, *Persuading The People, British Propaganda in World War II,* The British Library (TBL) (London, BTL, 2016), pp179, ISBN: 978 0 712356541.
12. Welch, David, *Persuading The People, British Propaganda in World War II,* The British *Library (TBL) (London, BTL, 2016), pp179, ISBN: 978 0 712356541.*
13. The Independent, www.independent.co.uk/news/people/obituary-dame-freya-stark.
14. Harry Ransom Center, www.norman.hrc.utexas.edu/fasearch/findingAid.cfm.
15. *IWM* Collections, *Showboat,* K7174.
16. *IWM* Collections, *The Muslim Community in Cardiff,* D15285.
17. *The National Newspaper,* Louis Allday, October 13, 2016.
18. www.germanhistorydocs.ghi-dc.org/about.cfm; Speech to the Press on the *Establishment of a Reich Ministry for Popular Enlightenment and Propaganda,* March 15, 1933.
19. *Deutsches Rundfunk Archiv* (DRA), Nr. C 1117 (77' 50"); reprinted in Helmut Heiber, ed., Goebbels-Reden. Volume 1, 1931-1939. Düsseldorf, 1971, pp. 90, 94, 95, 106-07. Address to the Officials and Directors of the Radio Corporation, Berlin, House of Broadcasting, 25th March, 1933.
20. *DRA,* Nr. C 1117 (77' 50"); reprinted in Helmut Heiber, ed., Goebbels-Reden. Volume 1, 1931-1939. Düsseldorf, 1971, pp. 90, 94, 95, 106-07. Address to the Officials and Directors of the Radio Corporation, Berlin, House of Broadcasting, 25th March, 1933.
21. Source of English translation: Jeremy Noakes and Geoffrey Pridham, eds., Nazism, 1919-1945, Vol. 2: State, Economy and Society 1933-1939. Exeter:

University of Exeter Press, 2000, pp. 188, 191-92

22. Hippler, Fritz Dr, *'Der Ewige Jude' 'The Wandering Jew,'* Scr Eberhardt Taubert, 1941.

23. *Ibid.*

24. *Ibid.*

25. *Ibid.*

26. Tye, Larry, *Bernays, Edward L, The Father of Spin: Edward L Bernays and the Birth of Public Relations,* (Holt Books, 1998), p89.

27. *British Library,* www.bl.uk/world-war-one/articles/the-legacy-of-world-war-one-propaganda, Prof Jo Fox, Professor of History, Durham University.

Chapter Six

1. *The Guardian,* Julian Borger, Diplomatic Editor, Thursday 21 May, 2009.

2. *Ibid.*

3. *League of Nations,* Palestine Mandate, Article Two.

4. *The Balfour Project,* Britain in Palestine 1917-1948, 2016.

5. TNA, Anglo-American Commission on Palestine, Sir Norman Brook Report to British Cabinet, 26th April 1946, CAB/129/9.

6. TNA, Palestine Future Policy, Memorandum by Secretary of State for the Colonies, 16th January 1947, CP (47) 32, CAB 129/16.

7. www.opendemocracy.net/opensecurity/james-renton/forgotten-lessons-palestine-and-british-empire.

8. Charters, David A, *The British Army and Jewish Insurgency in Palestine 1945-1947,* (Palgrave McMillan, 1989), p92.

9. TNA, COI 733/451/1.

10. Herf, Jeffrey, *Nazi Propaganda for the Arab World,* (Newhaven & London: Yale University Press 2009), p101, 266, ISBN 978-0-300-16805-1.

11. Herf, Jeffrey, *Nazi Propaganda for the Arab World,* (Newhaven & London: Yale University Press 2009), p143, 266, ISBN 978-0-300-16805-1.

12. www.tandfonline.com

13. Hansard, 17.12.1945.

14. Charters, David A, *The British Army and Jewish Insurgency in Palestine 1945-1947,* (Palgrave McMillan, 1989), p92.

15. Kennedy, Greg, and Tuck, Christopher, EDS, *British Propaganda and Wars of Empire: Influencing Friend and Foe 1900-2010,* (Routledge 2016), p83/84.

16. Counterpunch: https://www.counterpunch.org (accessed September 2017).

17. *The Guardian*/ books/31 May 2001.

18. www.theweek.co.uk/63394 .

19. Department for International Development, www.devtracker.dfid.gov.uk/countries/PS.

20. British Israel Communications and Research Centre, July 2017, bicom.org.uk.

21. *The Daily Telegraph,* www.telegraph.co.uk/news/2016/06/13.

22. *Ibid.*

23. Buttu, Diana, briefing at Unite the Union, London, 25th January 2019

24. Malki, Dr Riad, APPG Parliamentary Group on Palestine, House of Commons, 16th May 2019.

25. Burroughs, William S, *Interzone,* (New York: Viking Press 1989), p49.

Chapter Seven

1. BBC News, 26th July 1956.

2. Heikal, M, *Nasser, the Cairo Documents,* (London, New English Library Ltd,

1972) ISBN 450012239.
3. Heikal, M, p79.
4. Heikal, M, p77.
5. Shaw, Tony, *Eden, Suez and the Mass Media*, (London, IB Tauris, 1996) ISBN 978 1 84885 091 0, p4.
6. Shaw, Tony, p5.
7. BBC, *'Suez, A Very British Crisis,'* BBC, June 2004.
8. Heikal, M, p87.
9. Herf, J, *Nazi Propaganda for the Arab World*, (London, Yale University Press, 2009), ISBN 978 0 300 16805 1, p260.
10. *Jerusalem Centre for Public Affairs*, article, Johann von Leers, CIA Report of 12 March 1959, CS-3/390,421.
11. Herf, J, p 265.
12. Heikal, M, p78.
13. *Ministry of Information*, www.ministry-of-information.com/eden-and-suez.
14. *Ministry of Information (MOI)*, www.ministry-of-information.com/eden-and-suez.
15. TNA CAB/129/78 Middle East Oil.
16. *Ibid.*
17. BBC, *'Suez, A Very British Crisis,'* BBC, June 2004.
18. *MOI*, eden-and-suez.
19. *Ibid.*
20. Shaw, Tony, p27.
21. *MOI*, eden-and-suez.
22. The US National Library of Medicine *'Anthony Eden's (Lord Avon) Biliary Tract Saga,'* John W. Braasch,: ncbi.nlm.nih.gov/pmc/articles/PMC1356158.
23. BBC, *'Suez, A Very British Crisis,'* BBC, June 2004.
24. *IWM*, *'The Anglo-French Aggression Against Egypt,'* Egypt Today, 1956, IWM Collection, COI 582.
25. *IWM* COI340.
26. *IWM* Content: *'Showing of Films on Suez.'*
27. *The Atlantic Archive*: atlantic.com/archive.
28. Eden, A, *Full Circle*, (Houghton Mifflin, 1960).
29. The Atlantic, Chalmers Roberts, April 1960.
30. Eden, Suez and the Mass Media, Tony Shaw, IB Tauris & Co, 1996, p1X.
31. BBC, *'Suez, A Very British Crisis,'* BBC, June 2004.
32. www.gov.uk/government/history/past-prime-ministers/anthony-eden.

Chapter Eight
1. Wikipedia.
2. https://www.gov.uk.government/news/firmin-sword-of-peace-awarded-to-15-uk-psychological-operations-group (accessed June 2018).
3. www.sofrep.com/81669/special-air-services-secret-war-oman-part-2.
4. RealClearDefense,http://www.realcleardefense.com/articles/2017/05/08.
5. *Ibid.*
6. Beelman, Maud S, *'The Dangers of Disinformation in the War on* Terrorism,' Coverage of Terrorism Women and Journalism: International Perspectives, from Nieman Reports Magazine, Winter 2001, Vol. 55, No.4, p.16.
7. Beelman, Maud S, *'The Dangers of Disinformation in the War on* Terrorism,' Coverage of Terrorism Women and Journalism: International Perspectives, from Nieman Reports Magazine, Winter 2001, Vol. 55, No.4, p.16.

8. Paddock Jr, Col Alfred H, USA Ret, *'No More Tactical Information Detachments'*: *US military psychological operations in transition, Psychological Operations, Principles & Case Studies,* (US Department of Defense).

9. *Ibid.*

11. Goldstein, Col Frank USAF, Jacobowitz, Col Daniel W USAF Ret, *Psychological Operations, An Introduction,* (US Department of Defense).

12. *Ibid.*

13. *Ibid.*

14. American Forces Information Service, the 1991 Defense Almanac

15. Goldstein Col Frank USAF, Jacobowitz, Col Daniel, USAF, *PsyOp in Desert Shield/Desert Storm,* (US Department of Defense).

16. *Ibid.*

17. *Daily Mirror,* 15th January 2016

18. *ABC News,* http://abcnews.go.com/Politics/john-mccain-pow/story?id=3257463

19. US Special Operations Command: *'Post-operational analysis; Iraqi psychological operations during Operations Desert Shield/Storm'* SOJ9, 1992.

20. Goldstein Col Frank USAF, Jacobowitz, Col Daniel, USAF, *'PsyOp in Desert Shield/Desert Storm,'* (US Department of Defense).

21. *Ibid.*

22. Nato.int/docu/review/2003/issue2/english/art4.html.

23. *Ibid.*

24. *Ibid.*

25. Alvarez, Steven, J, *Selling War – A Critical Look at the Military's PR Machine,* (Lincoln, Potomac Books, 2016), p xiii.

26. The Men Who Stare At Goats, Jon Ronson, Picador/Simon & Schuster, 2004.

27. BBC News 2004

28. Beck, William J. *Senior Officer Debriefing Program: Report of Lieutenant Colonel William J Beck* (Washington DC: Department of the Army, Office of the Adjutant General, 31 January 1969, pps 12-13

29. *Gizmodo,* 'How The Military Could Turn Your Mind Into The Next Battlefield,' gizmodo.com/how-the-military-could-turn-your-mind-into-the-next-bat-1673214050.

30. *Ibid.*

Chapter Nine

1. *TNA,* Britain 1906-1918, Propaganda, Gallery 6.

2. *TNA,* Education, Propaganda, 1906-1918, Gallery 6, case studies.

3. *Ministry of Information,* https://www.ministry-of-information.com.

4. *TNA,* CAB/128/10, Rt Hon Herbert Morrison MP, Lord President of the Council.

5. *BBC News,* Government ad agency COI to be closed down, 23 June 2011.

6. Government Communication Service (GCS), gcs.civilservice.gov.uk/wp-content/uploads/2017/08/6.3149_CO_GCS-Comms-Plan_FINAL_WEB.pdf).

7. *Ibid.*

8. *Financial Times,* Comment, 16th December 2017.

9. www.statista.com/statistics/189788/global-outsourcing-market-size.

10. *Ibid.*

11. *The Register,* https//www. theregister.co.uk/2017/05/02/ .

12. *Soldiers of Misfortune?* Blackwater USA, Private Military Security

Contractors, Iraq War, (US Department of Defense, Progressive Management Publications), p13.

13. *Soldiers of Misfortune?* Blackwater USA, Private Military Security Contractors, US Government Department of Defense, Progressive Management Publications, p7.

14. *Los Angeles Times*, Mark Fineman, August 29, 1990.

15. Rampton S & Stauber J, *Weapons of Mass Deception, True Lies*, (Constable & Robinson 2003), p70.

16. Rampton S & Stauber J, p71.

17. MacArthur, John R. Jr *Second Front: Censorship and Propaganda in the Gulf War*, (Berkeley, Calif, University of California Press, 1992), p84.ISBN 978-0-8090-8517-0.

18. Rampton S & Stauber J, p74.

19. Sheldon Rampton and John Stauber, *How To Sell a War, In These* Times, 4th August, 2003.

20. *Rendon Group*, https://www.rendongroup.com (accessed August 2108).

21. *Rolling Stone Magazine*, 'The man who sold the war,' 21st November 2005.

22. *Democracy Now*, https://www.democracynow.org www.democracynow. org.

23. *Ibid.*

24. *Ibid.*

25. Corpwatch: https://www.corpwatch.org/article/information-warriors .

26. USA Today: https://www.usatoday.com/story/news/nation/2012/11/19.

27. *Democracy Now*, https://www.democracynow.org .

28. *The Bureau of Investigative Journalism*, 'How a British PR firm helped shape the War on Terror,' 10th October, 2016/youtube.com

29. Bureau of Investigative Journalism – Ref. 6916.

30. *Sunday Times*, 2nd October 2016.

31. *The Guardian*, 4th September 2017.

32. Paul, R, *'Liberty Report,'* 3rd October 2016.

33. Mazzetti M, Borzou Daragahi, *Los Angeles Times* , 30th November 2005.

34. MSNBC, *'Hardball with Chris Matthews,'* December 1, 2005.

35. Alavarez, Steven J, *Selling War, a critical look at the Military's PR machine* (Lincoln, Potomac Books, 2016), ISBN: 9781612347721.

36. *Ibid*, p278.

37. *Ibid*, p280.

38. www.foreignpolicy.com/2013/07/14/John Hudson, July 14, 2013; US Repeals Propaganda Ban, Spreads Government-Made News to Americans.

39. Campen, Alan D, Colonel, *Information, Truth & War, The First Information War,'* (AFCEA International Press, Virginia, October 1992, ISBN 0-916159-24-8, p 90

Chapter Ten

1. *Vice News*, 'The Spread of the Caliphate: Islamic State,' Vice News 14th August 2014, YouTube.

2. *Ibid.*

3. *Ibid.*

4. *Associated Press* (AP), 17th October 2017.

5. *Der Spiegel*, Christopher Reuter, 18th April 2015.

6. *Ibid.*

7. *Daily Express*, 15th February 2017.

8. ICSR Findings, *'Media Jihad, the Islamic State's Doctrine for Information*

Warfare,' 2017.

9. BBC, https://www.monitoring.bbc.co.uk, 23rd November 2017.

10. *Ibid.*

11. Adorno, T, *Freudian Theory and the Pattern of Fascist Propaganda,* (The Essential Frankfurt School Reader, 1982), p126.

12. *Washington Post,* Greg Miller, Souad Mekhnnet, 20th November 2015.

13. *Ibid.*

14. McHugo J, *A Concise History of Sunnis & Shi'is,* (London, Saqi Books, 2017), p204.

15. *The World Today,* Radicalisation, Sarah Marks and Daniel Pick, February/March 2017.

16. The Daily Beast, Katie Zavadski, 6th April 2017, *'The Boston Nerd Who Edited ISIS Magazine Is Dead'.*

17. *Brookings Institute,* official IS media content: https://www.brookings.ed/wp-content/uploads/2014/12/en who's who.pdf.

18. The Daily Beast, Katie Zavadski, 6th April 2017, *'The Boston Nerd Who Edited ISIS Magazine Is Dead'.*

19. www.bbcnews.co.uk/19th September 2017.

20. Vox-Pol, *'Disrupting Daesh: Measuring Takedown of online terrorist material and its impacts,'* Network of Excellence 2017.

21. *Ibid.*

22. *#Greenbirds: Measuring Importance and Influence in Syrian Foreign Fighter Networks,* ICSR, Joseph A Carter, Shiraz Maher, Peter R Neumann 2014

23. . *Ibid.* 2017

25. Author interview, ICSR 17th October 2017

26. London Tigers, https://www.londontigers.org (accessed 30th July 2018).

27. Global Coalition, https:// www.the global coalition.org.

28. *Ibid.*

29. Europol, www.europol.europe.eu/newsroom/news/Islamic-state 27/04/2018.

30. jihadology.net, Aaron Y Zelin (accessed 20th January 2019).

Chapter Eleven

1. *'Public Diplomacy before Gullion, The Evolution of a Phrase,'* Nicholas J. Cull, Routledge Handbook of Public Diplomacy, 2009.

2. https://www.nancysnow.com, (accessed 15th May 2018).

3. *Ibid.*

4. *Daily Telegraph,* www.telegraph.co.uk/news/worldnews/1579085.

5. Washington Institute, www.washingtoninstitute.org/policy-analysis/view/inside-u.s.-public-diplomacy-toward-the-middle-east, 16th January 2013.

6. *Ibid.*

7. UNESCO, World Arabic Language Day, 18th December 2012.

8. www.alaraby.co.uk/english/comment/2018/7/18/arab-views-of-us-low-support-for-palestinians-high.

9. www.youthpolicy.org/mappings/regionalyouthscenes/mena/facts.

10. Rugh, W, Northeastern University, Boston, MA, USA, *'American soft power and Public Diplomacy in the Arab world':* (Palgrave Communications, Rugh W ,2017).

11. www.usnews.com/news/best-countries/articles/2017-04-11/Devon Haynie, News Editor, April 11, 2017.

12.

13. Medical Aid for Palestinians.

14. *The Independent*, 30th January 2005.

15. *Attitudes towards the Arab world – a poll among UK residents, Arab News,* You Gov, Council for Arab-British Understanding, 16-17 Aug 2017; total sample size 2,142 adults.

16. OECD, https://www.oecd.org/dac/financing-sustainable-development/development-finance-data/ODA-2016-detailed-summary.pdf.

17. www.gov.uk/government/uploads/system/uploads/attachment_data/file/660062/SID-2017b.pdf.

18. *BBC Panorama*, BBC One, 4th December 2017

19. *Ibid.*

20. World Economic Forum, https://www.weforum.org/agenda/2016/06/the-world-continues-to-spend-enormous-amounts-on-violence-and-little-on-building-peace.

21. *BBC News*, 23rd January 2018.

22. *The Times*, Oliver Wright and Francis Elliot, 3rd August 2017.

23. *'Jihadism after the Caliphate': Terrorism and Counterterrorism in Europe,'* King's College London 22nd March 2018.

24. *Test.*

25. *Foreign Policy*, Qatar Won The Saudi Blockade, Hassan Hassan, 4th June 2018.

26. *Times of Israel*, Qatar Pays for Outreach to US Jews, JTA, 8th September 2017.

Bibliography

Adorno, Theodor, *Freudian Theory and the Pattern of Fascist Propaganda*, (The Essential Frankfurt School Reader, 1982), p126.

Alvarez, Steven, J, *Selling War – A Critical Look at the Military's PR Machine*, (Lincoln, Potomac Books., 2016), p xiii.

BBC, *'Suez, A Very British Crisis,'* BBC, June 2004.

Beck, William J. *Senior Officer Debriefing Program: Report of Lieutenant Colonel William J, Beck* (Washington DC: Department of the Army, Office of the Adjutant General, 31 January 1969, pps 12-13.

Beelman, Maud S., *'The Dangers of Disinformation in the War on* Terrorism,' Coverage of Terrorism Women and Journalism: International Perspectives, from Nieman Reports Magazine, Winter 2001, Vol. 55, No.4, p.16.

Bernays, Edward L, *Crystallizing Public Opinion, Introduction*, Stewart Ewen, (New York: Ig Publishing) , ISBN 978-1-935439-26-4.

Bernays, Edward L, *Autobiography of an Idea*, (New York, Simon and Schuster, 1965).

Brown, John, *'Public Diplomacy & Propaganda, Their Differences,'* American Diplomacy, Foreign Service Despatches and Periodic Reports on US Foreign Policy, 2008.

Burroughs, William S, *Interzone*, (New York: Viking Press 1989), p49.

Campen, Alan D, Colonel, *Information, Truth & War, The First Information War,'* (AFCEA International Press, Virginia, October 1992, ISBN 0-916159-24-8, p 90.

Charters, David A, *The British Army and Jewish Insurgency in Palestine 1945-1947*, (Palgrave McMillan, 1989), p92.

Creel, George, *How We Advertised America*, (New York: Harper & Brothers, 1920), Second Lines.

Cull, Nicholas J, *'Public Diplomacy before Gullion, The Evolution of a Phrase,'* Routledge Handbook of Public Diplomacy, 2009.

Curtis, Adam, *'Century of The Self, Part 2': 'The Engineering of Consent,'* interview with Edward L Bernays, (BBC2, March 2002).

D'Amato, David, *Libertarianism*, Mussolini and the Press, pub 28th January 2016.

Davies, Nick, *Flat Earth News*, (Chatto & Windus, 2008), p69. ISBN: 9780701181451.

Ewen, Stuart, *Crystallising Public Opinion*, Introduction, (New York, Ig Publishing).

Freud, Sigmund, *Group Psychology and The Analysis Of The Ego*, (printed by Amazon) ISBN: 9781500715427.

Gardner, Brian, *Allenby*, Allenby and Lawrence, (London, Cassell & Co, 1965), p207.

Goldstein, Col Frank USAF, Jacobowitz, Col Daniel W USAF Ret, Psychological *Operations, An Introduction*, (US Department of Defense).

Heikal, M, *Nasser, the Cairo Documents*, (London, New English Library Ltd, 1972) ISBN 450012239.

Herf, Jeffrey, *Nazi Propaganda for the Arab World*, (London, Yale University Press, 2009), p74, ISBN 9780300168051.

Hippler, Fritz Dr, *'Der Ewige Jude' 'The Wandering Jew,'* Scr Eberhardt Taubert, 1941.

Hitler, Adolf, *Mein Kampf*, Volume 2, Propaganda & Organisation,' Chapter 11, 1926.

IWM, 'The Anglo-French Aggression Against Egypt,' Egypt Today, 1956, IWM Collection, COI 582.

Jawahirriyah,W, *The Storyteller of Jerusalem*, 2015, (Interlink Books, January 2014), p353, ISBN: 978-1566569255.

'Jihadism after the Caliphate': Terrorism and Counterterrorism in Europe,' King's College London 22nd March 2018.

Kennedy, Greg, and Tuck, Christopher, EDS, *British Propaganda and Wars of Empire: Influencing Friend and Foe 1900-2010*, (Routledge 2016), p83/84.

Keohane, Robert O and Nye, Joseph S, *Power and Interdependence in the Information Age*, Foreign Affairs, Vol. 77, No. 5, September/October 1998, p. 86.

Knightley, P, *The First Casualty*, (Andre Deutsch, 2003), p486, ISBN 0-801880-300.

Lasswell, Harold D, *Propaganda Technique In The World War, The Matter In Hand*, (New York: Peter Smith, 1927) p9. ISBN 978-1-61427-506-0.

Le Bon, Gustave, *The Crowd*, Study of the Popular Mind, the Era of Crowds, (Aristeus Books 2014) ISBN 9781502303264.

Lippmann, Walter, *Public Opinion*, Leaders and The Rank And File, (Jefferson Publication 5th December 2015). ISBN-13 978-1512179316.

MacArthur, John R. Jr *Second Front: Censorship and Propaganda in the Gulf War*, (Berkeley, Calif, University of California Press, 1992), p84.ISBN 978-0-8090-8517-0.

McHugo J, *A Concise History of Sunnis & Shi'is*, (London, Saqi Books, 2017), p204.

'Media Jihad: the Islamic State's Doctrine for Information Warfare,' ICSR, 2017.

Paddock Jr, Col Alfred H, USA Ret, *'No More Tactical Information Detachments': US military psychological operations in transition, Psychological Operations, Principles & Case Studies*, (US Department of Defense).

Ponsonby, Arthur, *Falsehood in Wartime, Propaganda Lies of the First World War*, (Chatto & Windus, 1928). ISBN: 978 0939484393.

Post, Jerrold, Prof, *Yasser Arafat, Psychological Profile and Strategic Analysis*, International Policy Institute for Counter-Terrorism, 2002

Rampton S, Stauber J, *Weapons of Mass Deception, Liberation Day*, (USA Jeremy P Tarcher, Penguin 2003), p5, ISBN 1-84119-837-4.

Reynolds, David, *'The Long Shadow,'* BBC, 16th January 2015.

Rogan, Professor Eugene, *The Fall of The Ottomans*, A Global Call To Arms, (Penguin Books 2016), p72.

Ronson, John, The Men Who Stare At Goats, Picador/Simon & Schuster, 2004.

Rubin, Barry; Schwanitz, Wolfgang, *Nazis, Islamists and the Making of the Modern*

Middle East, (Yale University Press, March 2014) ISBN: 978-03001-40903.

Rugh, W, Northeastern University, Boston, MA, USA, *'American soft power and public diplomacy in the Arab world'*: (Palgrave Communications, Rugh W ,2017).

Said, Edward, *Orientalism*, (London, Routledge & Keegan Paul 1978), p3, ISBN 978-0-141-18742-6.

Shaw, Tony, *Eden, Suez and the Mass Media*, (London, IB Tauris, 1996) ISBN 978 1 84885 091 0, p4.

Soldiers of Misfortune? Blackwater USA, Private Military Security Contractors, Iraq War, (US Department of Defense, Progressive Management Publications), p13.

Stewart, Rory, 'The Legacy of Lawrence of Arabia,' (BBC, October 2016).

Stuart, Sir Campbell, *Secrets of Crewe House, the Story of a Famous Campaign*, Foreword, (Hodder & Stoughton, September 1920).

The British Library (TBL), 10R/L/MIL/7/1873, *'Report on the Treatment of British POWs in Turkey, 1918,'* Lord Justice Younger.

Thomas, Lowell, *With Lawrence in Arabia*, (Hutchinson & Co, 1924).

Trotter, Wilfred, *Instincts of the Herd in Peace and War*, England Gegen Deutschland, (Trs Marco Pedulla, Independently Published). ISBN: 9781520332611.

Tye, Larry, Bernays, Edward L, *The Father of Spin: Edward L Bernays and the Birth of Public Relations*, (Holt Books, 1998), p89.

Urban, Mark, *Generals: Ten British Commanders Who Shaped the World*, (Faber & Faber, June 2006) ISBN: 978-0571224876.

US Special Operations Command: *'Post-operational Analysis; Iraqi Psychological Operations during Operations Desert Shield/Storm'* SOJ9, 1992.

Von Ludendorff, Erich, *My War Memories 1914-1918*, (London, Hutchinson & Co).

Welch, David, *Persuading the People, British Propaganda in World War II*, The British Library (TBL) (London, BTL, 2016), pp179, ISBN: 978 0 712356541.

About the Author

Vyvyan Kinross has spent over 30 years in the PR and communications business. Latterly he has specialised in advising governments on how to set up and manage their information and communication capacity, most recently working in Abu Dhabi, UAE and the Occupied Palestinian Territory. In 2013, he was a Senior Advisor in Public Administration & Organisational Capacity Development at the United Nations Office for Project Services (UNOPS) Copenhagen, as an expert in PR & corporate communications systems in fragile and post-conflict states.

Since 2014, Vyvyan has been a Member of the Executive Board for the Council of Arab British Understanding (CAABU), an NGO active in UK Parliament working to advance Arab-British relations. Vyvyan is a graduate in Modern Arabic Studies from the University of Durham.